# Advanced Praise for *Objectives and Key Results: Driving Focus, Alignment, and Engagement with OKRs*

"Providing value to your organization is about business outcomes, not technology. This book is a must-read for anyone looking to align resources to focus on what matters most to their business. The insights and techniques you will acquire reading this book will put you on a fast track to providing clarity of purpose."

*Roger Fugett*
*CIO, CareerBuilder*

"Even after implementing OKRs three years ago at SHC, this book helped me reflect on how we can continue to improve our approach and benefit even more from the tremendous value of OKRs. If you're new to OKRs, read this book. If you've already implemented OKRs, read this book."

*Holly Engler*
*Director Strategic Talent Management,*
*Sears Holdings Corporation*

"A great read! OKRs are critical to driving operational rigor and alignment—and every company can benefit from this approach. Applying the right technologies and the right processes together can truly revolutionize the way we work. If you care about driving business results, innovation, employee engagement, and alignment, this book is a must read."

*Kris Duggan*
*CEO, BetterWorks*

"Niven and Lamorte have done a great job putting together this comprehensive guide to OKRs. They offer an interesting and practical approach that is sure to save you time in figuring out what works best for your organization."

*Henrik-Jan van der Pol*
*Founder & CEO, Perdoo*

"Written by two renowned experts in the field, this is the essential OKRs handbook. As an OKRs coach, I can tell you with confidence that you don't want to miss this one."

*Felipe Castro*
*Founder, Lean Performance*

"Setting objectives and measuring performance against those objectives are critical to every organization's success for many, many reasons. This book is a must-read for any organization that wants to do these things *right*."

*Randall Bolten*
*CFO and author of* **Painting with Numbers**

"A scorecard is great for an executive, a dashboard for a department, but what about individuals? Enter the OKRs—objectives and key results—a new lightweight technique popularized by Intel and Google that focuses and motivates employees to achieve at high levels. This book explains what OKRs are, how they work, and how they can transform organizations."

*Wayne W Eckerson*
*Founder & Principal Consultant, Eckerson Group*

"When I discovered OKRs, I realized that someone had codified the methods that the best executives use to create consistently superior performance. When I read this book, I realized that Niven and Lamorte had explained what OKRs are, why OKRs lead to success, and how to implement OKRs in a practical, efficient manner. CEOs of companies large and small should read this book!

*Mark Mitchell*
*Entrepreneur & Angel Investor*

# Objectives and Key Results

Founded in 1807, John Wiley & Sons is the oldest independent publishing company in the United States. With offices in North America, Europe, Asia, and Australia, Wiley is globally committed to developing and marketing print and electronic products and services for our customers' professional and personal knowledge and understanding.

The Wiley Corporate F&A series provides information, tools, and insights to corporate professionals responsible for issues affecting the profitability of their company, from accounting and finance to internal controls and performance management.

# Objectives and Key Results

## Driving Focus, Alignment, and Engagement with OKRs

**PAUL R. NIVEN**
**BEN LAMORTE**

WILEY

Published by John Wiley & Sons, Inc., Hoboken, New Jersey.
Published simultaneously in Canada.

For general information on our other products and services or for technical support,
please contact our Customer Care Department within the United States at (800)
762-2974, outside the United States at (317) 572-3993 or fax (317) 572-4002.

Wiley publishes in a variety of print and electronic formats and by print-on-demand.
Some material included with standard print versions of this book may not be included
in e-books or in print-on-demand. If this book refers to media such as a CD or DVD that
is not included in the version you purchased, you may download this material at
http://booksupport.wiley.com. For more information about Wiley products, visit
www.wiley.com.

*Library of Congress Cataloging-in-Publication Data is Available*

ISBN 978-1-119-25239-9 (Hardcover)
ISBN 978-1-119-25558-1 (ePDF)
ISBN 978-1-119-25566-6 (ePub)

Cover image: background: © Pali Rao / iStockphoto
Cover design: Wiley

Printed in the United States of America

SKY10033873_032122

*To my wife, Lois, for always believing in me
and offering the inspiration to reach
beyond the limits of what I think is possible.
-P.N.*

*To my wife, Ariana, for the limitless, unconditional love and
for encouraging me to focus on my dreams.
-B.L.*

# Contents

Introduction     xiii

Acknowledgments     xix

**Chapter 1: Introduction to OKRs**     1

    The History of OKRs     1
    What Are Objectives and Key Results (OKRs)?     6
    Objectives     8
    Key Results     8
    Organizational Challenges, and Why You Need OKRs     13
    Benefits of OKRs     20
    Notes     26

**Chapter 2: Preparing for Your OKRs Journey**     29

    Why Are You Implementing OKRs?     29
    Executive Sponsorship: A Critical Component of Your
        OKRs Implementation     31
    Where to Develop Your OKRs     33
    Special Cases     36
    An OKRs Development Plan     37
    Key Lessons for Successful Transformation     41
    The Building Blocks of OKRs: Mission, Vision, and Strategy     42
    Roadmap Strategy     53
    Notes     59

**Chapter 3: Creating Effective OKRs**     61

    Omaha     61
    Creating Powerful Objectives     62
    Tips for Creating Objectives     64
    Objective Descriptions     68

Characteristics of Effective Key Results    69
Tips for Creating Key Results    73
Types of Key Results    76
Scoring OKRs    80
How Often Do We Set OKRs?    85
How Many OKRs Do We Have?    86
Do OKRs Stay the Same from Quarter to Quarter?    88
Can OKRs Change *during* the Quarter?    89
The Process to Set OKRs    90
Notes    95

**Chapter 4: Connecting OKRs to Drive Alignment**    **97**

A Critical Link    99
Connecting OKRs    99
How to Connect OKRs    100
Creating Alignment    108
Confirming the Alignment of Connected OKRs    113
Closing Thoughts on Connecting    114
Notes    115

**Chapter 5: Managing with OKRs**    **117**

The Cycle: Monday Meetings, Mid-Quarter Check-Ins, and
     Quarterly Reviews    118
Updating OKRs at the End of the Quarter    128
Software and OKRs    129
Let's Play 20 Questions!    137
Notes    138

**Chapter 6: Making OKRs Sustainable**    **141**

Don't Think of OKRs as a Project    141
Who Owns the OKRs Process?    142
OKRs and Performance Reviews    144
OKRs and Incentive Compensation    147
Top 10 OKRs Issues    151
How Not to Implement OKRs . . . and Where Consultants
     Can Help    156
Concluding Thoughts    159
Notes    160

**Chapter 7: Case Studies in OKRs Use** **161**

    Flipkart 162
    CareerBuilder 167
    Zalando 171
    Sears Holdings Corporation (SHC) 175
    GoNoodle 185
    TaxSlayer 190
    Note 194

**About the Authors** **195**
**Index** **197**

# Introduction

## WHY WE WROTE THIS BOOK

Any company embarking on an OKRs implementation will realize very soon after the work begins that it is much more than a "measurement project." The ultimate goal is improved performance through the identification of objectives and key results that are refreshed frequently in order to ensure agility in a business world where the pace of change is ever accelerating. However, to achieve success with OKRs, there are numerous processes and tasks that must be seamlessly executed. Generating support and enthusiasm from executives, determining where to deploy OKRs, mastering the nuances of effective OKRs, connecting OKRs throughout the company, reporting results, capturing key learnings, and ingraining the methodology into the culture of the organization are just some of the requirements of an effective rollout.

As we write this, the OKRs field is still relatively nascent in terms of standard practices and proven procedures. It is an emerging discipline, and while implementations are growing by the day, and consultants and software providers are coming forward in attempts to plug knowledge gaps, no definitive how-to guide exists for organizations anxious to implement OKRs without falling prey to potential pitfalls that can derail this or any change effort. This book is our answer to that challenge. It was written to fill the void that currently exists between knowledge and practice. Organizations wishing to reap the benefits of OKRs must first be made aware of—and properly equipped to overcome—the challenges associated with an undertaking of this magnitude. Based on our global consulting experience with OKRs as well as the extensive research we've conducted, these pages will act as your comprehensive guide through the entire OKRs terrain. We're confident the tools and techniques profiled in this book will propel the success of those currently engaged with OKRs and compel more executives to launch OKRs programs in their own organizations. Before we outline how the book is organized, let us share with you our backgrounds and experience with the topic.

**HOW WE GOT STARTED WITH OKRs**

## Ben

"When you go for a hike with your family, it's fine to just walk and enjoy the scenery, but when you're at work you need to be crystal clear about the destination. Otherwise you're wasting your time and the time of everyone who works with you."

Those words changed Ben's life. The source of that wisdom was former Oracle Chief Financial Officer Jeff Walker. Walker shared this advice with Ben in a personal conversation and later expanded on the principle in a keynote he delivered to a group of planning professionals in Palo Alto in 2011. During the talk Walker explained objectives and key results (OKRs). He discussed how businesses must outline their desired future in the form of objectives—aspirational and qualitative statements designed to move the organization forward in a desired direction. Each objective is then translated into an underlying set of measurable key results. If the objective asks, "What do we want to do?" the key result asks, "How will we know if we've met our objective?" Ben was immediately struck by the potential power of OKRs and sensed that the framework would become critical to his work, but at that point didn't know how it would manifest. He was soon to find out.

Ben was approached by an organization to assist them with a KPI (key performance indicators) project. He accepted the assignment and found himself eagerly awaiting the strategy document that was to be supplied by the company's CEO. When it arrived, Ben felt overwhelmed. The strategy slide decks and documents were stuffed with ideas and good intentions, but the materials contained a confusing mix of key pillars (corporate priorities), core values, and business metrics. Ben struggled with how to approach the project, and it wasn't until arriving at his hotel room the night before meeting with the CEO and CFO that he recalled the advice of Jeff Walker. With that in mind, Ben condensed the strategy document into a single page, translating the key pillars into objectives, and assigning key results to each. The next day, he used this organizing framework of OKRs to share his understanding of the organization's strategy. After his overview, the executives fell quiet and asked for a moment of privacy. Ben left the room convinced he had misinterpreted the strategy and would quickly be dispatched to the airport for the next plane home. Two minutes in the hallway felt like two hours, but when he was summoned back into the room he was relieved to see a smile on the face of the CEO, who said: "We want you to help us create this type of document for every business unit and department in the company!" After helping close to 50 teams at the company draft and refine their OKRs, and later witnessing their success with the method, Ben knew he had found his calling. Hundreds of hours coaching teams and managers later, here we are.

## Paul

Paul has been working in the performance measurement and strategy execution space for close to two decades. He was introduced to the concepts through interactions with a company looking to improve its performance. In Paul's case, the company was in a fast-changing industry with nimble competitors emerging rapidly and customers demanding improved service with no price increases. A new strategy was created: one that if effectively implemented would deliver enhanced strategic skill sets across the company, see the overhaul of key business processes, drive value for customers, and ultimately produce breakthrough financial results. But could they make it happen? Key to their execution was the identification of measures they would use to hold themselves accountable for achieving each plank of the strategy. It took time, but by focusing on a core set of metrics to learn about what was, and was not, working with the strategy, the company ultimately delivered on its promises to customers, employees, and shareholders alike. The real "Aha" for Paul came in the form of employee surveys conducted before and after the development and use of strategic measurement. Beforehand, just a small percentage of employees said they understood the company's strategy and how they could contribute. However, after the use of strategic measurement, the percentage jumped nearly fivefold to a large majority of employees. Like Ben, Paul saw the value of applying measurement to strategy and set out to help organizations harness that power.

Some readers may be familiar with Paul through his work and books on the Balanced Scorecard, a popular framework that translates strategy into objectives, measures, targets, and strategic initiatives, using four distinct yet related perspectives of performance: financial, customer, internal processes, and learning and growth. The framework has been embraced by legions of organizations around the globe, and while it is unquestionably effective, many companies have struggled in implementing, and fully maximizing the benefits of, the scorecard model. One of the chief issues organizations raise is the model's increasing complexity. The Scorecard's taxonomy has swollen over the years since its founding in the early 1990s, and many experts have layered on increasingly convoluted schematics that have added even more moving parts to what was originally conceived as an easy-to-apply approach to measuring an organization's strategy. The end result is that, for many organizations, despite its benefits the Balanced Scorecard appears too cumbersome to be rolled out to an entire organization, one comprised of teams yearning for simple, yet powerful methods to ensure their work is focused on what matters most and leads to the execution of the company's strategy. Enter OKRs.

Paul was searching for a "lighter-weight" system that would still provide the very real benefits desired by his clients who wished to extract the most value from their strategies. He discovered OKRs through his research and quickly learned of the work Ben was doing in the field. The two met and bonded over their mutual desire to help improve organizational performance and the belief that OKRs, while seemingly simple, can deliver outsized value to any company wishing to improve focus, drive alignment, and improve engagement. They began working together with clients in 2015.

 **HOW THE BOOK IS ORGANIZED**

*Objectives and Key Results* is composed of seven chapters. The first six will lead you through an OKRs implementation in more or less chronological order, while the final chapter showcases the work of a number of global organizations currently benefiting from OKRs.

In the opening chapter we share the history of OKRs, followed by definitions and examples of both objectives and key results. Modern organizations face many crucial challenges that OKRs are well-suited to overcome. The chapter explores some of the more pressing topics. Chapter 1 concludes with an overview of the many benefits of OKRs. Before you can implement OKRs, you must ensure your organization is ready to embark on the journey ahead. Chapter 2 explores how to prepare for the creation and use of OKRs. The first question posed is, "Why are you implementing OKRs?" The critical topic of executive sponsorship is discussed, including how to gain sponsorship. Considerations on where to develop OKRs are presented, followed by a comprehensive plan for developing OKRs. The chapter concludes by defining the strategic context for OKRs using a mission, vision, and strategy. In order for OKRs to deliver benefits, they must be crafted with care and possess a number of key characteristics. Chapter 3 outlines how to create effective OKRs. Types of key results are examined, followed by a discussion of health metrics, and the scoring of OKRs. The chapter ends with a review of our CRAFT (create, refine, align, finalize, and transmit) process for creating OKRs.

OKRs must be created throughout the organization in order to drive engagement, accountability, and focus. We call this "connecting OKRs," and it is the subject of Chapter 4. Processes and tips for connecting OKRs both vertically and horizontally across the organization are explored. To gain the maximum value from OKRs, they must be regularly monitored both during, and at the conclusion of, each cycle. Chapter 5 explores the cycle of OKRs reviews and how software can enable OKR success. The OKR review cycle consists of three primary mechanisms, each of which is discussed: Monday meetings, mid-quarter check-ins, and quarterly reviews. The second half of the chapter examines the use of software in the implementation and management of OKRs. To ensure the long-term success of OKRs, they must be ingrained into the culture of the organization. Chapter 6 examines how to make OKRs sustainable. Many companies will consider OKRs a "project," but that is a mistake. The chapter opens by arguing why you should consider OKRs an ongoing process. Any company using OKRs must determine whether to link them to performance reviews and/or incentive compensation. These potential links are explored in detail in the chapter, with pros, cons, and recommendations. The chapter concludes with the top 10 issues to consider before, during, and after creating OKRs and analyzes how and if to leverage consultants for your OKRs implementation.

Chapter 7 shares the stories of six global organizations currently using OKRs to great advantage. Profiled in the chapter are: Zalando, Flipkart, Sears Holdings, TaxSlayer, GoNoodle, and CareerBuilder. We're confident you'll both enjoy and learn from the reflections offered by these exceptional and innovative organizations.

Companies at any stage of OKRs development will benefit from the advice offered in this book. Those launching OKRs efforts will, of course, derive benefits from the detailed tools and techniques guiding them from initial design to the creation of a robust management system. Those organizations that currently employ OKRs will also benefit from a review of the topics presented here. The processes and exercises chronicled can serve as a checkpoint or audit of their own program to ensure it is operating at peak effectiveness. And for those of you who are currently utilizing another form of strategic management system, we invite you to consider the many advantages offered by OKRs. Wherever you are on your OKRs journey, we thank you for allowing us to serve as your guides.

Paul R. Niven and Ben Lamorte
San Diego and San Anselmo, California, May 2016

# Acknowledgments

THIS BOOK IS PRIMARILY CONCERNED with connecting goals to the larger strategic picture and focusing on what is most important. Therefore, it's only fitting that we begin by recognizing the many people who contributed to this book, ensuring that we remained strategic and focused on what matters most in relating the story of OKRs. We've been exceedingly fortunate to enjoy the support of clients, colleagues, friends, and family. Outlined below are some of the many people we've been honored to work with and learn from—individuals whose lessons and insights helped shape this book.

We'd like to thank John Doerr, a leading Silicon Valley investor, for recognizing the power and potential of OKRs and introducing the concept to Google. We extend a shout-out to Rick Klau for creating the Google Ventures workshop video detailing how Google uses OKRs, and who was kind enough to take time to discuss OKRs with us. Thanks to Sid Ghatak, Jennie Lindeman Fimbres, Craig Heldman, Bobby Wilson, and the entire Metrics360 team. What began as an exercise in key performance indicators quickly evolved into the OKRs project that got us started. We'd like to thank our early OKR coaching clients who took the time to provide extensive feedback after OKR coaching sessions. These early clients include Terrell Chafin and Ken Heaps of Latham & Watkins, Richard Kip at University of California Santa Barbara, Chris Mason and Holly Engler at Sears Holdings Corporation, and Gary Mynchenberg of ZIN Technologies who hosted one of our first OKR workshops in Cleveland, Ohio. Our first International OKRs project took us to Berlin where we enjoyed many nights along the Spree River, collaborating with the team at Zalando. We'd like to thank Christoph Lange, Robert Gentz, Frauke von Polier, Maren Kroll, Katrin Mueller, Rami Sowan, Steven Bianchi, Edouard Yendell, and all the Zalandos who sat through our full-day OKRs Expert Training sessions. Thank you Willem-Jan Jansen and Grant Bryce of eBay Classified Group for connecting us to the Kijiji team in Toronto. We are indebted to John Herbold, Scott McQuigg, and the GoNoodle team for proving that it is in fact possible to launch a successful OKRs project across an entire organization in just a few weeks! We thank Devin Sherman, Brian Rhodes, Scott Rhodes, Thomas Sherrouse, and the TaxSlayer team for their southern hospitality and putting in the extra work to draft OKRs prior to our workshops in Georgia. We'd like to thank Sonia Madan for setting up our memorable OKRs workshop with Roger Fugett and the early OKR adopters at CareerBuilder along with Sabrina Pickeral and Andy Krupit for coordinating workshops in Chicago and Atlanta where CareerBuilder somehow managed to learn about OKRs and create drafts for roughly 30 teams in just a few days!

Although we cannot name every client, we do want to acknowledge some clients who often came to our minds as we developed material for this book, including Reiko Imai of ShopStyle, Jim Ricitelli, Thomas Spoonholtz, and Brian Elbogen at FirstREX, Alicia Raymond at OfferPop, Ben and Moisey Uretsky at Digital Ocean, and Roger Corn from OpenX.

In addition to these clients, we've benefited tremendously from the relationships and input from colleagues and friends. Vincent Drucker didn't simply provide us with guidance about what his father, Peter Drucker, might have had to say about OKRs, his mentoring forced us to carefully consider long-term planning at the team level in addition to the company level. In addition, Vincent reinforced our belief that OKRs should be framed positively and enabled us to expand OKR scoring by balancing the stretch concept with a commitment level. Conversations with OKRs experts around the world, especially Christina Wodtke, Felipe Castro, and Dan Montgomery, inspired us over numerous discussions regarding the theory and implementation of OKRs. Thanks to Kris Duggan and Paul Reeves at BetterWorks for giving Ben the opportunity to contribute to some of the early OKR training materials, hosting Goal Summit, and introducing us to Donald Sull. We'd like to thank other software vendors in the OKRs space, including Henrik-Jan Van der Pol, founder of Perdoo, and Chris Pieper of Alliance Enterprises, for their passion and commitment to ensuring OKRs can be connected and made visible throughout an entire organization. Other business partners and friends that have been instrumental in our thinking include Jay Forbes from MTS, Greg Foster of Vizen LLC, Sandy Richardson of Collaborative Strategy, Joe Clark of Prana Business, and Tor Inge Vasshus of Corporater. Finally, we would like to thank our parents, Bev and Jean Niven (posthumously), and Mario and Suellen Lamorte, for their love and support.

# CHAPTER ONE

# Introduction to OKRs

## THE HISTORY OF OKRs

We're fans of the BBC television show *Connections*, which premiered way back in 1978, and was later reprised in 1994 and 1997. The program demonstrated how major discoveries, scientific breakthroughs, and historical events were *"built from one another successively in an interconnected way to bring about particular aspects of modern technology."*[1] What the show made clear is that there is a long and interesting history behind virtually everything. So it is with OKRs. While we think of the model as relatively new—most of us would pin its origination to Google's adoption in the 1990s—it is actually the result of a successive number of frameworks, approaches, and philosophies whose lineage we can track back well over a hundred years. At the turn of the twentieth century, organizations were much enamored with the work of Frederick Winslow Taylor, a pioneer in the nascent field of Scientific Management. Taylor was among the first to apply scientific rigor to the field of management, demonstrating how such an approach could vastly improve both efficiency and productivity.

In another development, in the 1920s, researchers discovered what would later be termed "The Hawthorne Effect." At a factory (Hawthorne Works) outside of Chicago, investigators examined the impact of light on employee performance. The studies suggested that productivity improved when lighting increased. However, it was later determined the changes were most likely the result of increased motivation due to interest being shown to employees. While these and many other advancements were casting a light on how companies could enhance productivity through monitoring discrete activities, for the most part employees themselves were an afterthought. That all changed, however, with the work of Peter Drucker.

Considered by most people (ourselves included) to be the father of management thinking, Peter Drucker set the standard for management philosophy and the theoretical foundations of the modern business corporation. Many of his more than 30 books are considered classics in the field. It is one book, his 1954 release, *The Practice of Management*, which is of particular significance to those of us interested in OKRs. In the text, Drucker tells the story of three stonecutters who were asked what they were doing. "*I am making a living*" was the response of the first cutter. The second continued hammering as he answered, "*I am doing the best job of stonecutting in the entire country.*" Finally, the third answered confidently, "*I am building a cathedral.*"[2] The third person is clearly connected to an overall aspirational vision, while the first is focused almost exclusively on providing a fair day's work for a fair day's pay. Drucker's primary concern was with the second stonecutter, the individual focused on functional expertise, in this case being the best stonecutter in the county. Of course, exceptional workmanship is something to be esteemed and will always be important in carrying out any task, but it must be related to the overall goals of the business.

Drucker feared that in many instances, modern managers were not measuring performance by its contribution to the company, but by their own criteria of professional success. He writes, "This danger will be greatly intensified by the technological changes now underway. The number of highly educated specialists working in the business enterprise is bound to increase tremendously . . . the new technology will demand closer coordination between specialists."[3] Did we mention he wrote this in 1954! Prescient as always, Drucker recognized the surge in specialized roles that were to become the hallmark of the modern corporation, and sensed immediately the danger that change posed should these specialists be focused on individual achievement rather than the goals of the enterprise.

In response to this challenge, Drucker proposed a system termed *management by objectives*, or MBO. He introduces the framework this way:

> Each manager, from the "big boss" down to the production foreman or the chief clerk, needs clearly spelled-out objectives. These objectives should lay out what performance the man's own managerial unit is supposed to produce. They should lay out what contribution he and his unit are expected to make to help other units obtain their objectives. Finally, they should spell out what contribution the manager can expect from other units toward the attainment of his own objectives.... These objectives should always derive from the goals of the business.[4]

Readers will forgive Drucker's exclusive use of the masculine pronouns; again, he was writing this in the 1950s. He went on to suggest that objectives be keyed to both short- and long-range considerations and that they contain both tangible business goals and intangible objectives for organizational development, worker performance, attitude, and public responsibility. This last point is yet another example of Drucker's considerable foresight. It would be another four decades before the inclusion of intangible "assets" was formally included in a corporate performance management system (the *Balanced Scorecard*).

Already somewhat of a renowned management guru, Drucker's words carried significant weight in the boardrooms of corporate America and thus resonated with executives, who then raced to create MBO systems within their firms. Unfortunately, as is often the case with any type of managerial or organizational change intervention, implementations varied widely in form, often straying far afield from Drucker's original intentions for the model. Perhaps the biggest mistake committed by firms eager to gain the benefits offered by MBOs was transforming what was originally envisioned as a highly participative event into a top-down bureaucratic exercise in which senior managers shoved objectives down into the corporation with little regard of how they would be executed. Many also damaged the integrity of the model by making it a static exercise, often setting objectives on an annual basis, despite the fact that even 50 years ago businesses faced pressure to react quickly to market and environmental changes. But, rather than adopt a more frequent cadence, when it came to objective setting most companies chose the "Set it and forget it" pattern we so often see in organizations to this day.

Drucker's expectation was that organizations would use MBOs to foster cross-functional cooperation, spur individual innovation, and ensure all employees had a line of sight to overall goals. In practice, that rarely occurred and eventually MBOs became the subject of substantial criticisms. However, those with keen business acumen saw the underlying power of Drucker's words and recognized the value inherent in the process. Enter Andy Grove.

A Silicon Valley legend, Andy Grove served as CEO of Intel Corporation from 1987 to 1998 and shepherded the company through its remarkable transformation from a manufacturer of memory chips into the planet's dominant supplier of microprocessors. An astute student of business, Grove recognized the latent power in the MBO system and inserted it as a key piece of his management philosophy at Intel. However, he made a number of modifications to the model, transforming it into the framework most of us would recognize today. In Grove's thinking, a successful MBO system need answer just two fundamental questions: (1) Where do I want to go (the objective) and (2) How will I pace myself to see if I am getting there?[5] That second question, simple as it may seem, turned out to be revolutionary in launching the OKRs movement by attaching what would come to be known as a "key result" to an objective.

A guiding principle in Grove's use of objectives and key results was driving focus. As he put it:

> Here, as elsewhere, we fall victim to our inability to say "no"—in this case, to too many objectives. We must realize—and act on the realization—that if we try to focus on everything, we focus on nothing. A few extremely well-chosen objectives impart a clear message about what we say "yes" to and what we say "no" to—which is what we must have if an MBO system is to work.[6]

He didn't stop at limiting the number of objectives, however. Grove modified the Drucker model in a number of important ways.

First, he suggested setting objectives and key results more frequently, recommending quarterly or in some cases monthly. This was in recognition of the fast pace of the industry in which he found himself, but also reflected the fundamental importance of adopting fast feedback into an organization's culture. Grove also insisted that objectives and key results not be considered a "legal document" binding employees to what they proposed and basing their performance review solely on their results. He believed OKRs should be just one input used to determine an employee's effectiveness.

Another important ingredient of success at Intel was ensuring OKR creation was a mix of top-down and bottom-up involvement. As noted earlier, Drucker assumed this mechanism in his rendering of the model, but many organizations, fixed in a purely hierarchical mindset, abandoned it. Not so with Grove. He intuited the critical nature of employee involvement in fostering self-control and motivation.

Finally, Grove understood the importance of introducing the concept of stretch into OKRs. In his words:

> When the need to stretch is not spontaneous, management needs to create an environment to foster it. In an MBO system, for example, objectives should be set at a point high enough so that even if the individual (or organization) pushes himself hard, he will still only have a 50-50 chance of making them. Output will tend to be greater when everybody strives for a level of achievement beyond his immediate grasp, even though trying means failure half the time. Such goal-setting is extremely important if what you want is peak performance from yourself and your subordinates.[7]

At this point in our story, we're just one degree of separation from Google and the OKRs boom we're witnessing today. John Doerr represents that link in the chain. Now a partner at the venerable Silicon Valley venture capital firm Kleiner Perkins Caulfield and Byers, Doerr started his career at Intel and enthusiastically soaked up the many management lessons Andy Grove was only too pleased to volunteer. Among them, of course, was objectives and key results. Doerr recognized the value and potential of the model and continues to share it with entrepreneurs to this day.

Two of his early students were Larry Page and Sergey Brin, who you may know as the founders of Google. Here's how John Doerr recalls the introduction of OKRs at Google:

> Shortly after we invested, we had our board meetings around a ping pong table above the ice cream parlor on University Avenue, and Larry called an all-hands meeting because I'd shown him this OKR thing . . . I went through a slide presentation that I still have today . . . and Larry and Sergey—so smart, so aggressive, so ambitious, so interested in not just making but achieving moonshots, embraced the system and that was thirty or so people and to this day I think they're part of the culture, they're part of the DNA, at Google they're part of the language the actual words that you use. Larry embraced it for himself, for the company and he uses it as a tool to actually empower people. People think it's about accountability and it does achieve that as a byproduct. It's really a way to build a social contract in your organization that says I'm going to sign up to do this amazing stuff.[8]

From those modest beginnings at a board meeting above an ice cream parlor, the OKR model has become the performance management tool of choice throughout all of Google.

We live in a Google universe today. As an example of the behemoth's place in the business zeitgeist, if you were to type "Google" into the search bar on Amazon (books only) you'd get 17,882 results as of March 2016. If someone were to write a book sharing how often Google changes the paper towels in their restrooms it would most likely rocket to number one. Given their place in the popular culture you might assume that OKRs began their ascendance immediately upon Google's adoption of the program. However, it wasn't until 2013 and the release of a video by Google Ventures partner Rick Klau that the model and the movement really began to gain inexorable momentum.[9] The Klau video has now been viewed over 300,000 times, and while that might not seem like an extraordinarily high number when sleeping-kitten videos easily attract millions of views, it is an achievement when you consider the program runs close to an hour and a half. That's a serious commitment, but one many organizations were willing to make in order to emulate the performance paradigm at Google.

As of today, OKRs have been embraced by thousands of organizations around the world. The nexus of OKR activity is often assumed to be Silicon Valley, with high profile companies like LinkedIn, Twitter, and Zynga serving as passionate proponents of the framework, but in reality, OKRs have been embraced by organizations large and small around the globe. What we've shared represents the life of OKRs to this point. We look forward to companies like yours contributing to the next phase of their development.

##  WHAT ARE OBJECTIVES AND KEY RESULTS (OKRs)?

Here is our definition:

> OKRs is a critical thinking framework and ongoing discipline that seeks to ensure employees work together, focusing their efforts to make measurable contributions that drive the company forward.

We doubt anyone is going to put that on a t-shirt any time soon. But it's important to specifically define the model so that as you begin working with, and sharing it with your teams, you possess a shared understanding of what exactly you mean when you say "OKRs." One of the biggest problems we see when organizations launch any kind of a change program is simply terminology, or, more precisely, not being specific with their terminology.

Confusing your words can lead to the transmission of mixed signals to employees and result in less than desirable outcomes for the organization. Thus, it's imperative that you use consistent definitions for OKRs terms and concepts. We recommend that you employ what we outline in this book. However, in the end it really doesn't matter what you call the concepts—remember Shakespeare's admonition: *"What's in a name? That which we call a rose by any other name would smell as sweet."* The key is using your chosen terms with unwavering consistency throughout the organization to ensure there is true consensus on the point, and the terms and concepts are communicated clearly to all stakeholders. Everyone has to be operating from the same playbook should you expect OKRs, or any new initiative, to be understood, accepted, and able to produce results. Back to our definition, let's break it down into more reasonable bite-sized chunks:

- *Critical-thinking framework:* The end in mind with OKRs is accelerating performance, but you don't get there simply by monitoring your results each quarter. In the preceding history lesson we introduced the work of Peter Drucker. One of our favorite "Drucker-isms" is this: "The most serious mistakes are not being made as a result of wrong answers. The truly dangerous thing is asking the wrong questions."[10] When examining OKR results your challenge is to go beyond the numbers and, like a business anthropologist, dig deeper into what they're telling you so that you can unearth the stimulating questions that may lead to future breakthroughs. OKRs, when implemented with rigor and discipline, facilitate this model of critical thinking.
- *Ongoing discipline:* OKRs represent a commitment—of time and effort. Earlier, we warned against the danger of "set it and forget it" goal setting. To ensure you benefit from OKRs, you must commit to actually (as common sense as this sounds) using the model. That entails updating OKRs each quarter (or whatever cadence you choose), examining results carefully, and modifying your ongoing strategy and business model as necessary, based on results.
- *Ensure employees work together:* We've already noted the importance of cross-functional collaboration and the value of teams in creating organizational success. OKRs must be structured, and used, to maximize collaboration and alignment. One of the ways this is facilitated is through the inherent transparency of OKRs, which are shared widely so that everyone, from top to bottom, can see objectives and key results from throughout the organization.

▦ *Focusing their efforts:* OKRs are not, and should never be, considered a master checklist of tasks that need to be completed. The aim of the model is identifying the most critical business objectives and gauging accountability through quantitative key results. Strategy pundits are fond of noting that strategy is as much about what not to do as it is about what to do. So it is with OKRs. You must be disciplined in determining what makes the final cut.

▦ *Make measurable contributions:* As we'll explain shortly, key results are typically (and almost exclusively) quantitative in nature. Whenever possible, we want to avoid subjectivity and note with precision how the business is advancing based on achievement of our OKRs.

▦ *Drive the company forward:* The ultimate arbiter of success is achievement of your goals. Follow the advice on these pages and we're confident OKRs will light that path for you.

Now you can make six t-shirts! With the methodology sufficiently dissected, let's turn our attention to what comprises objectives and key results.

## OBJECTIVES

An objective is a concise statement outlining a broad qualitative goal designed to propel the organization forward in a desired direction. Basically, it asks, "What do we want to do?" A well-worded objective is time-bound (doable in a quarter) and should inspire and capture the shared imagination of your team.

As an example, we're creating a series of collateral materials for this book, and one of our objectives this quarter is: "Design a compelling website that attracts people to OKRs." The objective is concise (just nine words), qualitative (no numbers here—that's the province of the key result), time-bound (we're confident we can create a design this quarter), and inspirational (it's exciting to engage our creativity in producing a site that people will find both helpful and aesthetically appealing).

## KEY RESULTS

A key result is a quantitative statement that measures the achievement of a given objective. If the objective asks, "What do we want to do?" the key result asks, "How will we know if we've met our objective?" In our previous definition, some may quibble with the use of the word *quantitative*, arguing that if a key result measures achievement, then by its very nature it's quantitative. Point taken, but we want to err on the side of too much information here to ensure that you recognize the vital importance of stating your key results as numbers.

The challenge, and ultimately value, of key results is in forcing you to quantify what may appear to be vague or nebulous words in your objective. Using our example objective of "*Design a compelling website that attracts people to OKRs,*" we're now committed to designating what we mean by "compelling" and "attracts." As you'll discover with your own key results, there are no given translations of words like *compelling* and *attracts* into numbers; you must determine what the words mean specifically to you in your unique business context. Here are our key results (most objectives will have between two and five key results—more on that later in the book).

- 20 percent of visitors return to the site in one week.
- 10 percent of visitors inquire about our training and consulting services.

The high-wire act you must balance with key results is making them difficult enough to force a good deal of intellectual sweat to achieve, but not so challenging as to demoralize your team because they appear impossible. In Exhibits 1.1, 1.2, and 1.3 you'll find more examples of objectives and key results for corporate, team, and individual levels.

That's all we're going to say about the mechanics of OKRs for now. Which may leave you thinking, "*Hmm, this seems pretty easy; do I really need to read the rest of this book?*" The answer is yes, of course you do.

Many seemingly simple frameworks are actually "deceptively" simple. The basic principles can be grasped quickly, and thus there is a temptation to eschew further study in favor of diving in and working with the model. However, you do so at your significant peril. There are many subtleties and "finer points" to the OKR approach that must be mastered should you hope to garner the benefits promised by the system. For example, a short list of considerations (we'll cover all these topics and more in the pages ahead) includes: Where to build your OKRs (corporate level or business unit), who will sponsor the implementation, choosing from the types of key results available, aligning OKRs with your strategy and vision, aligning cross-functional teams, reporting results to ensure rapid feedback and learning, and many more. So, please do strap yourself in and join us for the rest of this ride. We promise to make it as smooth a trip as we can.

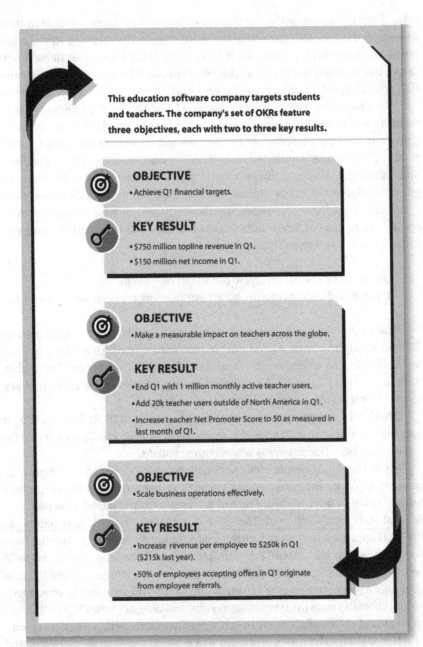

This education software company targets students and teachers. The company's set of OKRs feature three objectives, each with two to three key results.

**OBJECTIVE**
- Achieve Q1 financial targets.

**KEY RESULT**
- $750 million topline revenue in Q1.
- $150 million net income in Q1.

**OBJECTIVE**
- Make a measurable impact on teachers across the globe.

**KEY RESULT**
- End Q1 with 1 million monthly active teacher users.
- Add 20k teacher users outside of North America in Q1.
- Increase teacher Net Promoter Score to 50 as measured in last month of Q1.

**OBJECTIVE**
- Scale business operations effectively.

**KEY RESULT**
- Increase revenue per employee to $250k in Q1 ($215k last year).
- 50% of employees accepting offers in Q1 originate from employee referrals.

**EXHIBIT 1.1**    Examples of Company-Level OKRs

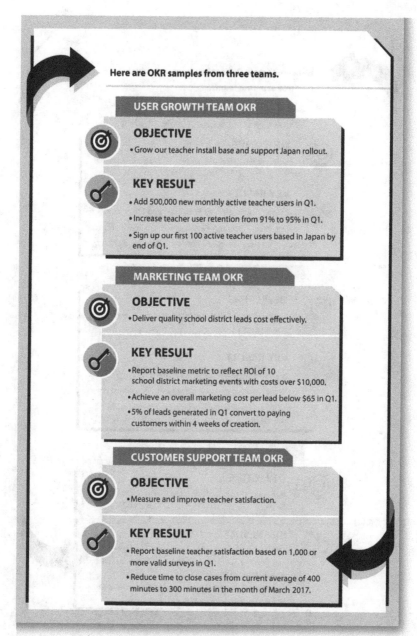

Here are OKR samples from three teams.

**USER GROWTH TEAM OKR**

**OBJECTIVE**
- Grow our teacher install base and support Japan rollout.

**KEY RESULT**
- Add 500,000 new monthly active teacher users in Q1.
- Increase teacher user retention from 91% to 95% in Q1.
- Sign up our first 100 active teacher users based in Japan by end of Q1.

**MARKETING TEAM OKR**

**OBJECTIVE**
- Deliver quality school district leads cost effectively.

**KEY RESULT**
- Report baseline metric to reflect ROI of 10 school district marketing events with costs over $10,000.
- Achieve an overall marketing cost per lead below $65 in Q1.
- 5% of leads generated in Q1 convert to paying customers within 4 weeks of creation.

**CUSTOMER SUPPORT TEAM OKR**

**OBJECTIVE**
- Measure and improve teacher satisfaction.

**KEY RESULT**
- Report baseline teacher satisfaction based on 1,000 or more valid surveys in Q1.
- Reduce time to close cases from current average of 400 minutes to 300 minutes in the month of March 2017.

**EXHIBIT 1.2** Examples of Team-Level OKRs

**Here are sample OKRs taken from individuals on three separate teams.**

### NEW SALES REPRESENTATIVE OKR

**OBJECTIVE**
- Build initial pipeline and ramp up on sales process.

**KEY RESULT**
- Deliver 5 demos without pre-sales support to prospects.
- Document outcomes of initial sales calls with 25 prospects.
- Add $500,000 to pipeline with potential to close in 2017.

### MARKETING ANALYST OKR

**OBJECTIVE**
- Improve inbound lead generation from the blog and landing pages.

**KEY RESULT**
- 10 new inbound leads originating from new blogs posted.
- 5 new landing pages with 8% or greater conversion rate.
- 10 existing landing pages with at least 2% improved conversion based on A/B testing.

### PRODUCT DESIGNER OKR

**OBJECTIVE**
- Make our core product user interface easier for teachers to use.

**KEY RESULT**
- Obtain a baseline to report and monitor the trend in number of requests from teacher users for features that already exist in the system.
- Improve teacher satisfaction rating on product usability to 9.0 (up from 8.5 last year).

**EXHIBIT 1.3**  Examples of Individual-Level OKRs

## ORGANIZATIONAL CHALLENGES, AND WHY YOU NEED OKRs

In the process of writing this book, we conducted an extensive amount of research, which translates primarily into an abundance of reading—books, white papers, articles, blog posts, and so on. They all differ based on their unique subject matter, but the one common denominator amongst virtually all of them can be found within the opening sentence or two. Invariably, the case is made that we live in the most volatile of times. The very foundations of our corporate thinking are challenged, forcing us to swiftly extend the frontiers of knowledge to stay one short step ahead of the change monster bearing down upon us. With this book, we wanted to do something a little different by allowing you to breathe a little deeper as we begin our journey together, because in some ways economic life, at least in the developed world, is actually less turbulent than it's ever been. In the United States, for example, the volatility of gross domestic product (GDP) growth decreased from 3 percent in the period of 1946 to 1968 to just 1.2 percent from 1985 to 2006. Both inflation and corporate profit growth also saw similar reductions in volatility during the period.[11] Today's technological wonders can make our heads spin, but they're really no more destabilizing than the advent of railroads, telephones, automobiles, mass production, or radio were in their day.

So we can all exhale just a bit: It still takes the planet 24 hours to complete one full rotation. But, here's the bad news, or more appropriately the reality—and the opportunity, should you choose to seize it—the pace of change both within companies and in entire industries *is* accelerating at a rapid, dare we say unprecedented, pace. As just one example of many, consider adoption rates on smartphones. In June 2007, the first touchscreen operated iPhones were offered for sale, followed shortly thereafter by Android-powered phones. As a category smartphones rocketed from 10 percent market penetration to 40 percent, faster than any other consumer technology in history.[12] And thank goodness for smartphones, huh? What else would we do every 4.3 minutes if we couldn't look at our phones? That's right, we—and by that, we mean the collective we: Paul, Ben, you, and everyone else on the planet—check our phones an average of two-hundred and twenty-one times a day.

Let's start by looking at a number of key challenges all modern organizations face. Some of the topics may be familiar to you, whereas others represent the very latest research and organizational thinking. While each of these is significant in its own right, we're confident an objectives and key results (OKRs) implementation will put you in good stead in overcoming all potential obstacles, paving the way for you to thrive despite the roadblocks our ever-changing global business market puts in front of you.

## Executing Strategy

In a recent survey, more than 400 global leaders identified exceptional execution as the number one challenge facing business leaders in Asia, Europe, and the United States. Execution topped a list of some 80 items, including innovation, geopolitical instability, and top-line growth (which we'll discuss later in this section).[13] As noted above, this was a recent survey, but the findings aren't surprising or novel, as execution has been front and center on the radar screens of executives for years, primarily as a result of frustratingly low execution percentages around the globe. Estimates vary, but most peg the rate of successful execution at a best case of 25 to 35 percent, while less optimistic pundits propose a stunningly low 10 percent.

Organizations spend thousands of hours meticulously crafting strategic plans they feel will vault them past their competition, and the rewards of turning strategy into action are certainly enviable indeed. One study suggested a 35 percent improvement in the quality of strategy implementation for the average firm was associated with a 30 percent improvement in shareholder value.[14] Given the substantial treasure at the end of the execution rainbow, it's not surprising that firms would focus their attention on it, and feel the costly sting of frustration when execution eludes most of them.

Why is execution so difficult to attain in practice? Researchers and authors Sull, Homkes, and Sull offer five myths of execution that shed significant light on the subject:

■ *Myth One: Execution equals alignment:* A practically unassailable truth in business ideology is the value of generating alignment: more colloquially, having everyone row in the same direction. The idea of creating alignment through shared objectives has been advocated by revered thinkers (see, for example, the work of Peter Drucker mentioned earlier) and corporate titans alike for decades. Alignment in itself is undoubtedly a worthy goal; however, the problem often lies in how organizations go about creating it. For many firms the process, while well intentioned, quickly devolves into a top-down exercise in which senior executives offer a number of seemingly critical objectives and force them into the organization with little regard for how they will be translated at lower levels. Execution suffers in these cases because individual business units and departments create objectives that align with the high level objectives from above, but neglect to consider other groups within the firm. Most work today is cross-functional in nature (as we'll discuss later in this section), and forced cascading often obscures this fact by creating silos that act solely in their own best interests.

▪ *Myth Two: Execution means sticking to the plan:* Perhaps the former heavy-weight boxing champion of the world, Mike Tyson, said it best when he offered this nugget regarding his opponents' strategy when facing him: *"Everyone has a plan until they get punched in the mouth."*[15] The punch line (pun intended): Strategic plans don't always survive contact with the real world that is your business. Part of the typical strategic planning process at most firms involves the creation of a portfolio of strategic initiatives aimed at ensuring the strategy's success. These initiatives entail the allocation of human and financial resources and once set in place, firms are often loath to alter them in any way. In order to execute strategy, companies must be agile in their approach: constantly sensing changes in the environment and making sometimes subtle and other times large-scale modifications to their strategy as a result. This also means having the flexibility of shift-ing both personnel and financial resources to take advantage of emerging opportunities. Those with a fixed mindset, unwilling to alter plans seem-ingly set in stone, will pay a heavy execution penalty.

▪ *Myth Three: Communication equals understanding:* Given today's access to simple and cost-effective modes of electronic communication, even the smallest of companies can lavish significant communication on their employees. And they do! Not only via electronic means, in fact senior leaders in most organizations spend substantial face time communicating strategic directives. Sadly, the message rarely sinks in. In one survey of managers from 250 companies around the globe, only half could name even their company's most important objective.[16] While that may seem a demoralizingly low number, other studies have suggested even poorer recognition of company priorities. One survey found that only one in seven people, a scant 15 percent, could name one of their company's most important goals.[17] Although many possible explanations for this lack of comprehension exist, one we witness frequently is the proclivity of organizations to bury their employees in jargon. It's not uncommon for a company to have core values, strategic priorities, mission statements, vision statements, codes of conduct, core competencies, and a dozen other potential candidates for a fun game of buzzword bingo. Employees are understandably confused, don't know what matters and truly warrants their focus, and thus pay little attention to *any* of it!

▪ *Myth Four: A performance culture drives execution:* If asked to describe competition in their industries today, most executives would likely reach for adjectives such as: fierce, intense, and brutal. The margin for error is slim, and thus a relentless drive toward a performance culture would seem to make great sense when attempting to distinguish yourself from rivals. In some cases, however, performance is so prized a virtue that failure in any form is completely anathema and avoided at any and all costs. "Mistakes" and missteps are hidden from view, the blame game is played with great zeal, and the organization quickly falls behind. As with most things, balance must be adhered to when it comes to shaping a culture. While performance is important, organizations would do well to also value agility, teamwork, collaboration, and calculated risk-taking. Driving execution is dependent on frank discussions of so-called failures, which in reality are really data points to be studied, learned from, and improved upon in the future.

▪ *Myth Five: Execution should be driven from the top:* We're all aware of the visionary CEO who, through sheer force of will and utter brilliance, can guide a company through even the most perilous of corporate journeys. But they are few and far between, and probably more myth than reality. In practice, vesting exclusive execution power in the hands of the CEO will most likely result in poorer performance, manifested by slow decision making—thus possibly missing key opportunities as they arise—and the escalation of often petty conflicts that waste scarce executive time. The responsibility for execution must be distributed throughout the enterprise, which, of course, requires that you properly negotiate the hurdles present in the previous four myths.

## Organizing to Meet New Realities

It's no secret that the demographics of the global workforce are changing dramatically, becoming simultaneously younger and older, as well as more diverse. Millennials, those born between the early 1980s and early 2000s, now account for half of the workforce, and that percentage is increasing rapidly. Their career desires have been well-documented: an environment that promises constant learning, a work experience that offers meaning and purpose, and a dynamic and rewarding career path. At the other end of the age spectrum are the baby boomer generation, an enormous cohort whose numbers are decreasing, but who still retain immense organizational knowledge and capabilities. Many baby boomers are now working into their 70s and even 80s, while facing the challenges of new roles as mentors, coaches, and subordinates of younger colleagues. Finally, given the globalization of modern business, our workforces exhibit more gender and cultural diversity.

Given these and myriad other forces conspiring to challenge leaders, many organizations are altering their structures from the traditional, hierarchical, and functional models to flexible and interconnected teams. In Deloitte's *2016 Human Capital Report*, 92 percent of respondents rated organizational design as a top priority, while nearly half (45 percent) state their companies are either in the middle of a restructuring or planning one.[18]

To visualize the change in design taking place, it may be helpful to think of your favorite movie. Virtually all films are created by individuals and small teams of experts (writers, producers, set designers, cinematographers, costume designers, etc.) that band together during the production and then move on to new assignments once the film is complete. We're witnessing something very similar in corporations: Networks of teams are formed to tackle specific business problems, and once the challenge has been successively resolved, the team disbands and its members are reassigned to other squads. The challenges these teams take on are directly aligned with the overall objectives of the firm, thus ensuring a link to execution. We feel that OKRs are very well suited to this growing trend in organizational thinking, and will discuss our rationale in the benefits section.

## The Challenge of Sustaining Growth

"Grow or Die" is a much-repeated mantra throughout corporate conference rooms here in the United States, and around the world. Ask executives to name their top priorities and, in addition to execution as we chronicled above, you're sure to hear the word *growth* spring enthusiastically from their lips. In fact, estimates suggest that over 90 percent of strategic plans aspire to growing revenue. The idea of growth is very enticing, not only because in many cases corporate survival depends on it but also because most executives are extremely sanguine when it comes to the growth prospects facing their firms. In one survey of 377 executives, respondents saw opportunities everywhere: 50 percent cited "tremendous opportunity" in the North American market, 65 percent in Europe, and more than 85 percent in Asia.[19]

It's great to be optimistic, but often painful when reality rears its pragmatic head (think of that punch from Mike Tyson). Despite the opportunities for growth that executives around the globe wish to seize upon, very few firms are able to sustain profitable growth in the long (or even medium) term. In the decade ending in 2010, just 9 percent of companies in one study achieved even a modest rate of growth (5.5 percent) while also earning their cost of capital. Another study of this important topic obtained very consistent results: Only 8 percent of nearly 5,000 companies in the sample grew their revenues by at least 5 percent year after year.[20]

What causes so many organizations to stumble, or perhaps more fittingly, collapse, along the road to growth? Interestingly, as already noted, it's not a lack of opportunity that forestalls the potential of growth. Actually, when asked, more than 75 percent of executives will cite factors relating to organizational effectiveness, such as: excess complexity (recall our discussion in the execution section regarding the overwhelming number of concepts employees are subjected to and expected to comprehend), risk-averse cultures (possibly due to an overwhelming focus on performance as we documented), and difficulty achieving sufficient focus. OKRs can assist you in overcoming each of these difficulties.

## The Threat of Disruption

Interested in starting a new company? Here's a sobering statistic that just may dampen your enthusiasm: Recent research suggests that the expected life of a new American company is on the order of six years.[21] That doesn't give you much time to make an impact. And even if you are fortunate enough to beat the odds of survival, just keeping your head above water may be challenging because you'll most likely be under the constant threat of disruption.

When most of us think of disruption, innovative firms like Uber or Airbnb come quickly to mind. However, strictly speaking, Uber, for example, is not a disruptive innovation. Disruption describes a process whereby a smaller player with fewer resources is able to successfully challenge established incumbent businesses. They do so by targeting overlooked segments, offering more suitable functionality (frequently at a lower price). Incumbents typically ignore this move, and eventually new entrants move upmarket delivering the performance customers require, while preserving the advantages (chiefly lower cost) that drove their early success.[22] Technically, Uber did neither of these, but that certainly hasn't stopped it from forever altering the taxi industry.

Rather than disruption, we could term the changes Uber and others are employing as "business model innovations," but regardless of the terminology employed the fact remains, there are hungry (nay, starving) companies that you've never heard of, who are at this very moment plotting to steal your market share. No industry is immune to this assault. Take shipping companies. They face a very unanticipated threat: 3D printing. As more manufacturers have the option to print parts and products in finished form onsite, shipments by air, sea, and roadway will plummet. It is estimated that as much as 41 percent of the air cargo business, 37 percent of ocean container shipments, and 25 percent of truck deliveries are vulnerable to 3D printing.[23] Given the undeniable threat, it's vital that organizations embrace agility and possess the ability to swiftly modify their business model based on new information. Once again, we believe OKRs will prove beneficial in this task.

## Employee Engagement

The business press is replete with stories relating the "war for talent" among corporations striving to stock their ranks with the best, brightest, and most highly engaged employees. It's a simple fact that no organization can succeed without skilled and motivated teams working in alignment with overall objectives. Of all the adjectives appearing in the last two sentences the one that has the greatest hold on executive attention is engagement. To put it bluntly, we're currently facing an engagement crisis.

Before we present the litany of statistics to bolster this point, let's define the term, because there is much confusion about what engagement is and is not. First, what it's not. Engagement does not represent employee happiness and it's much bigger than employee satisfaction. Kevin Kruse, author of *Engagement 2.0*, defines engagement as the emotional commitment an employee has to the organization and its goals.[24] This emotional commitment means engaged employees actually care about their work and the company. They don't work just for a salary, or for a promotion to the next rung on the ladder, but work passionately on behalf of the organization's goals. When employees care—when they are truly engaged—they use discretionary effort.

Here's a simple, but telling, example we observed at a client organization. We were scheduled to meet with the CEO of a small fast-food chain in Southern California. The meeting location was one of its restaurants, and we arrived quite early. None of the employees knew who we were, so there was certainly no incentive for them to try and impress us in any way. At one point, we noticed an employee rushing across the floor towards the door. Our first thought was that someone had attempted to leave without paying, but in fact we were wrong. As he approached the door the employee bent over and picked up a discarded napkin. He placed it in the trash and went back behind the counter to assist the next customer. You could say he was simply doing his job, but again, no one was watching. He could have easily left the trash on the floor, but he took the discretionary step of leaving his station to keep the restaurant clean.

Unfortunately, the engagement numbers in the United States and around the world are dismally low—Gallup reports only 13 percent of the global workforce is highly engaged. In the United States, the number is about 30 percent. And this produces a real penalty—by some estimates, low engagement costs $17,000 per employee per year in lost productivity, absenteeism, and so on. Seventeen thousand doesn't sound that big, so let's amplify it by extrapolating that to the entire U.S. workforce. We're then looking at approximately $450 billion to $550 billion in lost productivity each year. But we believe there may be an even bigger cost—the inability to contribute effectively to strategy execution. Disengaged employees are not willing to expend the discretionary effort necessary to sense new opportunities, take calculated risks, or propose business model innovations that may keep their firms ahead of rivals.

The good news is that organizations recognize what is at stake in this battle, and have significantly expanded efforts to enhance engagement. Annual employee satisfaction and engagement surveys are being phased out, replaced by employee listening tools such as pulse surveys, anonymous social tools, and perhaps most importantly regular check-ins with, and feedback from, managers.[25]

We've laid out some considerable challenges on the previous pages. Fortunately, as we've alluded to, OKRs can assist in overcoming these hurdles, and launch you on a trajectory of sustained success. Let's look at some of the many benefits of the OKRs approach.

##  BENEFITS OF OKRs

The very act of instituting and utilizing a formal measurement and monitoring practice is beneficial, as evidenced by a recent study of 30,000 U.S. businesses conducted by the U.S. Census Bureau's Center for Economic Studies. According to the authors, companies that had structured management practices focused on performance monitoring and targets had significantly better financial results than those that didn't use such measures.[26] So simply putting an OKRs program in place is upping your odds of fiscal success. The rewards to your bottom line will justifiably please you, the board, and your bean counters, but outlined next are a number of additional, also critical, benefits you can expect from a well-constructed OKRs implementation.

## OKRs Are Easy to Understand—Increasing Buy-in and Use

Here in California, where we live, there is a very popular burger restaurant called In-N-Out. If you've ever had the pleasure of savoring their offerings, which are absolutely a cut above most fast food, your mouth is probably watering as you read this. One of the many reasons In-N-Out has captured such a frenzied base of raving fans is the simplicity of the menu, which consists of burgers, fries, shakes, and beverages. That's it. Not like many restaurants, whose menu boards are so crammed with items you need 20/15 vision just to read them.

Consider OKRs the "In-N-Out of managing your performance." One of the biggest benefits the framework features is its sheer simplicity, and that begins with the taxonomy. Basically just three words: objectives and key results. Other approaches to managing performance and executing strategy are awash in jargon, which has the potential to confuse employees already under siege from missions, visions, core values, and KPIs, as we noted when discussing execution myth three (Communication equals understanding).

We've worked with clients who, after just a short introductory training session, are immediately using the terms correctly and creating meaningful objectives and key results. Again, as noted in the previous section, there is much more to the model, and we'll cover it all in depth, but in order to have your team buy into and support any program a critical first step is mastery of the vocabulary. OKRs make that easy. Here's how Rick Klau of Google Ventures describes it:

> When OKRs are working well in your company, it's as if everyone has acquired fluency in a new language. Every employee is familiar with a common vocabulary, and understands how this vocabulary describes what's most important to the company (and what's not). After just a couple of quarters relying on OKRs to set and manage goals, people inside a company develop three distinct superpowers: the ability to predict the future, the ability for the company's founders or CEO to be a part of every important discussion, even (especially) when they're not there, and the ability to say no.[27]

## A Shorter Cadence Fosters Agility and Change-Readiness

While there is room for customization with every implementation, most OKRs practitioners will set goals quarterly. This frequent establishment of priorities is vital. As the pace of change within, and outside, businesses accelerates, it's essential that new information be captured, analyzed, and transformed into knowledge that can be used to innovate and potentially alter the strategy or business plan. Doing so is immensely difficult if you're setting just annual goals—There is such a lag between the inciting incident that may have the potential to rock your business to the core, and your reaction to that event, that you're left completely flat footed and unprepared.

Frequent goal setting also establishes a discipline within the organization that may be lacking. Learning, and making proactive decisions, is incumbent upon regular, focused reviews of what is taking place in your company and its surrounding environmental milieu. By updating your OKRs each quarter, you're building an organizational muscle that will become stronger with use, allowing you to be ready for the inevitable forces of change and disruption.

Finally, recent evidence suggests that more frequent goal setting has a positive impact on financial results. Deloitte reports that companies that set quarterly goals were nearly four times more likely to be in the top quartile of performers.[28]

## OKRs Demand Focus on What Matters Most

Perhaps the scarcest resource in any company is employee mindshare. Think of the intense competition vying for a chunk of that real estate in today's 24/7 world: company goals, unit goals, individual achievement goals, the meeting you're late and unprepared for, industry trends, career concerns, family issues, social media, the score from last night's game, and so on. No doubt we live in a world of excess access, to everything. But one thing that must rise above the cacophony of competing voices is knowledge and understanding of what's most important for the company (and each employee's contribution to that) right now. OKRs demand that you isolate just the most fundamental priorities and dedicate your focus to that limited subset of potential variables involved in running any company.

When Dick Costolo, former CEO of Twitter, was asked what he learned from Google that he applied to Twitter he answered: "The thing I saw at Google that I definitely have applied at Twitter are OKRs—objectives and key results. Those are a great way to help everyone in the company understand what's important and how you're going to measure what's important. It's essentially a great way to communicate strategy and how you're going to measure strategy."[29]

As an executive or manager, you're faced with a constant barrage of choices that can be summed up in two words: yes or no? Do we build a new factory offshore? Do we hire that star engineer with the bad reputation? Do we green-light the new marketing campaign? There is a ceaseless procession of questions that must be answered in the affirmative or negative. By putting a spotlight on your absolute priorities, you're winning on two fronts: identifying what matters most, and by default, providing yourself with the appropriate ammunition to say no to the many initiatives that, while tempting, are not in line with your goals.

## Transparency Promotes Cross-Functional Alignment

Earlier in the chapter we discussed how organizations are redesigning the way work gets done by vesting small teams with the authority and challenge of overcoming specific problems, and then disbanding once the task has been completed. Regardless of the business problem a team is trying to solve, it's a virtual guarantee that a potential solution does not reside with just one team, but does in fact depend on the cooperation of another group (or groups) within the firm. Therefore, in our networked world it's imperative that teams have visibility into other teams' performance goals. OKRs encourage this transparency throughout the organization.

An effective OKR program works on several levels: There are corporate-level objectives and key results in place. Departments or business units (your structure or nomenclature may differ) have OKRs, and individuals may have OKRs. The composition of OKRs at each level is not confined to their provincial interests. On the contrary, a well-developed set of OKRs should include objectives and key results that foster (and demonstrate) collaboration with other teams on whom you rely, or conversely, rely on you to drive results. OKRs should ideally be transparent throughout the organization, meaning everyone is able to see what others are measuring and provide feedback and input. This transparency fuels collaboration, alignment, and ultimately, the execution of strategy.

## OKRs Facilitate Focused Conversation and Drive Engagement

There is an oft-quoted career adage that says people don't leave companies, they leave managers. This has been accepted human resources wisdom for quite some time, and companies have, naturally, attempted to remedy the situation by crafting leadership development programs, offering sensitivity training, and engaging in 360-degree feedback. These and other interventions have been designed to improve the employee-manager relationship and mitigate the risk of talent heading out the door. There's just one problem. The old adage isn't true, at least not according to a survey of over 7,000 LinkedIn members across five countries.

According to the respondents, the primary reason for playing the free agent card is lack of advancement opportunities. Three times as many people cited that rationale over a poor relationship with their supervisor as cause for leaving.[30] The good news for OKRs users is that whether people are tempted to start circulating resumes because of a sour relationship with a supervisor or because they see no upward mobility in the company, using OKRs can reduce the likelihood of either.

OKRs are not a top-down exercise with goals handed down, as if on stone tablets, to lower-level units and departments who are expected to dutifully execute, regardless of their opinion. In fact, an important distinction of this model is its focus on inclusivity. It is expected that individuals will have a legitimate say in the objectives and key results chosen, reflecting a mix of top-down and bottom-up goal setting. Having the opportunity to meaningfully contribute to what you will be held accountable for goes a long way in enhancing engagement. And later, when results are tabulated, the chance to engage in a meaningful discussion, conducted in a spirit of inquiry, also boosts morale and demonstrates to superiors an employee's readiness for the next level on the corporate ladder. This phenomenon has been demonstrated at Sears Holding, where OKRs have been in place since 2014. Employees who use OKRs are three and a half times more likely to be promoted.[31]

## OKRs Promote Visionary Thinking

Carol Dweck is a Stanford professor known for her work on motivation, and more specifically, mindset. She posits that people can be divided into two camps. Some individuals believe their success is a result of innate ability, and are said to have a "fixed" mindset. Others feel success is a result of hard work, tenacity, and determination. They are said to possess a "growth" mindset. Fixed mindset individuals fear failure because they feel it's an assault on their basic abilities, while those with a growth mindset embrace failure, recognizing it as a simple data point, and an opportunity for learning and improvement.

In our experience working with clients around the globe, and being somewhat liberal in our use of the concept, organizations may be similarly classified using this distinction. Those who "suffer" from a fixed mindset will often forgo opportunities that involve risk, motivated primarily by a fear of failure. Whereas, other organizations, embodying the growth paradigm, relish failure, embracing a spirit of fail fast and learn quickly. We believe that in order

Summary of benefits you can expect from a
well-constructed OKRs implementation

**COMMUNICATION**
Easy to understand system increases buy-in and use.

**AGILITY**
Frequent cycles foster agility and change-readiness.

**FOCUS**
OKRs ensure everyone is clear about what matters most.

**TRANSPARENCY**
Making measurable goals visible promotes cross-functional
alignment.

**ENGAGEMENT**
Most OKRs originate bottom-up so teams and individuals
own their goals.

**VISIONARY THINKING**
OKRs stretch our thinking about what's possible.

**EXHIBIT 1.4**  Why OKRs?

to compete in today's global economy it is incumbent upon all companies to adopt a growth mindset, and doing so means stepping out of any predefined comfort zone and creating audacious goals. Any OKRs that simply mimic the status quo are not only going to be ineffective, but will likely alienate talented employees looking for meaning and purpose in their work. Objectives and key results are meant to stretch the organization, challenging your teams to fundamentally rethink the way work gets done. The benefits of OKRs are summarized in Exhibit 1.4.

## NOTES

1. *Connections* (TV Series). *Wikipedia: The Free Encyclopedia.* Accessed March 7, 2016.
2. Peter Drucker, *The Practice of Management* (New York: HarperBusiness re-issue edition, 2010).
3. Ibid.
4. Ibid.
5. Andrew S. Grove, *High Output Management* (New York: Random House, 1983).
6. Ibid.
7. Ibid.
8. https://www.youtube.com/watch?v=MF_shcs5tsQ. Accessed January 25, 2016.
9. You can watch the video at: https://www.youtube.com/watch?v=mJB83EZtAjc.
10. Quoted in Robert Simons, "Stress Test Your Strategy," *Harvard Business Review* (November 2010).
11. Matthew Stewart, *The Management Myth: Why the Experts Keep Getting it Wrong* (New York: W.W. Norton & Company, 2009).
12. Jacob Weisberg, "We Are Hopelessly Hooked," *New York Review of Books* (February 25, 2016).
13. Donald Sull, Rebecca Homkes, and Charles Sull, "Why Strategy Execution Unravels—And What to Do about It," *Harvard Business Review* (March 2015): 58–66.
14. Brian E. Becker, Mark A. Huselid, and Dave Ulrich, *The HR Scorecard* (Boston: Harvard Business School Press, 2001).
15. www.brainyquote.com/quotes/quotes/m/miketyson382439.html.
16. Donald Sull and Kathleen M. Eisenhardt, *Simple Rules* (New York: Houghton Mifflin Harcourt, 2015).
17. Chris McChesney, Sean Covey, and Jim Huling, *The 4 Disciplines of Execution: Achieving Your Wildly Important Goals* (New York: Free Press, 2012).

18. *Global Human Capital Trends 2016* (Westlake, TX: Deloitte University Press, 2016).

19. Chris Zook and James Allen, *Repeatability: Build Enduring Businesses for a World of Constant Change* (Boston: Harvard Business School Press, 2012).

20. Rita Gunther McGrath, "How the Growth Outliers Do It," *Harvard Business Review* (January–February, 2012): 110–116.

21. Christopher G. Worley, Thomas Williams, and Edward E. Lawler III, *The Agility Factor: Building Adaptable Organizations for Superior Performance* (New York: Jossey-Bass, 2014).

22. Clayton M. Christensen, Michael Raynor, and Rory MacDonald, "What Is Disruptive Innovation?" *Harvard Business Review* (December 2015): 44–53.

23. Seven Surprising Disruptions, www.strategy-business.com/7-Surprising-Disruptions.

24. Kevin Kruse, *Engagement 2.0: How to Motivate Your Team for High Performance* (Create Space Independent Publishing, 2012).

25. *Global Human Capital Trends 2016* (Westlake, TX: Deloitte University Press, 2016).

26. J.C. Spender and Bruce A. Strong, *Strategic Conversations: Creating and Directing the Entrepreneurial Workforce* (Cambridge, UK: Cambridge University Press, 2014).

27. Rick Klau, "Superpowers at Work: OKRs," *Re: Work* (December 21, 2015).

28. Stacia S. Garr, "High-Impact Performance Management," Bersin by Deloitte, (December 2014).

29. "Bring OKRs to Your Organization," Re: Work, https://rework.withgoogle.com/guides/set-goals-with-okrs/steps/bring-OKRs-to-your-organization/. Accessed January 5, 2016.

30. Jena McGregor, "Why People Really Leave Their Jobs," *The Washington Post*, March 18, 2014, online edition.

31. From internal Sears presentation shared with the authors.

2

# Preparing for Your OKRs Journey

 **WHY ARE YOU IMPLEMENTING OKRs?**

In the previous chapter, we used the phrase *excess access*. Bestselling author and researcher Marcus Buckingham coined the term to describe our current state of affairs in which we have access to literally everything, all the time.[1] At home, at work, and at play, we're constantly bombarded by waves of information: news, entertainment, marketing messages—the litany of stimuli is unending. When time and attention are among our scarcest resources, one of the great challenges of early twenty-first century life is determining how to sort through the barrage, in an attempt to separate the signal from the noise.

Therefore, the first question you must answer when embarking on an OKRs implementation is simply, "Why are we going to use OKRs, and why now?" If you're unable to answer that to the satisfaction of your team, it's unlikely they'll push aside mountains of current priorities and devote the necessary commitment to make OKRs (or any type of change) successful. This is not surprising when you consider the surfeit of programs in place at most businesses of even modest scale. We recently worked with a subsidiary of an international corporation and on the first day of our work it was clear there was confusion regarding where OKRs would fit in with their already crowded performance management process. When we asked what other frameworks were in place they noted goals programs, individual performance plans, leadership development, and balanced scorecards. Employees around the room wondered aloud whether OKRs would simply add a layer of complexity rather than distinguishing itself by creating real value. This story leads to an important task for you: Before starting with OKRs, create an inventory of what systems you're currently using to manage performance and critically examine where OKRs fit in. Ideally, you want one system only—one version of the truth. Any more and you're simply adding complexity and confusion.

Here are a few possible answers to the "Why OKRs" question that you should definitely *not* communicate at your town hall meeting announcing the implementation: "We're going from good to great!" "We want to be on the cutting edge of performance." "Because Google did it." The first two explanations are nothing but empty platitudes that will most likely mean very little to employees, and probably not even resonate with the person or team who crafted them. The words are nebulous and open to interpretation, whereas what you desire when sharing why you're implementing OKRs is a specific rationale. The last option, "Because Google did it," is perhaps the most pernicious. There is a very good chance that you are considering the adoption of OKRs as a result of what you've heard or read about Google, LinkedIn, Zynga, or other high-profile users. However, you're not Google or any of those other companies. It's perfectly reasonable to hope to gain some of the benefits those organizations garnered from the approach, but it's still vital that you specify your unique motivation.

OKRs should solve a specific business issue you face. One distinct possibility is using the program, at least in part, to drive awareness of overall company goals and strategy. We've already lamented the fact that most employees can't list their company's most important objective. Here's another illustration of that fact. In a study, researchers found that 15 percent of employees could not identify even one of the top three goals identified by their leaders as key to success. The remaining 85 percent named what they felt was the primary goal, but it frequently bore little resemblance to what their executives had presented. The study went on to suggest that the further you are from the top of the organization, the lower the clarity and awareness of corporate aspirations.[2] Perhaps not surprisingly, given the low level of goal awareness, even those who did espouse recognition of the primary corporate goal reported low levels of commitment relating to its achievement. About half of respondents said they were passionate about the goal, meaning almost half of all employees were simply going about their daily work with little drive or engagement. OKRs, as we demonstrated in

Chapter 1, propel focus on what truly matters and are thus an outstanding aid in overcoming the lack of goal awareness.

In the end, however, only you can determine exactly why OKRs are the right answer for your organization at this time. We urge you to take the time to carefully consider this question and develop a response that will resonate with your entire team from the C-suite to the shop floor. We would further suggest you wrap your rationale in a larger narrative of where you currently reside in your corporate orbit. Are you a scrappy newcomer hoping to gain market share? Or are you perhaps an incumbent, vulnerable to business model innovations on the part of competitors? Vividly outline the challenges you face, your strategy for meeting them, and how OKRs will be used as your guide throughout. Growth and change should be viewed as an imperative, not an option.

##  EXECUTIVE SPONSORSHIP: A CRITICAL COMPONENT OF YOUR OKRs IMPLEMENTATION

We both speak at industry conferences, and in addition to sharing our knowledge of OKRs and strategy with the audience we also enjoy listening to the other presenters and learning from their unique experiences. Of particular interest are individual companies telling their stories, outlining their implementation and lessons learned along the way. Of course every company will traverse a slightly different road and their tale will reflect the subtle nuances of their journey. However, one thing all companies that have achieved success in implementing a change program of any kind have in common is the massive safety net provided by a sponsoring executive who feels truly passionate about, and committed to, the endeavor.

We've already cataloged the immense amount of stimuli vying for our attention today, and with that demanding setting as a backdrop, it's understandable that no initiative will survive without executive sponsorship. When we're overloaded, we look for cues to help us cut through the clutter and focus on what truly matters. One such cue, a vital one, is what our executives (in particular, the chief executive) are devoting their time and attention to. There is an old saying, "If it interests my boss, then it fascinates me." Should senior leaders show knowledge of the change program, and support it in words and action, you can be certain employees will follow suit. If, however, leaders are visibly disinterested in the latest change program why should employees be expected to cede any of their valuable bandwidth to support it?

Writing in their book *Confronting Reality*, authors Charan and Bossidy state the case for executive sponsorship quite clearly:

> The usual reason for the failure of an initiative is that it was launched halfheartedly, or was beyond the ability of the organization to master. Here's what tends to happen: the leaders announce a bold new program and then walk away from it, leaving the job to others. With no clear impetus from the top, the program will wander and drift. An initiative, after all, is add-on work, and people already have full plates. Few of them can take it seriously if the boss doesn't. Eventually the effort bogs down and dies.... Real results do not come from making bold announcements about how the organization will change. They come from thoughtful, committed leaders who understand the details of an initiative, anticipate its consequences for the organization, make sure their people can achieve, it, put their personal weight behind it, and communicate its urgency to everyone.[3]

This quote should be formatted as a warning label and affixed to any document relating to a proposed change initiative circulating at your organization. The only thing missing is this coda: If you don't have sponsorship, do not proceed.

## Gaining Executive Sponsorship

If you're excited about the potential of OKRs to provide value to your company but don't possess the decision rights to approve an implementation, you'll require the support of at least one member of your senior leadership team, preferably the CEO. Here are a few tips we've seen organizations use to great effect in gaining executive traction for a change initiative:

▣ *Link OKRs to something the executive is passionate about:* There is little doubt that any executive is more likely to lend active and vocal support to a program that resonates with their personal passions and values. Your job is to find that hook and explain how OKRs will transform it from rhetoric to reality within the organization. Perhaps your CEO is fixed on the virtues of speed to market. You can note the swift cadence of OKRs and how they'll allow you to move quickly, provide feedback, and promote flexibility and agility in aid of accelerating the new product development cycle.

▣ *Provide OKRs education:* Before providing our support for any new program we must first feel it possesses legitimate value and meaning. That meaning and value are derived from a comprehensive understanding of the subject matter. Senior managers will follow this same path from knowledge to meaning to value and commitment, and therefore the first step is providing basic education on OKRs: Definitions, examples, benefits, and most importantly, why they should be used at your organization right now.

▪ *Involve executives in the OKRs implementation:* Most change experts would assert that we don't think ourselves into acting differently, but in fact, we act ourselves into thinking differently. The upshot: You're much more likely to support something that you're actively involved in creating because you are physically acting out the change. Therefore, we strongly suggest you ensure senior executives are part of your OKRs implementation, and the task is not delegated to a lower-level team. CareerBuilder, the largest online job website in the United States, provides a great example of a company committed to executive involvement. Its CIO, Roger Fugett, participated in all three days of recent OKR drafting workshops. He recognized that his presence was critical in order to align IT with the business. The attendance of the CIO made it obvious to workshop attendees that OKRs are to be taken seriously.

The colossal benefits of a truly engaged CEO were in evidence to us in a recent client engagement. The CEO was new to the organization, and although he had performed substantial due diligence before accepting the position, he was unsure what awaited him when he actually began inhabiting the CEO post. Sure enough, things were not quite what he'd hoped. As he confided to one of us, "The floorboards were a lot looser than I expected." Because he had used OKRs with great success at his two previous companies, one of his first actions was to institute an OKRs program from top to bottom throughout the organization. He didn't delegate, but sat in on all the corporate-level workshops and took precious time from his schedule to later review all lower-level goals. He shared articles on the topic, spoke about it at all-hands meetings, and even communicated it to outside audiences. Needless to say, everyone witnessed his passion for the implementation and fell in behind him very quickly. It's still early in their work, but thanks to the focus provided by OKRs, results are already beginning to show improvement.

## WHERE TO DEVELOP YOUR OKRs

At first glance, OKRs appear to be very simple: Determine what you want to do, and how you'll know when you've achieved your goal. However, the actual creation and overall implementation of OKRs will require serious deliberations on a number of topics. We described one earlier in the chapter when we examined your rationale for using the framework. In this section we'll look at another early implementation question: where you'll create OKRs. This section outlines the primary choices awaiting you.

## Company-Level Only

For many organizations, this will be the most logical choice. Starting at the top has a number of inherent benefits: It clearly communicates what the organization is most focused on, demonstrates commitment and accountability on behalf of the executive team, and provides the means for later development of OKRs at lower levels of the firm. This approach "eases" the company into OKRs, giving all employees the time to digest the idea and witness how it can help transform results. There is actually a scientific basis for the notion of *easing in*, which is called *future lock-in*. Behavioral scientists Todd Rogers and Max Bazerman coined the term to describe the proclivity of people to be more amenable to a change (assuming it aligns with their values) if it will be implemented at some point in the future.[4] Especially if you've had difficulty launching change efforts in the past, this alternative has merit because it will be less threatening to employees. You're only rolling out at the corporate level initially and employees will have time to adjust to the idea as you show early benefits.

The critical enabler of success should you choose this option is executive sponsorship. A lackluster rollout, followed by anemic interest on the part of executives, will doom OKRs from the outset. You'll require an enthusiastic champion (or champions) to create the initial momentum for the program and prove to the entire team that it isn't just another "flavor of the month," destined to soon disappear.

## Company and Business Unit or Team

A more ambitious approach is to launch OKRs at both the company and business unit or team level. By business unit or team, we're referring to any group that reports to a senior executive, your terminology may differ. The implementation won't be simultaneous. Rather, we would expect overall company-level OKRs to be created, and once they have been widely communicated, business units or teams will create their own OKRs that demonstrate their alignment to overall goals.

Most important with this method is ensuring that the company-level objectives have been carefully selected and are well understood, since they will provide the critical input for business unit or team OKRs. And once again, from the broken-record department, sponsorship at the executive level is vital. Additionally, this choice entails some significant prework in the form of deployment parameters. Before you allow units or teams to create OKRs, you'll want to ensure that you've outlined key principles such as any maximum number of objectives or key results, agreement on terminology, scoring, and so on. We'll be covering those topics in Chapter 3.

## Entire Organization

Ultimately, this is where you want to go, having OKRs at the company, business unit, and individual levels to ensure alignment from top to bottom; it's just a matter of how long it takes to get there. The risks enumerated in the previous paragraphs apply here, but are amplified since you're attempting to go even lower in the organization. Unless you have a very small organization, we would not recommend this be your first choice when you begin your OKRs effort. Having said that, it shouldn't take you years to reach this point. Once you've proven the concept at one level, go deeper and establish momentum until eventually your entire organization has embraced OKRs and they've become part of your culture. Only you can determine the right rhythm for your implementation.

## Pilot at a Business Unit or Team

In an attempt to limit downside risk, some organizations will choose to begin their OKRs program at the business unit or department level. They utilize a pilot approach to demonstrate proof of the concept, show quick wins, and generate enthusiasm for a broader rollout. The unit or team you choose will require a leader who deeply understands the inner workings of OKRs and believes in the ability of the framework to generate real business results (yet another way of saying sponsorship, but at a lower level). We've seen this approach pay dividends when the pilot group does indeed generate quick wins, capturing the attention of other groups eager to mimic their success. The danger in this choice is ensuring the pilot team selects OKRs that are achievable. Should they establish unreachable goals and fail miserably on their OKRs, this will undoubtedly scare off others who are afraid the program will simply shine a spotlight on their deficiencies.

## Use OKRs for Projects

This is another "ease your way into OKRs" approach. Rather than developing corporate-level OKRs or using the framework at the unit or team level, you might start by applying objectives and key results to your biggest projects. Ask what your objective is for investing in the project, and then establish key results to track the project and gauge success. This method helps socialize the concept, creates a fluency for the terminology, and will, hopefully, improve your project management discipline. We're presenting this as an option, but would not strongly endorse it as an adoption approach for most organizations. Any projects you're spending time and money on should necessarily be linked to your overall strategy (and vision and mission). With those conditions in place, you will be more likely to accelerate execution by applying OKRs at the corporate level, and eventually rolling out to the entire company.

 ## SPECIAL CASES

In this section, we've used the terms *team,* and *business unit.* However, defining the teams that will create OKRs is not merely an exercise of re-creating your organization chart. Let's look at two common cases, based on OKR implementations, which will help you get started defining your OKR teams.

### Two Teams Using a Single Set of OKRs

We often see a single set of OKRs work for two teams when they are aligned as business partners. For example, IT may be set up by vertical: IT for sales operations, IT for finance, IT for marketing, IT for product, and so on. In these cases, rather than each IT team setting up its own OKRs, or for each business team to set up OKRs, the combined team "IT for sales operations" defines a single OKR set. The business team drives the creation of OKRs, but their corresponding IT team is involved with the process to ensure OKRs are feasible and well understood. This ensures alignment from the start. This pattern can also emerge with other corporate groups such as Finance.

While IT and finance teams are commonly merged with other teams for purposes of creating OKRs, there are other sets of teams that, depending on your industry and structure, may be considered "one" as well. In the software space, product and engineering teams are highly dependent on one other. While each have independent team leads and appear as separate boxes in the organizational chart, if there are major dependencies between these two teams, you might consider merging them to create a single set of OKRs.

## Many Teams for a Single Set of OKRs

Some organizations have initiatives that require extensive contributions from a number of teams. One of our mid-sized technology clients faced this situation, and did not set OKRs by team at all. Rather, they defined a "squad" devoted to each of their five key initiatives. Each squad had its own set of OKRs and included individual contributors from various teams. So, one squad might consist of four engineers, two designers, a marketing analyst, a finance manager, and a product manager.

There are probably other implementation permutations we haven't documented here, but what we've presented is based on actual client implementations and our research. As noted previously, we feel you should ultimately aim for using OKRs throughout your organization, but of course be patient and flexible in your timing. The most important thing, as with any endeavors in life and business, is overcoming the forces of resistance and simply getting started! A summary of options for where to deploy your OKRs is presented in Exhibit 2.1.

## AN OKRs DEVELOPMENT PLAN

Do you know who "The Wizard of Westwood" is? If you guessed Harry Potter's next nemesis you'd be mistaken. The Wizard to whom we're referring was a mere muggle, but one possessing legendary skills as a basketball coach: John Wooden.

During his nearly three decades at the helm of the UCLA men's basketball team, Wooden racked up an unprecedented ten national championships. He elevated basketball strategy to new heights, but beyond his acumen for the game itself lay another secret to his success: planning. He described his philosophy this way:

> When I coached basketball at UCLA, I believed that if we were going to succeed, we needed to be industrious. One way I accomplished this was with proper planning. I spent two hours with my staff planning each practice. Each drill was calculated to the minute. Every aspect of the session was choreographed, including where the practice balls should be placed. I did not want any time lost by people running over to a misplaced ball bin.[5]

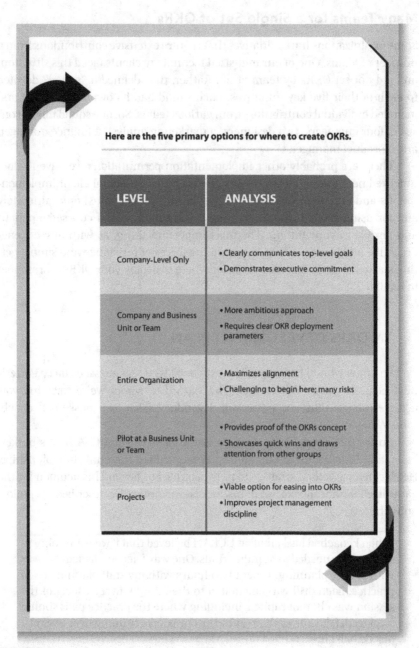

Here are the five primary options for where to create OKRs.

| LEVEL | ANALYSIS |
|---|---|
| Company-Level Only | • Clearly communicates top-level goals<br>• Demonstrates executive commitment |
| Company and Business Unit or Team | • More ambitious approach<br>• Requires clear OKR deployment parameters |
| Entire Organization | • Maximizes alignment<br>• Challenging to begin here; many risks |
| Pilot at a Business Unit or Team | • Provides proof of the OKRs concept<br>• Showcases quick wins and draws attention from other groups |
| Projects | • Viable option for easing into OKRs<br>• Improves project management discipline |

**EXHIBIT 2.1** Where to Deploy Your OKRs

This same commitment to detail will serve you well as you begin your work with OKRs. Given the many benefits we've touted, there is often a strong temptation to jump right in with both feet, immediately drafting OKRs without considering any of the questions we've proposed (why OKRs, who will sponsor, etc.) and will share throughout the book. But there is a potential price to be paid for that speed: confusion and mounting skepticism regarding your ability to deliver on the project.

Picture this: You're excited about getting started and immediately call a meeting of your executive team and their direct reports to build the corporate-level OKRs. There are some inevitable hiccups, maybe a lack of complete consensus on what you've constructed, but at the end of the day your walls are papered with sticky notes, and you arrive at a draft set of objectives and key results. We can guarantee that just before you adjourn and utter the words: Does anyone have any questions? Hands will go up. And at least a few people will ask: "What's next?" If you've barely thought through what was going to happen in the meeting you just had, there is no way you can competently offer up what's going to follow. That will often lead to skepticism and can quickly derail your implementation.

You don't need a phone-book-sized project plan delineating every conceivable step you'll take over the next 18 months, just a document that outlines the big chunks of your implementation so that you can monitor your progress and ensure you're leaving no stone unturned during the process. In the two sections that follow we've outlined the key steps comprising the planning and development phases of your implementation.

## Planning Phase

In this phase, you're laying the groundwork for a successful rollout. Here are the key steps to consider:

- Secure executive sponsorship for OKRs.
- Answer the question, "Why OKRs, and why now?"
- Determine where you'll begin with OKRs (corporate-level only, pilot, etc.).
- Create an implementation plan (see the development phase section).

## Development Phase

This plan supplies the concrete steps you'll take in creating your first set of OKRs, and reviewing initial results. Your development plan will, of course, depend on where you decide to build your OKRs. We'll assume you're going to begin with a set of OKRs at the corporate level only.

- *Provide OKRs education:* We've previously noted the seductive simplicity of OKRs, and that ease of understanding will often prompt organizations to skip this important step. However, consider this education with a capital E, during which you'll not only provide fundamentals on the model but share why you're choosing to use OKRs now, success stories from other firms, and what people can expect during the journey.

- *Develop or confirm the mission, vision, and strategy:* Your OKRs should be translated from your strategy, drive the achievement of your vision, and be in alignment with your overall mission. These are key enablers of success and as such should be solidly in place before you begin.

- *Create your corporate level objective(s) and key results:* There are several options for this step: using a small team, gathering input from employees through surveys that will later be used in a workshop, conducting executive interviews, or simply drafting objectives during a workshop. We'll explore this topic, and the attendant choices, in Chapter 3.

- *Present OKRs to the company:* We suggest using multiple media here: Share electronically, post to your intranet, and most important, communicate in person (perhaps at an all-hands meeting) so that you can facilitate a dialog surrounding the OKRs you chose and why.

- *Monitor OKRs:* You don't "set and forget" OKRs, but must monitor them during the quarter (or whatever cadence you choose).

- *Report results at the end of the quarter:* Score your OKRs and communicate the results with the entire organization. As with everything discussed above, we'll return to this topic with much more information later in the book.

We began this section with what we hope was inspiration provided by one of the greatest basketball coaches of all time, and will end with another "inspirational" quote, albeit one that is much more colloquial in nature. One of us had a co-worker early in our career that was obsessed with planning. The only picture adorning her office walls was a large framed print bearing the words: "Fail to Plan and You Plan to Fail." By following the steps noted in the previous sections you will be turning that on its head and planning to succeed!

## KEY LESSONS FOR SUCCESSFUL TRANSFORMATION

We supplied a definition of OKRs back in Chapter 1, but beyond the taxonomy you must remember that OKRs are really a change and transformation effort. And, unfortunately, it's well documented that organizations struggle with change. In one of many studies on the topic, Michael Beer and Nitin Nohria of Harvard Business School estimate failure rates as high as 70 percent.[6] Therefore, it's critical that you adhere to the latest findings in the field of change research in order to tip the scales in your favor. One recent survey (and study) from the global consulting firm McKinsey uncovered four key managerial actions that prove most effective in driving successful transformation initiatives.[7] Each is briefly discussed below in the context of OKRs.

The first is role modeling, exemplified by leaders who "walk the walk" and demonstrate desired behaviors to a staff, hungry for cues from their executives. This finding corroborates our earlier discussion of the importance of securing executive sponsorship for your OKRs engagement.

Fostering understanding and conviction is the second key action. It asserts that if employees understand the rationale for a change they're asked to make, they are more likely to act in support of the changes. This action can be fostered by creating a "change story" that communicates why the change is necessary, what people can expect, and what tools will be provided to help them during the change. As with executive sponsorship, we noted the importance of "Why OKRs?" earlier in the chapter.

The next action is reinforcing change through formal mechanisms. Structures, systems, and processes represent formal mechanisms you can use to support employees' efforts to embrace new mind-sets and behaviors. For example you might revise your employee performance review system to partially incorporate individual OKR results. This creates an alignment between the change (OKRs) and a formal system (performance reviews).

Developing talent and skills is the final key action noted in the McKinsey survey. It suggests that when employees have the skills they need to act in a new way they're more likely to make the desired changes. This action highlights the importance of having an actual strategy in place, as it will dictate what skills are ultimately necessary for execution. Once you assess current (and anticipated) skill strengths and gaps, you can intervene with a set of targeted development opportunities.

There is no magic formula that will guarantee either the effective design or success of a transformation initiative. However, we're confident that if you take the time and effort to rigorously apply the advice offered in this chapter you will be laying a very solid foundation for your OKR program, one that will position you well for the actual construction of objectives and key results, which we'll turn our attention to in Chapter 3.

## THE BUILDING BLOCKS OF OKRs: MISSION, VISION, AND STRATEGY[8]

One of the biggest strengths of OKRs is their emphasis on a shorter cycle. More frequent review cycles lead to rapid learning, increased opportunities to make progress, and even a feeling of winning at work. However, the emphasis on a short cycle can also be problematic. Are OKRs too short-sighted? How can OKRs be strategic if they look out just a single quarter? Some critics suggest that OKRs resemble a tactical rather than strategic framework. To overcome these potential deficiencies, you must create context for OKR setting.

OKRs should never be created in a vacuum, but must be a reflection of the company's purpose, its desired long-term goals, and its plan to successfully defend market space. In other words, they should translate your mission, vision, and strategy into action. In the sections that follow we'll share background information on each of these OKR raw materials, discuss why they're important, and supply you with tools to either assess your current versions or create entirely new editions.

Entire books have been written about these subjects, in the case of strategy, hundreds if not thousands. This is a book about OKRs, we recognize that, and therefore we understand if you're hesitant to invest the time in the following sections. However, as noted above, if your OKR investment is to be a profitable one, the objectives and key results you establish must propel your company toward its desired future state. That ideal future is captured in the mission, vision, and strategy (see Exhibit 2.2). Therefore, we urge you to read the sections that follow and utilize the advice offered to ensure a solid foundation for your OKRs program.

### Mission

Anyone encountering your company, whether it's a customer, current or potential employee, or strategic partner, will undoubtedly have a number

**Creating OKRs in the context of your mission, vision, and strategy ensures alignment.**

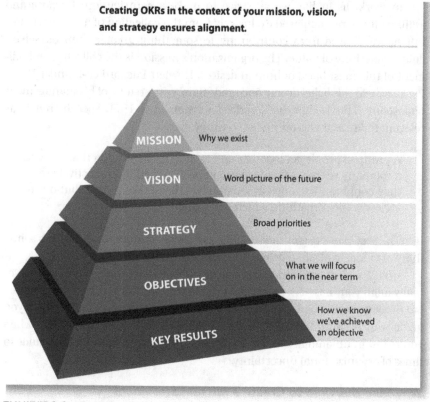

**EXHIBIT 2.2**   Creating Context for OKRs

of questions in mind. Who are you as an organization? Why do you exist? It is the mission of your organization that provides the answers to these vital questions.[9]

A mission statement defines the core purpose of the organization, its *raison d'etre*, why it exists. The mission also reflects employees' motivations for engaging in the company's work. In the private sector, which is strongly influenced by shareholder concerns, a mission should provide the rationale for a company's existence beyond generating stockholder wealth. Even in today's Wall Street driven, meet-the-numbers-or-else markets, the mission statement should describe how an organization is indeed serving the public interest; why it matters—the true responsibility of any organization.

In work, as in life, we all strive to make a contribution. Purpose and fulfillment are not achieved exclusively from the collection of a paycheck, but rather are derived from contributing to something greater than ourselves, doing something of value. The organization's mission is the collective embodiment of this most basic of human desires. Hewlett-Packard co-founder David Packard held this belief deeply and made it the cornerstone of his management philosophy. This is how he described mission in a 1960 speech that is as relevant today as it was over a half century ago:

> A group of people get together and exist as an institution that we call a company so they are able to accomplish something collectively that they could not accomplish separately—they make a contribution to society . . . do something which is of value.[10]

The best of our organizations offer us the opportunity to accomplish something of value, to attain true meaning and fulfillment through work.

Unlike visions and strategies that may be achieved over time, you never really fulfill your mission. It acts as a beacon for your work, constantly pursued but never quite reached. Consider your mission to be the compass by which you guide your organization. And just as a compass can lead you to safety when you're lost in unfamiliar terrain, a powerful mission can serve as your guide in times of organizational uncertainty.

## Why Take the Time to Create a Mission Statement

Before we go any further, we should acknowledge the Dilbert-esque response that mission (and vision) often engenders in change-weary corporate veterans and newcomers alike. Some see it as nothing but corporate whitewashing, vacuous words that in the end add little or no value to the organization. We disagree. Particularly with OKRs, we believe mission is truly critical to your implementation.

Earlier, we noted that OKRs must not be created in a vacuum. You require context for the exercise should you hope to gain the benefits the approach has to offer. The immediate context will be provided by your specific strategy (which we'll discuss shortly), but OKRs must also lead you to the achievement of your vision (see the next section) and be consistent with your mission. Consider for a moment the tremendous value and alignment you create when developing OKRs that truly translate your mission. Now you have a tool that can act as your compass and guide the actions of your entire employee team. Your challenge is to elevate the mission beyond embellishments to a coffee mug and take advantage of the power it can offer.

## Effective Mission Statements

Now that we know what they are, let's look at some of the attributes that make for an effective and enduring mission statement.

- *Be simple and clear:* Peter Drucker has said one of the greatest mistakes organizations make is to turn their missions into "hero sandwiches of good intentions."[11] We've read thousands of pithy quotes over the years but this may very well be our all-time favorite. It's short, colorful, and most important, 100 percent accurate. We have yet to share this nugget of sage advice with an audience and not have the entire room nod in unison or chuckle somewhat apologetically, as if to say, "Okay, you got us on that one." As admirable as your intentions may be, they aren't necessarily practical. You can't be all things to all people and still expect to maintain the focus necessary to accomplish specific goals. The mission must mirror your chosen field of endeavor.
- *Inspire change:* Although your mission doesn't change, it should inspire great change within your organization. Since the mission can never be fully realized it should propel your organization forward, stimulating positive change and growth. Consider the mission of Wal-Mart: Saving people money so they can live better.[12] Retailing may look vastly different in 100 years than it does today, but you can wager safely that people will still want to save money.
- *Be long-term in nature:* Mission statements should be written to last 100 years or more. Although strategies will surely change during that time period, the mission should remain the bedrock of the organization, serving as the stake in the ground for all future decisions.
- *Easy to understand and communicate:* Buzzwords really have no place in a mission statement. It should be written in plain language, which is easily understood by all readers. A compelling and memorable mission is one that reaches people on a visceral level, speaks to them, and motivates them to serve the organization's purpose.

If you've never created a mission statement, Exhibit 2.3 provides a simple template that can help you get the ball rolling within your organization.

**We exist to** *(primary purpose, need served, or problem solved)*

_____

_____

_____

**For** *(primary clients or customer)*

_____

_____

_____

**In order to** *(core services offered)*

_____

_____

_____

**So that** *(long-term outcomes determining success)*

_____

_____

_____

**EXHIBIT 2.3**   Simplified Mission Statement Template

### If You Already Have a Mission

Chances are, whether you know it or not, your company probably already has a mission statement. Perhaps it's proudly adorning office walls throughout your organization, or conversely, it may sadly be gathering dust on a shelf, or tucked out of sight in a desk drawer somewhere. If yours falls into the latter category, that is, you haven't seen, or heard much about your mission for a while—that's probably a good sign that it's time to reexamine it.

Start by evaluating your mission in the context of the attributes presented earlier in the chapter. Does your statement contain all of these attributes? Here are some additional questions to ask if you're uncertain about the efficacy of your current mission:[13]

- *Is the mission up to date?* Does it reflect what the organization actually does and is all about?
- *Is the mission relevant to all stakeholders?* Does a compelling reason for your existence present itself from a review of your mission?
- *Who is being served?* Should you rewrite the mission to more accurately reflect your current customer base?

Exhibit 2.4 contains sample mission statements from a diverse group of organizations.

### Mission Objectives and Key Results (MOKRs)

If you've read this far, but have flipped ahead and see multiple pages on vision and strategy awaiting you, we fully understand that you may feel a bit frustrated. That frustration likely stems from the distinct possibility that there is no way your executive team has the appetite to invest in mission and vision workshops along with a potentially protracted strategic planning effort. We'll share the essence of these topics in the sections that follow with the hope, and expectation, that you can create powerful versions of each with minimal time and effort. However, if you still don't think that's possible, we suggest you at least consider the shortcut concept of MOKRs, which as the acronym suggests, simply means creating a mission statement for the company and all teams developing OKRs, and using the mission to guide the development of OKRs.

Having a clear mission, and aligning OKRs—whether monthly, quarterly, or yearly— to it, helps ensure that work performed in the short term is meeting the long-term purpose of the organization. Exhibit 2.5 shows the use of MOKRs with a marketing team. In this example, marketing is focusing on two

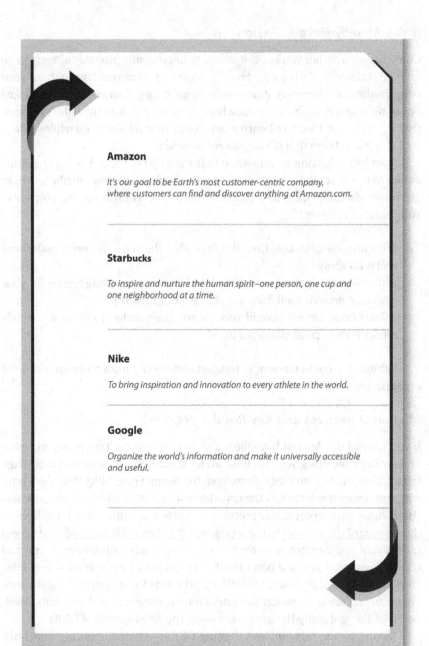

**Amazon**

*It's our goal to be Earth's most customer-centric company, where customers can find and discover anything at Amazon.com.*

**Starbucks**

*To inspire and nurture the human spirit–one person, one cup and one neighborhood at a time.*

**Nike**

*To bring inspiration and innovation to every athlete in the world.*

**Google**

*Organize the world's information and make it universally accessible and useful.*

**EXHIBIT 2.4**   Example Mission Statements

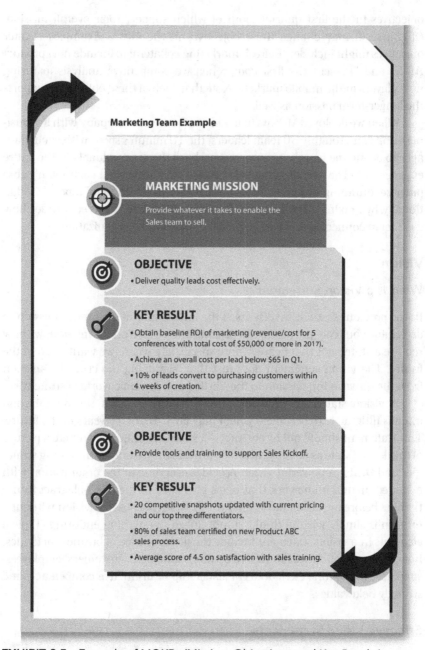

**Marketing Team Example**

**MARKETING MISSION**

Provide whatever it takes to enable the Sales team to sell.

**OBJECTIVE**

• Deliver quality leads cost effectively.

**KEY RESULT**

• Obtain baseline ROI of marketing (revenue/cost for 5 conferences with total cost of $50,000 or more in 2017).

• Achieve an overall cost per lead below $65 in Q1.

• 10% of leads convert to purchasing customers within 4 weeks of creation.

**OBJECTIVE**

• Provide tools and training to support Sales Kickoff.

**KEY RESULT**

• 20 competitive snapshots updated with current pricing and our top three differentiators.

• 80% of sales team certified on new Product ABC sales process.

• Average score of 4.5 on satisfaction with sales training.

**EXHIBIT 2.5** Example of MOKRs (Mission, Objectives, and Key Results)

objectives in the first quarter, both of which support their overall mission. Of course, it may change those objectives in the future. Examples of later objectives might include: "Refresh marketing collateral to include new product ABC," and "Present the first comprehensive competitive analysis featuring new players in the mobile market." Note that each of these objectives supports the longer-term mission as well.

When we deployed MOKRs in a mid-sized software company with five business units and roughly 50 team leaders, the 10 minutes spent with each manager to define the team's mission was perhaps the most valuable in the entire engagement. The exercise enabled the CFO to quickly read each team's core purpose, outlining how they fit into the larger organizational tapestry. Additionally, by making all of the mission statements public, it was easy to see how each team connected and was aligned throughout the organization.

## Vision

### What Is a Vision Statement?

In the previous section, we discussed the importance of a powerful mission to determine your core purpose as an organization. Based on the mission, we now require a statement that defines more specifically where we want to go in the future. The vision statement does just that, signifying the critical transition from the unwavering mission to the spirited and dynamic world of strategy.

A vision statement provides a word picture of what the organization intends ultimately to become—which may be 5, 10, or 15 years in the future. This statement should not be abstract—it should contain as concrete a picture of the desired state as possible, and also provide the basis for formulating strategies and OKRs. A powerful vision provides everyone in the organization with a shared mental framework that helps give form to the often-abstract future that lies before us. Vision always follows mission (purpose). A vision without a mission is simply wishful thinking, not linked to anything enduring. Typical elements in a vision statement include the desired scope of business activities, how the corporation will be viewed by its stakeholders (customers, employees, suppliers, regulators, etc.), areas of leadership or distinctive competence, and strongly held values.

### Effective Vision Statements

Without a clear and compelling vision to guide the actions of all employees, you may wind up with a workforce lacking direction and thus unable to profit from any strategy you create, no matter how well conceived. Let's look at some characteristics of effective vision statements:

- *Quantified and time-bound:* An organization's mission describes its reason for being: its core purpose. Typically these statements are composed of inspirational prose, but do not include numerical aspirations or timing of any kind. The vision, however, must include both in order to be effective. Visions are concrete representations of the future and, as such, they must provide specific details about the envisioned future state of the company. Although it will depend on the unique circumstances of each organization, many choose to wrap their vision in long-term financial goals of seemingly audacious revenue or profit targets. Others may include daring goals related to the number of customers served or geographies entered. Without numbers it will be impossible to measure progress toward the vision in your OKRs.

- *Concise:* The very best vision statements are those that grab your attention and immediately draw you in without boring you from pages of mundane rhetoric. Often the simplest visions are the most powerful and compelling. When Muhtar Kent assumed the CEO position at Coca-Cola in 2008, he was asked about his top priority moving forward. Without hesitation he replied, "Establishing a vision . . . a shared picture of success. We call it 2020 vision and it calls for us to double the business in 10 years. It's not for the fainthearted but it's clearly doable."[14] His vision is both succinct and powerful. Notice also, that his vision is both quantified and time-bound.

- *Consistent with mission:* Your vision is a further translation of your mission (why you exist). If the mission suggests solving problems for customers and one of your core values is constant innovation, we would then expect to see a reference to innovation in your vision statement. In the vision you're painting a word picture of the desired future state that will lead to the achievement of your mission, so ensure the two are aligned.

- *Verifiable:* Using the latest business jargon can render your vision statement nebulous to even the most trained eye. Who within your organization will be able to determine exactly when you became *world class*, *leading edge*, or *top quality*? Write your vision statement so that you'll know when you've achieved it. Notice again Muhtar Kent's specificity of doubling the business in 10 years. While the mission won't change, we would expect the vision to change, since it is written for a finite period of time.

- *Feasible:* The vision shouldn't be the collective dreams of senior management, but must be grounded in reality. To ensure this is the case, you must possess a clear understanding of your business, its markets, competitors, and emerging trends.

▓ *Inspirational:* Your vision represents a word picture of the desired future state of the organization. Don't miss the opportunity to inspire your team to make the emotional commitment necessary to reach this destination. The vision statement should not only guide but also arouse the collective passion of all employees. To be inspirational, the vision must first be understandable to every conceivable audience from the boardroom to the shop floor. Throw away the thesaurus for this exercise and focus instead on your deep knowledge of the business to compose a meaningful statement for all involved.

## Developing Your Vision Statement

"Back to the Future Visioning" is a fun exercise you can use to help develop your vision statement. The process can be administered either individually or with a group. In describing the method, we'll assume a group session. Distribute several 3 × 5 index cards to each of the participants. To begin the session, ask the members of the group to imagine they awake the next morning 5, 10, of 15 years in the future (your choice of time increment). In order to record their impressions of the future they've each been given a disposable camera to capture important images and changes they hoped might take place within their organization. At the end of each day's adventure, they must create a caption for the pictures they've taken during the day. Instruct the group to use the index cards you distributed to record their captions. By the end of the trip, they've cataloged the future in detail. Give the participants about 15 minutes to imagine their trip to the future and encourage them to visually capture as much as possible in their minds' eye. Ask the group: "What has happened with our organization, are we successful?" "What markets are we serving?" "What core competencies are separating us from our competitors?" "What goals have we achieved?" Record the captions from the index cards on a flipchart or laptop computer and use them as the raw materials for the initial draft of a vision statement.

We think you'll enjoy the exercise, but the outcome is very important. Your vision possesses the ability to reduce the gap between current and desired performance. The OKRs you draft throughout your company will be designed to close that performance gap, and hence vision is critical to the maximum utilization of OKRs.

## Strategy

We were able to capsulize our discussion of mission and vision on the preceding pages. However, strategy is such an enormous subject, with literally hundreds of books and thousands of articles and white papers available on the subject, that it is impossible to provide a cursory overview of the topic here. What we can say is that strategy is critical to your OKRs as it provides the initial context for creation. All OKRs should be directly translated from your strategy—your game plan for successfully creating or defending aggressively contested market space. Therefore, we would expect you to have a strategy in place before embarking on your OKRs implementation. If you're reading that and thinking, "Well, I think Jim (or Cindy or whoever your CEO is) knows what the strategy is," you're in trouble. Like a ship without a rudder, if you try to create a robust set of OKRs without the benefit of a widely communicated and understood strategy in place, you can be certain of drifting off course and steering your entire team into a fog of confusion.

If you're from a younger, more entrepreneurial company that embraces lean and agile concepts you may be tempted to skip this section, thinking old school strategic planning is anathema to your culture of pivots and rapid experimentation. That's simply not the case. A core strategy supplies boundaries, helping you determine what not to do when faced with a sea of opportunities, which is every bit as important as determining what to do. It also helps you choose viable opportunities, remain focused, align your entire organization, and make necessary commitments to execute.[15]

One of us (Paul) wrote a management fable on how to develop a strategy. In the final section of this chapter, we've provided a summary. Paul's model for creating a strategy is based on answering four fundamental questions. If you don't have a clear strategy in place, one that has been widely disseminated, and is comprehended by all, we strongly encourage you to convene your team and answer the questions below.

 ## ROADMAP STRATEGY[16]

Before writing his management fable on strategic planning, *Roadmaps and Revelations*, Paul reviewed hundreds of strategic plans, and scoured the literature from the likes of Michael Porter, Henry Mintzberg, Michael Raynor, W. Chan Kim, Renee Mauborgne, and many others. During the process, he constantly asked himself what core elements appeared again and again—what, in fact, represented the DNA of effective strategic planning? There are literally hundreds of approaches to strategic planning, but his investigation yielded a set of questions that appeared in one form or another in virtually all of the materials he discovered. Those core questions came to form the basis of *Roadmap Strategy*, a process he documented in the book. As you can see, the process draws its name from the book's title.

Exhibit 2.6 provides an overview of the process—you'll see the four fundamental strategy questions, and on the outer ring of the diagram you'll find what we call the four lenses, each of which will assist you in answering the fundamental strategy questions. At the center of the diagram is, of course, the word strategy, as the four questions and accompanying lenses are designed to drive strategy formulation.

**EXHIBIT 2.6**   The Four Fundamental Strategy Questions

## The Four Fundamental Questions You Must Answer When Creating a Strategy

Let's review each of the four questions, beginning with the first.

### What Propels Us Forward?

At this very moment your organization is being propelled in some direction by a force put in place through years of decisions made on everything from how you allocate your financial resources to whom you hire, to how you employ technology. What propels you forward represents, in many ways, your corporate identity; in other words if people were to say, "They are a _____ company," the blank in the sentence will often describe what propels you forward. Possessing a unique identity has been proven to boost TSR (total shareholder return). One study found that companies considered to have a "clear" identity—standing for something unique and consistent over time—have superior three-year TSR growth compared with companies that lack a clear identity.[17]

Most organizations will typically be propelled by one of six forces:

1. *Products and services:* Companies propelled by products and services may sell to many different customer groups, using a variety of channels, but their focus is on a core product or service. Consider Coca-Cola. It focuses exclusively on nonalcoholic beverages, with hundreds of global brands.

2. *Customers and markets:* Organizations dedicated to customers and markets may provide a number of product or service offerings, but they are all directed at a certain core audience. Johnson & Johnson's diverse wares have one thing in common: they're aimed at the needs of their core market, doctors, nurses, patients, and mothers.

3. *Capacity or capabilities:* Hotels focus on capacity. They have a certain number of rooms available and their goal is to fill them, simple as that. Airlines operate on the same premise, using available seats. Organizations propelled forward by capabilities possess expert skills in certain areas and will apply that toolkit of skills to any possible product or market.

4. *Technology:* Some organizations have access to a proprietary technology that they leverage to a number of different products and customer groups. Consider DuPont, which discovered nylon in the 1930s. DuPont went on to apply the technology to a varied range of offerings, including fishing line, stockings, and carpet.

5. *Sales and distribution channels:* The operative word with this focus is *how*, not *what* or *who*. Organizations that are driven by sales channels will push a diverse array of items through their selected channels. TV shopping networks are a great example. Where else can you buy makeup one hour and DVD players the next?
6. *Raw materials:* If you're an oil company, everything you sell is going to be derived from that black gold you pumped from the ground. You may have the skills and technology to mold the oil into a number of things, but all will be directly descended from the original raw material.

Some may view the six areas and claim they can, and must, do all in order to succeed in our hypercompetitive marketplace. We suppose in theory that's possible, but it will prove exceedingly difficult to go beyond simply skimming the surface of what each area has to offer if you attempt to pursue all six at the same time. Doing so will inevitably lead to bewilderment from an already skeptical employee audience, wondering which path to choose when presented with alternative opportunities. Ultimately, a focus on all is a focus on none, leading to suboptimal results. In order to truly capitalize on this principle, you must commit to one driving force for your organization and align your resources, human and financial, around that decision. Determine what propels you forward, and focus on optimizing it.

### What Do We Sell?

Regardless of which of the six areas propels you forward as an organization, you must sell something, some mix of products or services, to your customers in order to keep your business alive. The challenge inherent in this question is making the critical determination of which products and services you'll place more emphasis on in the future, and which you'll place less emphasis on.

Take for example, the American cable television channel, The CW. Parent companies Time Warner Inc. and CBS Corporation had high hopes when they launched the new network but it failed to deliver results and soon there were whispers it would be shut down. Recognizing that a strategic choice had to be made, CW returned to its ancestral roots and decided to focus on programs geared toward young women. Dawn Ostroff, former CW entertainment president, addressed the change, when she said, "We really needed to stand out in the marketplace and not be another broadcaster...It was important for us to differentiate and create a brand that hopefully will be a real legacy here." CW bet its future on shows such as *Gossip Girl*, the new *90210*, a new *Melrose Place*, and *Vampire Diaries*, all focused on content relevant to young women. That tradition continues today with *Jane the Virgin* and *Crazy Ex-Girlfriend*.

## Who Are Our Customers?

When determining whom you'll sell to, you are once again faced with a choice: Which customer groups (and geographies) do we place more emphasis on in the future, and which deserve less of our attention? The first step in answering this question is acquiring a clear understanding of your current group of customers by reviewing standard metrics such as Net promoter score, profitability by customer group, retention, and market share. It's also vital to experience things from your customers' point of view in order to glean insights not visible from within the walls of your corporate headquarters.

The upscale beauty company Estée Lauder, which controls 30 brands including the iconic MAC and Clinique, examined this question, and made strategic choices as a result. CEO Fabrizio Freda decreed that reducing the company's dependency on declining U.S. department stores, which accounted for nearly one-third of Estée Lauder's sales, was a top priority. A new geographical focus is in the works as well, as Estée Lauder plans to focus increasingly on emerging markets and Asia.

Often, responses to the questions, "What do we sell?" and "Who are our customers?" will be revealed in unison, as analysis on one leads to insights on the other, ultimately creating answers for both queries. Consider once again, The CW. By making the strategic choice to offer programs geared to young women (What do we sell?), it is simultaneously committing to young women as its core customer group.

## How Do We Sell?

This is perhaps the most crucial of the four questions, as it determines value proposition. In other words, how do you add value for customers, or to put it even simpler: Why would anyone buy from you? Despite the importance of the question, the choices awaiting you are limited and basic: You can either attempt to offer the lowest total cost of ownership to your customers or you can put forth a *differentiated* product or service.

Companies that compete on lowest total cost invest deeply in capabilities, processes, and assets that allow them to standardize their operations, and create a repeatable formula that results in low prices for the consumer. Think of Wal-Mart in the retail world or McDonald's in the fast-food industry.

Those who choose to compete based on differentiation will find two potential paths to follow. The first is differentiation based on cultivating deep and rich relationships with customers, so that your focus is not on a single transaction but on building something that last years, maybe even decades or a lifetime. This is known as customer intimacy. Nordstrom is a great example. Its customer service is legendary and keeps customers coming back for years.

Competing based on the superior functionality of your products offers the second choice of differentiation. Innovation, cutting-edge design and functionality, and the latest technology are all hallmarks of organizations such as Apple, which choose to sell based on product leadership.

As we noted, if we had to choose one question that is most critical for your team to achieve consensus on, this is it. In many ways, it represents the aggregation of your responses to the previous questions, and it will directly impact, in a significant way, every decision and investment you make going forward.

## The Four Lenses

So how do you answer these strategy questions? On the outer ring of the Roadmap Strategy diagram, you'll find what we call *the four lenses*. Think of each of these as just that, a lens through which to consider the question you're pondering, or a different perspective to adopt as you deliberate on your alternatives.

As you work through each of the fundamental questions, you can turn the "dial" on the outer ring to a different lens. We like to think of it as clicking the dial on a safe, although when you're rotating a safe's dial there is only one correct combination. With the four lenses, every combination of question and lens is a winner, because each challenges you in a new and enlightening way. Each is summarized below:

*Social/Cultural:* In *Roadmaps and Revelations*, a mentor character notes, "You've got to start with the heart." When discussing and debating the strategy questions, and developing possible responses, consider which potential answer most resonates with your passion as an organization. For example, if you're propelled by a proprietary technology, have a long and proud tradition of technological achievement, one which your employees are justifiably proud of, it may not make sense from a social and cultural standpoint to shift your focus to customers and markets, or any other alternative. The evidence suggesting that such a shift will lead to profound success had better be substantial to override what's in the hearts of your people.

*Human:* When debating alternative responses to the strategy questions, it's vital to be ruthlessly realistic about your team's skills and talents. You may wish to sell surfboards because three members of your team are avid surfers, but if your sales associates have never been to the beach, you've got very little chance of succeeding. In that case, to make the transition, you'd have to be willing to invest in training, perhaps consultants (surfer dude consultants?), and new hires to bridge the potential skills gap.

*Technological:* Technology has become a critical enabler of virtually every industry, and thus it must be carefully considered as you answer the four fundamental strategy questions. Will the answer you're contemplating require an investment in new technology? What about the current technology you employ: Will it become redundant? It's important to realize that the lenses impact one another. New technology may require new skill sets, the human lens. And technology is one of the most threatening things you can introduce, especially to seasoned employees, so you better have a good grasp on your cultural and social lens.

*Financial:* This is perhaps the most basic of the four lenses, but certainly not to be overlooked. Every decision you make when answering the four questions will most likely entail the allocation of resources, for example: training your people to cover a skills gap (Human lens), investing in new technology (Technological lens), or creating a communications campaign to support your chosen direction (Social/Cultural lens). And on the opposite side of the ledger, each decision must be examined in light of the potential revenue and profit that will result from pursuing that course of action.

We won't repeat the sorrowful statistics on strategy execution that we've previously shared, but we're certain you'll recall they are frightfully low. Perhaps one of the reasons the numbers are so poor is the fact that many companies, although they would be loath to admit this, really don't have a strategy. They may possess some sort of guiding idea or have a rudimentary business plan in place, but they've never taken the time and considerable intellectual effort to construct a real plan. Once again, if that describes your company, we urge you to gather your team and use the simple yet powerful questions above to discover your unique strategic formula.

## NOTES

1. Marcus Buckingham, *The One Thing You Need to Know* (New York: The Free Press, 2005).

2. Chris McChesney, Sean Covey, and Jim Huling, *The Four Disciplines of Execution: Achieving Your Wildly Important Goals* (Free Press, 2012; Kindle edition, location 483).
3. Ram Charan and Larry Bossidy, *Confronting Reality; Doing What Matters to Get Things Done* (New York: Crown Business, 2004).
4. Steve J. Martin, Noah Goldstein, and Robert Cialdini, *The Small Big: Small Changes That Spark Big Influence* (New York: Grand Central Publishing, 2014).
5. John Wooden and Jay Carty, *Coach Wooden's Pyramid of Success* (Ventura, CA: Regal, 2005), 34.
6. Michael Beer and Nitin Nohria, "Cracking the Code of Change," *Harvard Business Review* (May–June 2000): 133.
7. McKinsey & Company, "The Science of Organizational Transformations" (September 2015), www.mckinsey.com/business-functions/organization/our-insights/the-science-of-organizational-transformations#0.
8. Portions of this section are drawn from Paul R. Niven, *Balanced Scorecard Evolution: A Dynamic Approach to Strategy Execution* (Hoboken, NJ: John Wiley & Sons, 2014).
9. Michael Allison and Jude Kaye, *Strategic Planning for Nonprofit Organizations* (New York: John Wiley & Sons, 1997), 56.
10. James C. Collins and Jerry I. Porras, "Building Your Company's Vision," *Harvard Business Review* (September–October, 1996).
11. Peter F. Drucker, *Managing the Non-Profit Organization* (New York: Harper Business, 1990), 5.
12. http://panmore.com/walmart-vision-mission-statement-intensive-generic-strategies. Accessed November 11, 2013.
13. Thomas Wolf, *Managing a Nonprofit Organization in the Twenty-First Century* (New York: Fireside, 1999).
14. Muhtar Kent, "Shaking Things Up at Coca-Cola," *Harvard Business Review* (October 2011): 94–99.
15. David Collis, "Lean Strategy," *Harvard Business Review* (March 2016).
16. Paul R. Niven, *Roadmaps and Revelations: Finding the Road to Business Success on Route 101* (Hoboken, NJ: John Wiley & Sons, 2009).
17. Paul Leinwand and Cesare Mainardi, "What Drives a Company's Success? Highlights of Survey Findings," *Strategy&* (originally published by Booz & Company, October 28, 2013), www.strategyand.pwc.com/reports/what-drives-a-companys-success. Accessed March 16, 2016.

CHAPTER THREE

# Creating Effective OKRs

## OMAHA

We're not referring to the city in Nebraska, or the landing site of Allied troops in Normandy on June 6, 1944. Our Omaha is the phrase recently retired American football legend Peyton Manning uttered many times at the line of scrimmage over the last few years of his career. Even if you're not a football fan, we're confident you're aware of Peyton Manning—the National Football League's all-time leader in a trove of categories, including touchdowns thrown, passing yards, wins, and many more. Manning, who is famous for his meticulous preparation, would approach the line, survey the defense, and when he was ready, yell "Omaha." Then the ball would be snapped and the play was on. In order to maximize his team's chances for success, Manning never called for the ball until he was completely prepared to take advantage of whatever vulnerabilities the defense was displaying.

We're about to shout Omaha to you. Before you can begin using OKRs, and reaping the many advantages we touted in Chapter 1, you need to be prepared and able to create robust and effective objectives and key results. In this chapter we'll share with you how to do that. Then the game is truly on!

It is here that we'll show you exactly what goes into creating OKRs. Specifically, we'll outline the characteristics of quality OKRs, supply you with tips to make the job easier, and warn you of the pitfalls that can stand in the way of effective objectives and key results. Among the many other topics covered in the chapter are: The difference between OKRs and health metrics, how to score OKRs, how often you should set them, how many are appropriate, and of course how to specifically create them. In case you're wondering, Manning never revealed why he used the word Omaha, and appears to have taken the secret with him into retirement. But you know why we're using it. Ready? Omaha!

 ## CREATING POWERFUL OBJECTIVES

Recall our definition of objectives from Chapter 1: An objective is a concise statement outlining a broad qualitative goal designed to propel the organization forward in a desired direction. Basically it asks, "What do we want to do?" At face value, this is not what most of us would term an intellectually challenging concept. However, from our work with clients around the world, and in conversations with other thought leaders and consultants, it's clear that many organizations struggle to create high-value objectives. It's difficult to make the hard choices (which probably explains the fact that Americans devote more time to choosing a TV than to setting up a retirement account[1]), and often companies will default to choosing pedestrian objectives that do little in advancing their charge towards strategy execution.

One challenge faced by those new to OKRs is a lack of context for the exercise. "What exactly is a good objective?" they wonder. To assist you in overcoming that potential barrier, we'll begin by outlining a number of criteria you should keep in mind when constructing your objectives.

### Inspirational

A well-written objective is more than a short collection of words that string together to describe a business goal. Anyone could mash together a few pieces of business lingo that, taken in the aggregate, represent something you'd like to do. However, we're challenging you to create something bigger and much bolder. Your objectives should compel people to a higher standard of performance based on the inspirational power of the message. People should be forced to think differently based on the inherent challenge and inspiration of the objective. Upserve (formerly Swipely) is a company that uses artificial intelligence to help restaurants improve performance. CEO Angus Davis captured the essence of inspiration well, when he said:

> It's not enough to say you want to see 10 percent improvement when you know that's well within your reach. It means you'll just keep doing the same things, just working ever so slightly harder. But if I said to you, I need 50 percent improvement in what you're doing, you'd probably say, "Gosh, in order to do that, I'd have to completely solve this hard problem," or "I need to completely rethink how I'm addressing X or Y." That's what OKRs are supposed to do. When you aim higher, you think harder about the steps you need to take to really accomplish something.[2]

## Attainable

It's no accident that this item appears directly below our call for inspirational objectives. Finding the balance between inspiration and reality is one of the foremost trials of creating objectives that work. We encourage you to push the limits of employees' imaginations when setting objectives, but please do be cognizant of the fact that limits exist. If you cross the line, the damage can be especially deleterious to your company. In one aptly titled study, "Goals Gone Wild," the authors discovered several side effects of excessively demanding objectives, including corrosion of culture, reduced motivation, and the temptation to engage in risky or unethical behavior. Another study found that managers who believed they had been presented with a goal that was unattainable are more likely to abuse their subordinates. As the authors point out, it's the corporate equivalent of kicking the dog because of your troubles.[3] Although there is no steadfast rule for assessing the attainability of objectives, in the spirit of learning from the crowd, gathering feedback from a cadre of employees will assist in making the determination.

## Doable in a Quarter

We'll discuss the cadence for OKRs a bit later in the chapter, but assuming you're creating objectives each quarter, you'll want to advance something that can, indeed, be accomplished during the subsequent three months. If, after drafting an objective, the collective wisdom of the team suspects it will take a year to realize, then perhaps what you've developed is closer to a strategy or even a vision. While each have their place (as we argued in Chapter 2) objectives must be time-bound to the rhythm you establish, most likely quarterly. We recently worked with a client whose communications department developed this objective: "Increase sellers' success through communication." That actually resembles a mission; their core purpose as a department. Despite changes in the business model, they'll always want to increase sellers' success through communication. Clearly this is not something that can be accomplished over 90 days and forgotten.

## Controllable by the Team

Whoever drafts the objective, whether it's at the corporate, business unit, department, team, or individual level, must be able to control the outcome. OKRs that generate cross-functional coordination are critical (and we'll explore that topic in Chapter 4); however, when you create a new objective it is with the explicit understanding that you independently possess the means to realize it. If, at the conclusion of the quarter, your objective has not been reached and your first temptation is to say, "Well, sales didn't deliver, so we missed our objective," you're missing the spirit of the exercise.

## Provide Business Value

Our narratives will become shorter as the criteria become more obvious, like this one. Your objectives should be translated from your strategy and directed toward creating tangible value for the enterprise if achieved. If there is no promise of a business benefit at the end of the day, there is little need to expend the resources necessary to accomplish the objective.

## Qualitative

This one is especially brief. Objectives should represent what you hope to accomplish, and therefore, be expressed in words and not numbers. The use of numbers will be thoroughly covered with key results (see Exhibit 3.1).

## TIPS FOR CREATING OBJECTIVES

In the previous section, we laid out the characteristics you should strive for when constructing objectives. To help you get there, we've compiled a number of tips and practical suggestions to consider.

## Avoid the Status Quo

Our advice here is consistent with what we discussed in the preceding section on ensuring your objectives are inspirational and add business value. Your aim

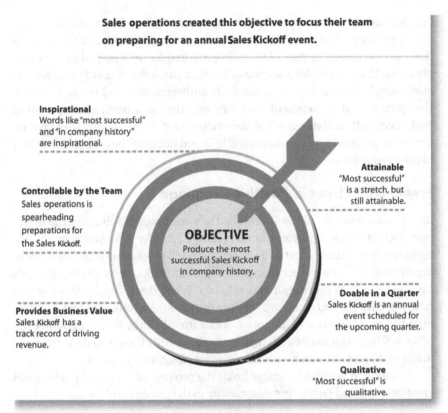

**EXHIBIT 3.1**  Anatomy of an Effective Objective

is to always identify new objectives that tug at the edges of your capabilities. Therefore, you should avoid those that simply recite what you're already doing, for example: "Maintain market share" or "Keep training employees." If you can accomplish an objective with virtually no change in the way you're working, it is most likely going to prove to be wholly ineffective in moving your business forward.

## Use Clarifying Questions

We've both been witnesses to the endless debates that often seem to be isolated exclusively to corporate meeting rooms. You've undoubtedly endured a few yourself: the kind in which words are swirling back and forth through the air, but little progress is being made on the task at hand. Often, the best way to cut the confusion is to simply and sincerely ask, "What do you mean by . . .?" When creating objectives, there will be an onslaught of ideas and concepts that may contain a nugget of value but are frequently wrapped in nebulous phrasing. If, for example, someone offers that you must "Create value for our customers," assume the role of an OKR anthropologist and try to ascertain the specifics of that comment. Are they referring to a particular segment of customers? All customers? What does value mean in this context? Escalating from abstractions to specifications will help you unearth the true objective that requires your focus.

## Frame Objectives in Positive Language

Ideally, your team should feel compelled to work towards achieving the objectives you set. Therefore, you should carefully consider how you frame them. Research demonstrates that we humans are much more comfortable approaching what we do want, rather than avoiding what we don't. As an example, let's say you want to improve your eating habits. When designing an objective you have two choices. You could say, "Reduce the amount of junk food I eat." Or, you might term it this way: "Eat more calories from healthy food." Choosing the latter will force you to research healthy foods, identify those you'd like to experiment with, and ultimately provide a greater likelihood of success.

Framing in positive language holds the promise of opening up additional creative space and facilitating adaptability in the pursuit of objectives.

## Use Simple Rules

A recent study experimented with approaches for sparking creativity among 180 Chinese high school students. The students were assigned two tasks—to complete a story and design a collage from stickers—and divided into three groups. The first group was simply given the assignment, while the second group received the additional instruction "please try to be creative." The third group received the assignment and simple but specific rules on how to complete the activity, such as "fold or tear the stickers to vary the shape and size of the materials." Four independent judges assessed creativity and found the third group, the one that received the simple but specific rules, was the most creative. The concrete guidance gave the students a starting point and channeled their creativity.[4] Brainstorming remains an extremely popular tool, but the truth is, starting from a blank canvas can overwhelm and actually inhibit our ability to create. Before you embark on creating objectives, draft your own set of simple boundaries. As a starting point, you might want to assemble a checklist that includes the items we presented in the previous section dealing with the characteristics of effective objectives.

## Start with a Verb

Very basic advice, but frequently ignored. An objective is a concise statement outlining a broad qualitative goal designed to propel the organization forward in a desired direction. That implies action, thus it's crucial that every objective begin with a verb to denote the action and desired direction. For reasons of simplicity and brevity, some organizations will truncate their objectives. For example, take the seemingly innocuous *customer loyalty*. As written, it is not an actual objective so much as a vague hope, offering little value in providing employees with direction on how to act in order to achieve it. Does the company want to maximize loyalty, build loyalty, leverage loyalty? Each of these is quite different and would drive diverse actions. Action verbs are what bring your objectives to life.

## What's Holding You Back?[5]

It was 1841 in London, and American portrait painter John Goffe Rand faced a frustrating challenge plaguing all artists of his day—keeping his oil paints from drying out before he could use them. The best solution available to Rand and his contemporaries was using a pig's bladder sealed with a string. To expose the paint, an artist would prick the bladder with a tack, but of course there was no way to completely seal the plug afterward, leading to the vexing problem of prematurely dry paint. Additionally, pig bladders were not the best travel companions, frequently bursting open and wasting what was then an expensive commodity. Rand studied the problem extensively and devised a solution—the tin paint tube. Although it was slow to catch on, it eventually proved to be exactly what Impressionists required to escape their studios and capture inspiration from the natural world around them. Thanks to Rand's portable invention, for the first time in history it was possible for a painter to produce a work onsite, whether in a café, a garden, or waterfront. The paint tube also revolutionized the use of color, since it was now practical and affordable to produce and carry dazzling new pigments such as chrome yellow and emerald green, allowing the artist to capture the full majesty of any moment. So important was this invention that Renoir declared, "Without colors in tubes there would be no Cezanne, no Monet, and no Impressionism."[6]

The moral of this story is the power of recognizing and overcoming problems to improve your situation, and that applies as much to objectives as it does to Impressionism paintings. When considering possible objectives ask yourself what problems are holding you back from executing your strategy. Taking an unvarnished look at the problems that separate you from the successful execution is a great starting point in the creation of objectives.

## Use Plain Language

We've emphasized this point elsewhere, but it bears repeating here as well. Given the many functional specialties represented in the modern business environment it would be very easy for experts to offer up objectives teeming with esoteric words and phrases that only they and their colleagues can decipher. While you don't want to shy away from using words that accurately convey the essence of the objective, you should err on the side of choosing language that everyone can immediately understand to generate widespread comprehension of the objective and why it's important. We also suggest sparing use of acronyms. Should you include any, ensure everyone is aware of their meaning.

 **OBJECTIVE DESCRIPTIONS**

Following the advice offered in the preceding section will ensure you select objectives that are poised to provide immediate value to your business. The last recommendation centered on using plain language to ensure everyone grasps the objective. However, our experience shows that, even when you attempt to make the objective as simple as possible (without dumbing it down), its meaning and relevance for your immediate business context may not be immediately apparent. For that reason, we suggest you write short descriptions for each objective.

Objective descriptions clearly articulate what is meant by the objective, ensuring all readers are literally on the same page as to what the objective encompasses. They aren't lengthy; a couple of sentences will almost certainly suffice in most cases. Included in the description is a summation of why the objective is important, how it links to a corporate-level objective, any specific dependencies, and internal customers it supports or relies on for achievement. Think of your description as the objective's rationale for being, like a note to the CEO justifying why this objective should exist.

If you're at all tempted to skip this step in the name of efficiency, let us share a very pragmatic reason for investing the relatively small amount of time necessary to create objective descriptions. Depending on your implementation schedule, you may create both objectives and key results in the same workshop. However, it's also possible that you'll split the tasks over two or more sessions, creating objectives first and allowing time to contemplate what you've developed, share with others for feedback, and make any necessary adjustments. Should you follow that path a funny thing tends to occur when you reconvene to draft the key results. You'll tee up the discussion of an objective, eager to assign key results when it dawns on you that you really don't remember what you meant when the objective was created. This is simply human nature, especially if some of your objectives are open to interpretation, for example, "Enhance Productivity." Some broad themes may linger from your discussion, but the specific nature and tone of what you meant may be a complete mystery, rendering it nearly impossible to write effective key results. To ensure this doesn't happen, we suggest you write draft descriptions immediately upon agreeing to the inclusion of an objective.

## CHARACTERISTICS OF EFFECTIVE KEY RESULTS

The previous sections took us deep into the world of objectives, examining criteria you should adhere to, and sharing tips on how to create them. But, of course, objectives are just one part of the OKR framework. In the pages that follow we'll examine their crucial counterpart, key results (see Exhibit 3.2).

In Chapter 1, we defined a key result as a quantitative statement that measures the achievement of a given objective. If the objective asks, "What do we want to do?" the key result asks, "How will we know if we've met our objective?" Sounds easy enough, especially since tracking results is something that comes almost naturally to most of us now, given the rise of Fitbits and other wearable devices. However, creating effective key results for your business, those that accurately gauge progress on your objectives, can sometimes prove elusive. Whether the problem stems from vague and difficult-to-quantify objectives or poorly conceived key results that simply don't accurately represent the objective, without sound metrics to hold yourself accountable you won't reap the benefits the OKRs framework promises. Therefore, as we did with objectives, in the space below we've outlined a number of criteria to adhere to as you build your key results.

### Quantitative

Objectives are always qualitative, representing a desired action, while key results are necessarily quantitative so that we can apply numbers to

**Here is one of the key results created by sales operations to reflect the objective from Exhibit 3.1.**

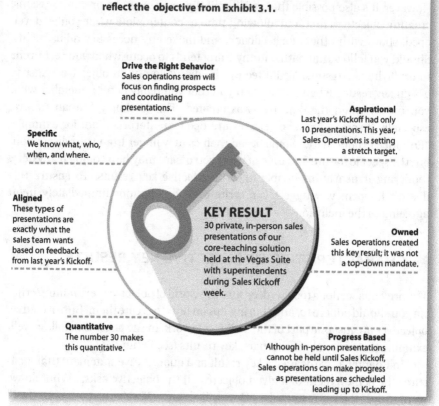

**Drive the Right Behavior**
Sales operations team will focus on finding prospects and coordinating presentations.

**Aspirational**
Last year's Kickoff had only 10 presentations. This year, Sales Operations is setting a stretch target.

**Specific**
We know what, who, when, and where.

**Aligned**
These types of presentations are exactly what the sales team wants based on feedback from last year's Kickoff.

**KEY RESULT**
30 private, in-person sales presentations of our core-teaching solution held at the Vegas Suite with superintendents during Sales Kickoff week.

**Owned**
Sales operations created this key result; it was not a top-down mandate.

**Quantitative**
The number 30 makes this quantitative.

**Progress Based**
Although in-person presentations cannot be held until Sales Kickoff, Sales operations can make progress as presentations are scheduled leading up to Kickoff.

**EXHIBIT 3.2**   Anatomy of an Effective Key Result

confidently determine whether or not we've met the objective. It could be a raw number (number of new visitors to your website), dollar amount (revenue from new products), percentage (percentage of repeat customers), or any other form of quantitative representation. Progress on a key result should never be a matter of opinion, and that's why numbers are so powerful. They scrub away any confusion as to whether you've hit your objective, providing clarity through objectivity. But numbers can do more than assess progress. As Niket Desai, Former Googler and now chief of staff at Flipkart, tells us in this story, they can also stimulate innovative thinking.

The company I was working with had a standard web-publishing model with three participants: the readers, the bloggers, and the advertisers. It found that every campaign led to more readers, which would grow the audience, which would then cause the advertisers to spend more money creating a cycle effect for rapid revenue growth. We learned that we needed more campaigns, but we also noticed most advertisers only ran one campaign. So our growth objective included two key results:

■ 50 percent of signups run a campaign within two weeks.
■ Increase the average campaigns per advertiser from 1 up to 5.

In order to increase the average number of campaigns, we had to think differently.

We came up with the idea to offer discounts on campaigns run within the first week, which led to many businesses running repeat campaigns. This greatly increased revenues, since companies were purchasing three to four full-priced campaigns after a single discounted one. The measurement aspect leads to a special type of focus that is more effective than making broad statements about improvement. It's hard for qualitative results to ever be substantial, and they are highly subjective.[7]

## Aspirational

The results of years of goal science research are quite clear and compelling: Setting the bar high leads to improved performance and enhanced satisfaction at work.[8] Conversely, should you decide to draft easy to attain results, you can expect achievement, but subsequent motivation and energy levels will most likely fall. So, when drafting your key results we urge you to stretch the limits in order to challenge your teams to think differently, as Niket Desai shared in the previous section. However, the obvious caveat (one we touched upon in the objectives segment on attainability) is ensuring the results are ultimately achievable. One way to walk this tightrope is through effective scoring of key results, a topic we'll explore later in the chapter.

## Specific

Clarifying terms and concepts, ensuring shared understanding, is critical when writing key results should you hope to foster communication among teams and avoid unnecessary and damaging ambiguity. Here's an example of what can happen when you don't specify exactly what you mean by the words comprising the key result. As part of their OKRs, the CEO of a company insisted on the key result of "100 percent of use cases are available on the new platform."

IT (information technology), which was the group in charge of putting the use cases on the new platform, didn't know what the CEO meant by *use cases*, so it put up what it could, based on its limited comprehension of his request. At the end of the quarter the CEO asked: How did we do? IT answered, "Great! We got all the use cases on there." Sure enough, what they posted had nothing to do with what the CEO was referring to when he said use cases. This waste of time, effort, and most likely engagement for OKRs could have been easily avoided with some simple dialog at the outset of the drafting process.

## Owned

In the previous example, we saw the problems that can occur when a key result is instituted by executive will, without the benefit of proper understanding by all involved. In that case, although IT accepted responsibility for the key result, it didn't in fact take "ownership" for it, and that is a critical distinction. Those responsible for delivering key results must be actively engaged in the process, principally in the creation. You will always be more prepared (and disposed) to execute on something that you helped create, since you molded your intentions based on a common understanding of the desired result, and your willingness to find innovative ways of achieving it. Most OKRs should originate from you, the OKR owner, and not from corporate mandate. In practice, we expect a mix of top-down and bottom-up OKR creation, something we'll discuss further in Chapter 4.

## Progress-Based

Harvard Professor Teresa Amabile has written extensively about what she terms "The Progress Principle." It suggests that:

> Of all the things that can boost emotions, motivation, and perceptions during a workday, the single most important is making progress in meaningful work. And the more frequently people experience that sense of progress, the more likely they are to be creatively productive in the long run. Whether they are trying to solve a major scientific mystery or simply produce a high-quality product or service, everyday progress—even a small win—can make all the difference in how they feel and perform.[9]

This finding has major ramifications for your key results. It's imperative that your key results be amenable to demonstrating progress frequently, at least every couple of weeks. If you won't know whether or not you've met the key result until the last day of the quarter, you're robbing yourself of the opportunity of enhancing motivation and engagement through frequent check-ins.

## Vertically and Horizontally Aligned

We'll have much more to say on the topic of alignment in Chapter 4. For now, we'll underscore the importance of ensuring your key results are vertically aligned by reviewing them within your team and leadership, and horizontally aligned by sharing and reviewing with teams upon whom you depend, or who depend on you.

## Drive the Right Behavior

There are a number of pithy statements relating to measuring performance; perhaps the best known being, "You get what you measure." That is often the case. Once you shine a metaphorical light on anything, you will necessarily be drawn to it, and increase the attention paid toward it. At times, the devotion to meeting targets you set can become single-minded and lead to dysfunctional decision making at best and unethical behavior if left unchecked. For that reason, we suggest you think carefully about the behavior each key result you generate may engender in people. Here's an example. A colleague of ours tells the story of a client in the fast-food industry who, despite the best of intentions, chose a measure that led to disastrous results. It seems this organization found its restaurants were disposing of a lot of cooked food at closing time, and obviously that was draining their profits. To put a stop to such a hindering practice it instituted an efficiency measure for each outlet, charting the quantity of food they disposed of each day. Clever managers, not wishing to be chastised for poor performance, quickly devised a method to ensure great scores on the measure. If their restaurant closed at midnight, they would not cook any food between 11:00 and midnight until a customer entered and ordered. That way, there was very little chance of having any refuse at the end of the day. Of course, customers did not share the zeal of "chicken efficiency" and soon began staying away in droves once they learned this restaurant had effectively taken the fast out of fast food. The measure was devised with noble motives, but drove a behavior that proved to be completely counter-productive.

## TIPS FOR CREATING KEY RESULTS

We've already thrown a lot your way in this chapter, and there is more to follow. If it feels like a fire hose aimed directly at you, try and reframe the experience from an assault by the water to being soothed by its coolness on a hot summer's day. Our intention is not to overwhelm but to equip you with all the information you require to create a set of OKRs that can transform your business. These sections encompassing criteria and tips comprise the essentials of capturing the most effective OKRs. Let's conclude this phase of our journey with some practical tips to keep in mind when developing your key results.

## Key, Not All

This exercise is not an excuse to demonstrate how overworked and overburdened you are by cataloging every conceivable action you're considering for the next quarter. On the contrary, it's a strategic endeavor focused on highlighting and maximizing the most critical value drivers of your business. If, for example, you hired 10 people last quarter, and intend to hire another 10 in the next, don't list "Hire 10 new people" as a key result. It's simply business as usual and, while the additional staff may aid productivity and ultimately accelerate the execution of your strategy, it's not a key result that demands any innovative thinking or stretch on the part of your teams. Maintain exclusive emphasis on identifying the key results that denote actual progress on your objectives.

## Describe Results, Not Tasks

Related to the item above, your goal is to isolate key results, not create a list of tasks or activities. To clarify our terms, when we say task we're referring to something that can typically be accomplished in a day or two; that would reside comfortably on a to-do list. "E-mail a prospect" or "Meet with the new VP of Sales," are tasks, not key results. Whereas, "Add twenty-five qualified opportunities to the pipeline" is a key result. It demands problem solving and focus to meet with success. To distinguish between a task and key result, look at the verb you assign. If you find yourself using "help," "participate," "assess" or other relatively passive verbs (passive in this context at least) you're most likely offering up tasks rather than key results.[10] If that's the case, move up the value ladder by asking, "Why are we helping, or participating, or assessing?" What is the outcome? Once you do that, a more solid key result featuring an action-oriented verb is likely to emerge.

## Use Positive Language

We shared this advice when discussing how to create objectives and it holds equally well here. Bigger is better with key results. Rather than offering "Lower error rate to 10 percent," consider the messaging power inherent in: "Increase accuracy to 90 percent." The positive framing will enhance motivation and increase commitment.

## Keep Them Simple and Clear

We once worked with a client that, because of the nature of their industry, had to demonstrate environmental stewardship to both their shareholders and community. Thus, it was inevitable that a key result would relate to environmental performance. The director of the group went off to deliberate and after some time suggested a key result that we'd like to share with you, but we can't. Not because of confidentiality, but because we have no idea what it meant. To this day, after much explanation, we still don't know what this ultra complex metric was intended to capture. And we're not alone; members of the company's leadership and the director's own team were equally dumbfounded as to its nature, meaning, and efficacy. Needless to say this key result was ultimately scrapped and replaced by something that, while perhaps not as sophisticated or arcane, was understandable by all. Creating robust key results doesn't mean you should require a PhD to decipher them.

## Open up to All Possibilities

When contemplating the best key result for an objective, a seemingly logical candidate may spring to mind with virtually no effort on your part. You're so confident that this is *the* absolute perfect key result for the objective that you eschew any further discussion and select it. This is a great example of the overconfidence bias in action. Stanford researchers observed the effect in practice at a fast-food chain whose executive team was focused on improving customer satisfaction and profitability. With little in the way of proof to back their claim, they steadfastly clung to the notion that employee turnover was the driver of happy customers, and thus selected it as a key metric and invested substantial sums of money to lower turnover. As the data accumulated, however, executives were shocked to discover that some stores with very high turnover reported both happy customers and increased profitability, while others with low turnover produced anemic results. With time and enhanced analysis, they found that what actually drove satisfaction and profitability was store manager turnover.[11] When you begin selecting key results, it's important to possess the humility to acknowledge that you don't have all the answers, and thus be open to numerous possibilities.

## Be Sure to Assign an Owner

There is a well-known phenomenon in the social psychology literature termed *diffusion of responsibility*. Distilled to its essence it suggests that people are less likely to take action or assume responsibility when others are present. The quintessential example is someone suffering a heart attack on a busy urban street with nobody stopping to help, because they all assume someone else will. In less dramatic fashion, key results may suffer the same fate if an owner is not assigned (i.e., since no one individual is ultimately responsible for the result, no action is taken and the goal languishes). Key result owners are not singularly accountable for the achievement of the key results, but are designated as the go-to person for information related to that particular key result. They also update the company on progress during, and at the conclusion of, the quarter.

One of our favorite quotes comes from a book titled *How to Think Like Leonardo da Vinci*. And who wouldn't want to think like one of the greatest polymaths in history? The book's author, Michael Gelb, has this to say about the task of making difficult choices: "The discipline of ordering . . . the discipline of choosing one over another, ranking one a level higher than another, and then articulating why you chose the way you did requires a depth and clarity of consideration and comparison that inspires richer appreciation and enjoyment."[12] We can think of no better way to describe the arduous, but ultimately rewarding, process of selecting objectives and key results of genuine value. Although it's a difficult assignment, the hard work of making the demanding choices will leave you with a richer appreciation of what you do select.

 ## TYPES OF KEY RESULTS

Depending on the maturity of your performance monitoring systems and the availability of data at your disposal, you may use more than one type of key result. In practice, we see three primary varieties. Each is outlined, with examples, below, and illustrated in Exhibit 3.3.

## Baseline Key Results

Consider a company that has just refreshed their strategy and decided to focus on forging strong and lasting relationships with customers as their value proposition. You may recall from Chapter 2's strategy discussion, that this is known as *customer intimacy*. An objective for this might be "Increase customer loyalty." The team then deliberates and decides that "20 percent of customers

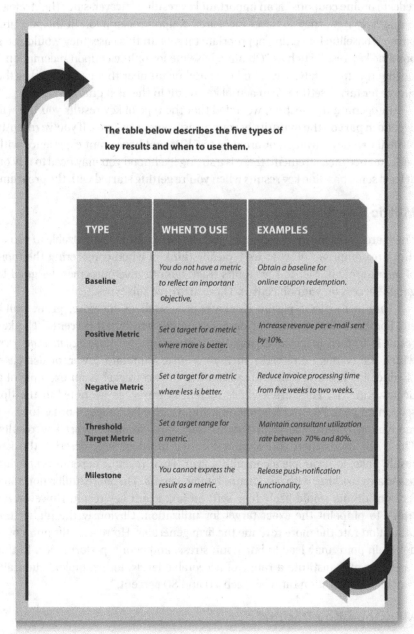

The table below describes the five types of
key results and when to use them.

| TYPE | WHEN TO USE | EXAMPLES |
|------|-------------|----------|
| Baseline | You do not have a metric to reflect an important objective. | Obtain a baseline for online coupon redemption. |
| Positive Metric | Set a target for a metric where more is better. | Increase revenue per e-mail sent by 10%. |
| Negative Metric | Set a target for a metric where less is better. | Reduce invoice processing time from five weeks to two weeks. |
| Threshold Target Metric | Set a target range for a metric. | Maintain consultant utilization rate between 70% and 80%. |
| Milestone | You cannot express the result as a metric. | Release push-notification functionality. |

**EXHIBIT 3.3** Types of Key Results

redeem online coupons" is an important key result. However, since the strategy is relatively new, they've never measured coupon redemption in the past and have no baseline for setting appropriate targets. In this case, they would use a baseline key result such as "Obtain a baseline for online coupon redemption." During the quarter, they will find the baseline number that can be used as the source for target setting of an actual key result in the next quarter.

In opening this section, we noted that the type of key results you use will depend in part on the maturity of your measurement systems. If you've recently pivoted to a new strategy, or are new to OKRs and have scant experience with performance measurement, there is a strong likelihood you may need to rely on at least some baseline key results when you're getting started with the program.

## Metric Key Results

These are by far the most common, and will be instantly recognizable to you as they are comprised of what we typically think of when considering the topic of measurement. Metric key results track quantitative outcomes designed to gauge success on your objectives. There are three sub-types.

*Positive metrics* typically employ words such as increase, grow, build, etc. For example: "Increase revenue per e-mail sent by 10 percent." The key result is framed in positive language. Conversely, we have *negative metrics*, which are composed of verbs such as reduce, eliminate, lower, or decrease. "Reduce invoice processing time from five to two weeks" is an example of a negative metric. They are a viable option; however, as we noted in the tips section on page 74, we recommend using positive language in order to foster motivation toward the goal. Finally, there are *threshold target* key results. These are used when you require a range to adequately describe the key result. Take, for example a consulting firm. Their revenue depends on having associates working with, and hence billing, clients. Therefore, utilization rates for consultants would likely represent an important key result. However, it's tricky to pinpoint the exact target for utilization. Obviously the higher the utilization rate the more revenue the firm generates. However, utilization over a certain point may lead to burn out, stress, and poorer performance. In this case, you may institute a range of acceptable levels, for example: "Maintain consultant utilization rates between 70 and 80 percent."

## Milestone Key Results

Occasionally, you may encounter things that, despite your best efforts, are very difficult to translate into a metric key result. This often occurs when you have a seemingly binary outcome at play; we either did it or we didn't. Did we ship the new product or not? Did we issue the report or not? However, yes or no, binary responses are not acceptable in an OKRs framework. You need to translate everything into numbers in order to properly assess your progress towards the objective. In these cases, a milestone key result may be appropriate.

All of the key result types we've shared thus far will benefit from scoring, but for milestone key results it is especially essential. You may wish to jump ahead to page 80 to review our guidance on scoring. With that as context you can return to this page. Outlined below is an example from a recent client that highlights the milestone key result approach.

The company's engineering group had this objective: To release push notification functionality in various countries. The release to various countries was the obvious key result but it appeared binary—either they did or didn't release the push notification. By applying scoring, they were able to transform this into a much more effective milestone key result. A score of 1.0 would be achieved should they release the functionality to all countries. Obviously this was an enormous stretch, and most likely not realistic. The still ambitious, but reachable, target of releasing the functionality in Canada and two additional countries was represented by a score of 0.7 and likely signified their most applicable target. Below that they instituted a 0.5 target level for releasing push notifications just in Canada. Finally, should they simply ensure push notification functionality passed QA and had scheduling tested in Canada they would receive a score of 0.3. By applying scores they were able to convert a potentially inadequate binary metric into one that stimulated progress and innovative thinking to meeting the targets.

## Health Metrics

In our discussion of baseline key results we used the hypothetical example of a company changing its strategy to one of customer intimacy. This fictional organization had an objective of "Increase customer loyalty" and a key result of "20 percent of customers redeem online coupons." Why would they want customers to redeem online coupons? To increase revenue of course. Not much of a brain teaser there, right? But it actually runs deeper than that. Coupons are just one method this company will likely engage in order to drive profitable revenue growth. Key to its strategy is loyalty, creating a genuine relationship with patrons, leading to a much higher lifetime value for each customer. Over time, the company might use in-store promotions, rewards programs, online marketing, and several other methods to drive loyalty. While the specific methods may change, it is ultimately interested in whether the interventions are leading to enhanced loyalty. Thus, it might utilize a metric like Net Promoter Score (NPS), which denotes the likelihood to recommend a product or service, to determine ongoing loyalty. The key word in that sentence was *ongoing*. It won't take the pulse of NPS just once and move on. It will be a critical and enduring metric as the company continues its efforts to execute strategy.

In this instance, NPS can be considered a health metric, which we define as something the company will monitor frequently (over years perhaps) because it is representative of successful execution of their strategy. You can probably think of several other metrics that would reside under the health banner. Employee engagement is an obvious candidate. Without engaged employees willing to provide discretionary effort to achieve goals you have little chance of success, regardless of the brilliance reflected in your strategic plan. Certain financial metrics will also likely fill your roster of health metrics: Revenue growth, net profit, and return on assets are all standard indicators of fiscal well-being and should be examined on an ongoing basis. Health metrics should derive directly from your strategy and be considered a complement to your OKRs. In fact, a good diagnostic test of OKRs is their ability to positively move the needle on a health metric. If you're considering the adoption of an objective and associated key results, but don't envision any line of sight toward an overall health metric (and thus your strategy), perhaps you should go back to the flip chart and try again.

##  SCORING OKRs

Let's say you've created the following key result, "Obtain 20 new customers this quarter." It's a stretch goal, one that excites the team, and everyone is eager to do their part in attracting new customers to the firm. At the end of the quarter, you've attracted 12 new customers. Is that great, good, or just okay? The answer to that question depends entirely on past results and your expectations for the future. If, during the preceding quarter you obtained just one new customer, then 12 looks like a staggering achievement. However, if 15 new customers came on board last quarter, then clearly 12 is unlikely to have people high-fiving in the hallways. To create effective key results that allow you to learn more about your business—and a primary purpose of any measurement is to do just that—you need to calibrate your expectations, creating a series of targets that specifically delineate exceptional, good, and mediocre performance. Scoring OKRs does just that.

Scores should be applied immediately after you agree on the wording for a key result. Doing so allows you to communicate expectations, enables continuous learning, and provides valuable clarity around what progress actually looks like for the key result. We suggest the following scale (see Exhibit 3.4):

1.0: An extremely ambitious outcome that may appear nearly impossible to meet. This is where you begin; all key results should be written as the 1.0 in order to foster breakthrough thinking. In our previous example of obtaining new customers, twenty is our 1.0 target. It may appear to be a shot for the moon if the company has never come close to attaining that level of performance in the past.

0.7: This level represents progress that is difficult, but ultimately attainable. To continue our example, securing 15 new customers could represent a valid 0.7 target level of performance because it's a lofty number well on the way to our stretch, but achievable based on past results.

0.3: We can phrase this the "business as usual" target level. It represents performance we can achieve with standard effort and little or no assistance from other teams. Our fictional company may believe acquiring five new customers is something it can do with minimal effort and therefore use that as the 0.3 level target. Considering the emphasis of OKRs is challenging teams to break from their current paradigms and devise new ways of working to meet inspirational goals, you may wonder why we would include a 0.3 target since it implies no extra effort to achieve. There is still learning value from this mediocre increment. If at the end of the quarter a team is only able to reach 0.3 on a key result (or results), you'll want to ascertain why. Did their priorities shift? If so, why? Were shared expectations unrealistic? Was the key result deemed irrelevant at some point? All of these queries, and many others, will reveal insights into how your teams work and the nature of setting effective key results you can draw upon in subsequent quarters.

Setting targeted levels of performance is one of the trickiest aspects of any form of monitoring system. Even if you possess years of baseline data to draw on or industry averages you can confidently apply, you must still use subjective judgment when making the final determination of what targets are suitable for you. The right numbers fall somewhere on the art versus science continuum, and your challenge is pinpointing their exact location. Our advice is to take advantage of any quantitative background material you have (baseline data, industry averages, customer requirements, etc.) but don't entirely shy away

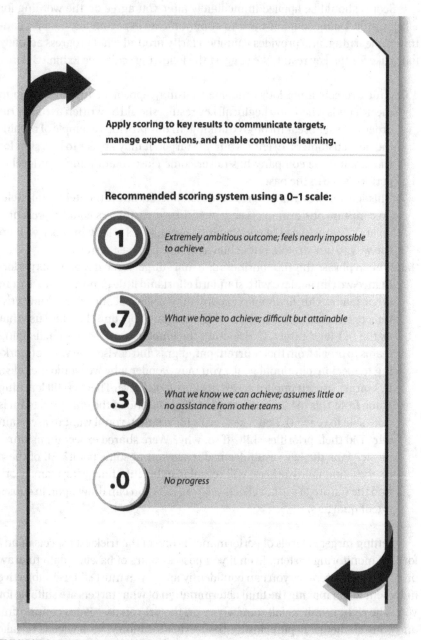

Apply scoring to key results to communicate targets, manage expectations, and enable continuous learning.

Recommended scoring system using a 0–1 scale:

**1** — *Extremely ambitious outcome; feels nearly impossible to achieve*

**.7** — *What we hope to achieve; difficult but attainable*

**.3** — *What we know we can achieve; assumes little or no assistance from other teams*

**.0** — *No progress*

**EXHIBIT 3.4** Scoring Key Results

from subjective evaluations and "gut feelings." Nobody should know your business better than you and, thus, professional judgment should be an important element to making final target decisions.

One final word on the scale presented above: The 1.0, 0.7, and 0.3 levels are what we recommend to our clients, and what we've encountered most frequently in practice. However, you may wish to alter the scale if doing so is consistent with your business practices or culture. Some organizations find 1.0 to simply be too small a number and feel a grander scale might impel greater drive towards the goal. Thus they'll use 100, 70, and 30, or in some cases 1000, 700, and 300.

## Mid-Quarter Check-Ins

You know that old saying, the only thing worse than bad news is bad news late? It definitely applies to key results. You'll grade your key results at the end of the quarter, determining whether you reached a 1.0, .7, or .3, but the last thing you want are surprises, especially in the form of poor performance. For that reason, we strongly recommend you check in with teams, assessing their progress throughout the quarter.

Our colleague, the OKR expert Christina Wodtke, has an easy-to-apply and practical suggestion to facilitate conversations during these mid-quarter check-ins. When setting key results at the beginning of the quarter assign a confidence level of 5 out of 10.[13] Remember, your 1.0 target must be ambitious, so a fifty percent chance of getting there should seem appropriate. With that as context, during the quarter you can assemble teams and ask where their confidence level currently resides. Has it jumped to 8 out of 10? Or, has it plummeted to 2 out of 10? Either way, the answers will be revealing and help you channel resources to either get the team back on track, or if they're surpassing expectations, assist others with their key results. We'll expand on this topic in Chapter 5.

## What to Expect When Grading Key Results

Speaking of Chapter 5, it also delves into reporting, and managing with, OKRs, but at this point you may be curious about what to expect when grading your key results for the first time. Is it an abject failure if you have nothing but zeroes across the board? Or, conversely, does meeting every 1.0 target mean you've left substantial value on the table by not setting the bar nearly high enough?

In our experience, those new to OKRs will tend to encounter one of two outcomes in their initial foray with the framework; either they will in fact have all ones, or at the opposite end of the spectrum, they're left scratching their heads because, despite their Herculean efforts, their reports are littered with zeroes. As we noted previously, establishing targets is a challenging affair, and most organizations have little experience doing so proficiently. Therefore, depending on their culture and past experiences, they will either declare wholly unattainable, dent-the-universe type targets, or at the other extreme, put forth goals that require virtually no effort to surpass. If either of these scenarios describes your company, don't panic, it's par for the course. What is most important when experiencing these initial bumps in the road is to exercise patience and trust in the process. With additional experience your dexterity in target setting will improve and you will in fact enjoy the many benefits OKRs have to offer.

Eventually, after a few quarters (more or less; every organization is different) your key result grades should begin averaging close to 0.6 to 0.7. Anything higher and perhaps your targets are not aggressive enough, meaning you're unable to take full advantage of the talent and potential your teams have to offer. On the other hand, results below 0.6 may indicate overly ambitious aspirations. If you're consistently falling short, you'll want to engage in a frank discussion with your teams about the attainability of their targets before they become demotivated and skeptical of the entire notion of OKRs.

## Should You Score and Grade Objectives?

The short answer is no. Recall once again the definition of an objective—a concise statement outlining a broad qualitative goal designed to propel the organization forward in a desired direction. The objective is designed to inspire the team to new heights of growth and innovation. The key results, through objective quantitative means, let us know whether or not we've achieved the objective.

Having said this, some organizations will attempt to score and grade objectives, employing various methods in their quest. One company decided an objective was either achieved or not. If each target on all the underlying key results was achieved, the objective was achieved. Otherwise, it was not. So if it had five key results, and achieved the targets on all but one, it did not achieve the objective. To us, this will lead to nothing but confusion, skepticism, and demoralization on the part of employees who may put their best efforts into achieving key results only to be told their work isn't good enough. Our recommendation is to focus on scoring and grading key results only.

## HOW OFTEN DO WE SET OKRs?

Compared to many other management disciplines, one of the refreshing aspects of the OKR approach is that, at this point at least, it can be considered an open source framework. It's not akin to generally accepted accounting principles (GAAP) that lay out the rules companies must absolutely follow when reporting financial results. There are no founding fathers or gurus laying down OKR guidelines as if on stone tablets, and this open-source environment is a great boon for organizations because it allows for customization and flexibility in implementation. There are a number of core principles (which we're sharing with you), but ultimately, our advice is descriptive, not prescriptive, meaning you can alter parts of the model to ensure a fit with your particular business context.

How frequently you set OKRs is one of the areas you might modify. The default answer to how often you create OKRs is, of course, quarterly. As we've previously noted, one of the chief virtues of the model is this rapid rhythm, which ensures enhanced communication and learning throughout each twelve-week period. However, quarterly may not represent the most fitting cadence for your business. Sadly, not all organizations recognize this inherent malleability of the model and we're aware of some that have abandoned OKRs because they falsely believed they must be set each quarter. Let's read what John Doerr, who you'll recall introduced OKRs to Google, has to say on the topic:

> The key for any team or any group is that you use this on a regular basis...you should pick what frequency is right for you. When Intel was doing them monthly National Semiconductor did them every four weeks so they had thirteen periods in their manufacturing year because they were primarily a manufacturing company...and that was right for their culture. Most companies are quarterly, but some of the more agile firms are saying no, we want to line them up with our sprints or our development schedules. A quarter is too long. Instead of every twelve weeks I'm going to set the timeframe to be every six weeks. Some places choose to do them quarterly and in parallel annually. So I've got a set of annual OKRs and then some quarterly ones that I update along the way as well.[14]

As Doerr correctly notes, the key is using OKRs on a regular basis, but of course the word *regular* may take on a different meaning for you than other companies. He also notes that some organizations will use a combination of both annual and quarterly OKRs. We call this a dual *cadence* approach. Within organizations using a dual cadence, the company defines a set of annual OKRs and typically breaks this down into a set of OKRs for each quarter. Teams may then create an annual and quarterly set of OKRs or decide to set OKRs only for the upcoming quarter. Among the benefits of the dual cadence is the aid of context provided by establishing annual OKRs. Teams and individuals then possess a direct line of sight from their own OKRs to what the company wishes to realize during the year. In this way, an organization is balancing long-term (annual) strategic priorities with the quarterly victories necessary to meet them. Dual cadence is just one option; there are many others, again depending on the situation in which you find yourself. What matters most, to quote Doerr's cogent guidance one more time, is using OKRs on a regular basis.

## HOW MANY OKRs DO WE HAVE?

The late screenwriter Nora Ephron left us with a number of Hollywood classics, including *When Harry Met Sally*, *Sleepless in Seattle*, and *Silkwood*. All three were Academy Award nominated for writing. Before she turned her talents to the screen, Ephron was a journalist, and perhaps her greatest gift in that world was the ability to capture the essence of a story. She learned the importance of identifying a story's core early on, at Beverly Hills High School from her Journalism 101 teacher Charlie Simms. Here's the enduring lesson Simms passed on to Ephron.

He started the first day of class much the same way any journalism teacher would, by explaining the concept of a *lead*. He explained that a lead (i.e., the leading sentence) contains the why, what, when, and who of the piece. It covers the essential information. Then he gave his students their first assignment: write a lead to a story. He then presented the facts of the story:

> Kenneth L. Peters, the principal of Beverly Hills High School, announced today that the entire high school faculty will travel to Sacramento next Thursday for a colloquium in new teaching methods. Among the speakers will be anthropologist Margaret Mead, college president Dr. Robert Maynard Hutchins, and California Governor Edmund 'Pat' Brown.

The students then hammered away on their manual typewriters outlining their lead. Each attempted to summarize the who, what, where, and why as concisely as possible: "Margaret Mead, Maynard Hutchins, and Governor

Brown will address the faculty on . . ."; "Next Thursday, the high school faculty will . . ." Simms reviewed the students' leads and put them aside. He then informed them that they were all wrong. The lead to the story, he said, was "*There will be no school Thursday.*" In that instant, Ephron realized that journalism was not just about regurgitating the facts but about figuring out the point. It wasn't enough to know the who, what, when, and where; you had to understand what it meant. And why it mattered.[15]

Ephron later noted that what Simms had taught her worked just as well in life as it does in journalism. We'd argue that it also works with OKRs. The day you set foot in a conference room with your team to debate and decide on your OKRs, you're searching for the business equivalent of the "lead." Just think of the universe of possibilities that awaits you when someone says, "*Okay, what are our most important objectives?*" You have customer concerns, shareholders or investors, the community, partners, vendors, employees, competitors, the list is endless. They are the organizational equivalent of the "why, what, when, and who." Your challenge is to cut through the clutter and pinpoint exactly what is most important to you, right now.

When it comes to the number of OKRs you produce, we recommend you adhere to the tried and true aphorism: less is more. This is a difficult exercise, we know, and not one every organization is initially ready to tackle. There are several factors conspiring to drive the number of OKRs to an unsustainably high count. Among them: the desire not to leave anything out ("*Everything is important to us right now!*"), the fact that it's always easier to list a multitude of things than zero in on the most critical, and the rise of software that places no upward limit on the number of objectives and key results you can enter into the system. There is a huge opportunity cost to increasing your inventory of OKRs, however. Primarily, lack of clarity and focus around what the company's priorities truly are. Employees today crave knowledge of what is most important so that they might align their actions toward those goals, which results in greatly enhanced meaning at work. Should you develop, say, 8 objectives and 20 key results, it will make it nearly impossible for employees, who are subject to the same laws of time as you and we are, to decide where to place their efforts.

As a species, we seem obsessed with maximizing . . . everything. Did you know the word *priority* entered the English language in the 1400s? It was singular then; meaning the very first or prior thing. It remained singular for the next five centuries. But in the go-go 1900s, we pluralized the word and began to speak of priorities. We felt, somehow, that by changing the word we could bend the reality and somehow be able to have multiple first things.[16] By sharing that anecdote, we're not suggesting you limit yourself to just one objective and a few key results, although for those brand new to OKRs, it is an option to ease into the process. We're simply restating the obvious principle that suggests if you try to do everything, you'll wind up making little progress on anything. As for an actual number range, if you examine the literature—and at this point the literature amounts primarily to blog posts and articles—the consensus seems to propose between two and five objectives, each with two to four key results. We believe that is the very high end of the scale, however, and once again urge you to conduct the organizational forensics necessary to isolate what matters most to your business. Find your lead!

## DO OKRs STAY THE SAME FROM QUARTER TO QUARTER?

Consultants are sometimes criticized (in good humor we hope) for not always planting a flag of certainty and telling clients exactly what they should do to cure whatever ails them. The truth is, as we can both attest, the answer to many questions posed to consultants is "*It depends.*" And that is the case with the question above.

Yes, some of your objectives may remain the same from quarter to quarter, especially those deemed particularly critical in light of current strategic or operational challenges. The same may be said of key results; some may remain for consecutive quarters and beyond. However, recall our discussion of health metrics on page 79. We described them as measures the company will monitor frequently, over years perhaps, because they are representative of successful execution of their strategy. You will likely have both objectives and key results that fall into this category of ongoing strategic significance. In the health metrics discussion we noted the objective of "Increase customer loyalty." We suggested that Net Promoter Score is a valuable ongoing indication of customer loyalty and, thus, may be elevated to health metric status, remaining unchanged until, perhaps, the company's strategic direction is altered.

In the same vein, "Increase customer loyalty" could be a *health objective,* one that is key to the translation of your strategy and unlikely to change in the foreseeable future. If you're pursuing a customer intimacy strategy, attempting to foster long-term relationships with your customers through outstanding service and support, then increasing loyalty will always be a critical desire. There is little point in adding it on your OKRs quarter after quarter, especially if you match it with the same key result. OKRs are about novelty, innovation, and creativity to spark breakthroughs. Repeating OKRs for years introduces a stale quality that is best avoided.

When you begin your OKR process, we recommend you generate a small number (a handful most likely) of objectives that are crucial to the execution of your strategy, and therefore unlikely to be modified any time soon. When drafting them, it might help to think in terms of the "pillars" of your business: Financial, Customers, Key Processes, and Employees. What is the core set of objectives necessary to successfully win in your marketplace? These are your health objectives. Next, decide on the key results that will gauge your success in meeting these objectives. Those, of course, represent the health metrics.

It's easy, very easy, to be sucked into the whirlwind of urgent problems and crises that face us when we set foot in the office each day. Easy, and in some ways seductive, because fighting fires feels good—you're crossing something off a list, getting things done. But this is often at the expense of what truly matters—executing your strategy. By creating a small set of health objectives and key results you're creating ongoing context for the OKR process each quarter. Constantly reminding yourself of what is most important and, at the end of the day, demands your utmost attention and care.

 ## CAN OKRs CHANGE *DURING* THE QUARTER?

Generally speaking, company-level OKRs will not be adjusted during the quarter. But, please welcome back our old friend, "It depends." There may be circumstances that demand a change in OKRs. One of us was working with the State of New Jersey just prior to Hurricane Sandy devastating parts of the state. In the weeks and months following the disaster, copious changes were made to their performance monitoring systems, reflecting the new reality faced by the many government departments required to provide services.

We're not suggesting, however, that a natural disaster is necessary to make modifications to your OKRs (at any level of the company) during a quarter. There are many other possibilities as well. For example: Perhaps you acquired a major new customer who initially demands intense resources from your teams. That could warrant the alteration of your current crop of OKRs. Or, you may decide to make a strategic pivot, which of course would dictate an update to the OKRs as well. What you cannot do is change objectives or key results simply because you feel they are too difficult, or you may have doubts about their efficacy.

Each quarter that you use OKRs, you're building a muscle, one that grows stronger as you introduce the discipline of setting, monitoring, grading, and most importantly learning from what the key results have to tell you.

Frequent alterations of OKRs during the quarter may be dressed up as "agility" or adaptive behavior, and in some situations that may be true. But, in most cases it's simply an unwillingness to commit to the rigor and discipline necessary to strive for better and better OKRs that push the frontiers of knowledge about what really drives your business.

 ## THE PROCESS TO SET OKRs

Throughout the chapter, we've provided numerous ideas, recommendations, and tips relating to the characteristics of effective OKRs. We're certain that at this point, you're anxious to put them into practice as you develop your initial set of objectives and key results. In this section, we'll guide you through the actual mechanics of creating OKRs. The exercise is conveniently represented by the fitting acronym *CRAFT*, which stands for Create, Refine, Align, Finalize, and Transmit (see Exhibit 3.5).

### Create

Some pundits would tell you that to complete this step, you gather your group together—whether it's the executive team if you're creating company-level OKRs, or your team if it's a team-level set—get out a fresh box of markers, stand at a flip chart, and yell, "Go!" to start a classic brainstorming session. Immediately, a brilliant chorus of ideas is shouted out so fast you can barely keep up. But we're not those pundits.

Large-group brainstorming is an accepted part of corporate workshop culture, but recent research has demonstrated many deficiencies with the process. Let's start with the number of people involved in most brainstorming exercises. The rationale is a noble one; involving crowds of people in the cause means they're more likely to buy in and support what's created. However worthy a principle that may be, it collides with the reality offered by social scientists who now conclude that the larger the group, the poorer the results. Author Susan Cain describes the phenomenon in her book *Quiet*.

> Some forty years of research has reached the same startling conclusion. Studies have shown that performance gets worse as group size increases: groups of nine generate fewer and poorer ideas compared to groups of six, which do worse than groups of four. The evidence from science suggests that business people must be insane to use brainstorming groups.[17]

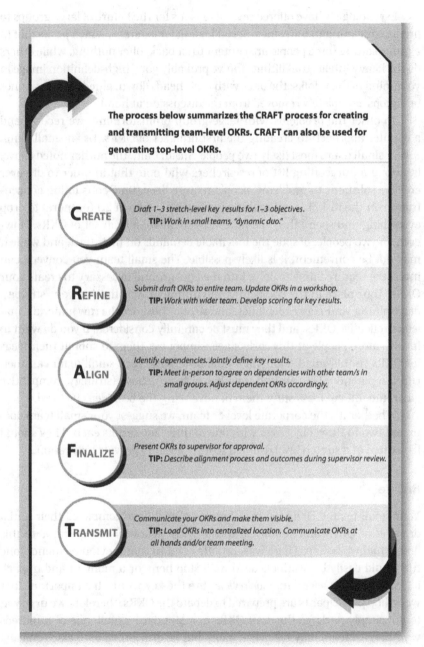

The process below summarizes the CRAFT process for creating and transmitting team-level OKRs. CRAFT can also be used for generating top-level OKRs.

**C**REATE
Draft 1–3 stretch-level key results for 1–3 objectives.
**TIP:** Work in small teams, "dynamic duo."

**R**EFINE
Submit draft OKRs to entire team. Update OKRs in a workshop.
**TIP:** Work with wider team. Develop scoring for key results.

**A**LIGN
Identify dependencies. Jointly define key results.
**TIP:** Meet in-person to agree on dependencies with other team/s in small groups. Adjust dependent OKRs accordingly.

**F**INALIZE
Present OKRs to supervisor for approval.
**TIP:** Describe alignment process and outcomes during supervisor review.

**T**RANSMIT
Communicate your OKRs and make them visible.
**TIP:** Load OKRs into centralized location. Communicate OKRs at all hands and/or team meeting.

**EXHIBIT 3.5** The "Craft" Process for Developing OKRs

Psychologists have offered several reasons for the failure of large groups to produce meaningful outcomes. Social loafing for example, which posits that in a group setting some people are content to sit back, offer nothing, while others do the heavy intellectual lifting. You've probably got a high-definition image in your mind of those folks: the ones with their heads down, glued to their phones or laptops, completely removed from the discussion at hand.

To offset the problems with large-group brainstorming, we recommend a counter approach to creating the first draft set of OKRs. Use a small team. A very small team, most likely two people. Susan Cain, the author noted above, is among a burgeoning list of researchers who note that in order to discover creative solutions to problems, people require deep, time-consuming concentration on the task. It's not realistic to expect a group of 20 (or more) to drop everything and spend the time necessary to create a draft set of OKRs. However, for two people, despite the inevitable demands on their time, and while it may not be convenient, it is likely possible. The small team you convene can invest the required time to delve into the background necessary to create your OKRs: Your place in the competitive environment, scrutinizing your strategy, determining your core capabilities, and so on. These are the raw materials that lead to effective OKRs, and they must be carefully considered. If you do want to involve more people at this early stage, simply ask them to submit their ideas for OKRs to this small team via e-mail or survey. Your small team can then run the potential list through the filter of issues above (strategy, competitive environment, etc.), assisting them in advancing the best ideas forward.

Whether it's the corporate level or team, we suggest your small team document two to three objectives with one to three key results each. They should be written at a stretch level (the 1.0 scoring level) to provide inspiration.

## Refine

Your small team ("Dynamic Duo," perhaps) will have completed their initial draft set of OKRs and submitted to the wider team for review prior to this first actual workshop. There was a subtle point in that previous sentence, one that could easily be overlooked, so we'll stop here for a moment and unpack it. *"Submit to the wider team for review"* are the key words. It's important that workshop participants are prepared to debate the OKRs; therefore we urge you to not simply package the draft OKRs in a standard e-mail, one of hundreds your harried team may receive in a day, but be distributed both electronically and by old-fashioned paper, accompanied by a letter from either the CEO or the team lead on the importance of the exercise.

In attendance for the workshop, we would expect the leadership team if you are working on your corporate-level OKRs, or the team-level leadership group if it's a team set of OKRs. The purpose of the session is to critically examine what has been prepared, have the small team explain their choices, generate debate (vigorous debate we hope), and ultimately come to agreement on the set of OKRs you'll use.

As part of the process, each key result should be scored using the scale discussed earlier in the chapter. You'll want to ensure your final list of OKRs adhere to the characteristics we presented and are a direct translation of your unique strategy. As for scheduling and timing, book an entire day with the goal of cancelling the afternoon component because you were able to complete the work in the morning. You may require the entire day, however, and that could be a very positive sign, indicative of spirited inquiry and debate. However, if you can end early, don't prolong things just to fit the allotted time. Nothing makes workshop participants cheerier than finishing early.

One last caveat, and this is based on our thousands of hours facilitating workshops with clients around the globe: Be realistic in your expectations of achieving full consensus on the OKRs. We can tell you unequivocally that it's virtually impossible. Why? For one reason, those people surrounding you in the conference room aren't robots or zombies (if they are, you've likely got a great *Walking Dead* script on your hands) but living, breathing human beings who bring a lifetime of unique experiences that shape their views and philosophies. It's exceedingly difficult to expect a group of people to reach full agreement on any topic, and in fact probably not completely advantageous. Dissenting voices can be helpful in ensuring the OKRs you do use have been carefully vetted and considered from all angles. What you must insist on, in the end, is *support* for what is created. Even if some members of your team aren't 100 percent in favor of a particular objective or key results, they must publicly support them. Otherwise you risk the possibility of them releasing the toxic venom of skepticism and lack of belief in the overall OKRs program. Encourage multiple voices and points of view but commit as a team to supporting and engaging with what you create.

## Align

Much of the work in modern organizations is cross-functional in nature—teams working together to solve problems or create new modes of working that will benefit multiple areas of the business. OKRs created at the team level must be created with this context front of mind.

The small team or dynamic duo we profiled in the previous steps should take your draft OKRs on a road trip around your organization, discussing dependent OKRs with other team leads. You'll be liaising with colleagues to discuss how some of your OKRs depend on their best efforts, while sharing with other teams how you are uniquely positioned to assist them in meeting their goals.

Scoring will often help you in assessing the level of dependency between you and another team. You'll recall that a score of 0.3 represents the minimum you feel your team can achieve without any assistance. Should there be a significant gap between your 0.3 and 0.7 target levels, that will most likely indicate a critical dependency. Your aim in meeting with other team leads is to come to agreement on the dependency and adjust targets in order to demonstrate the level of support required. For example, if you determine that one of your key results is highly dependent on another team's assistance, your aim in meeting with them is to ensure they acknowledge the dependency and pledge their support, which will then allow you to ratchet up your targets because you're confident they'll provide their backing when necessary. The converse is also true; other teams may rely on you to meet their targets and, thus, you'll work with them to show how you can help.

Although you shouldn't anticipate wholesale modifications to your OKRs during this step, it is possible that changes will be made. Seeing your goals through the fresh perspective of another team can often be revealing and illuminate potential shortfalls. Once you've assembled the updated OKRs, distribute them to the entire team for comments. Unless you receive significant pushback on any changes, an in-person meeting should not be necessary.

## Finalize

Once again, assuming you're creating OKRs at the team level, during this step the team lead and partner will confer with their superior (most likely a member of the senior executive team) to receive final approval to use the OKRs in the upcoming quarter. You can provide an overview of how you arrived at the OKRs, the due diligence performed in drafting them, and the cooperation agreements you've cemented with other dependent teams. It's also important to ensure that the executive understands the rationale behind the scoring targets you've chosen. The last thing you want when results begin to accumulate is mismatched expectations that lead to confusion and disappointment.

## Transmit

There are two components in this final step. First is the fairly rote necessity of loading your OKRs into a software system or whatever product (Google Sheets, Excel, etc.) you deem appropriate to track your results over time. A rote process indeed, but a vital one nonetheless. OKRs must be rigorously and formally cataloged and monitored to ensure integrity in the system. Calculations and ideas scrawled on the back of cocktail napkins may be the stuff of business lore, but won't be helpful quarter in and quarter out as you're attempting to outmaneuver competitors and successfully execute your strategy. There are numerous high-quality software vendors providing tools in this space, and when the time is right (software should always be regarded as an enabler, not a requirement), you might consider purchasing one. We'll have more to say on this topic in Chapter 5.

The second task is transmitting the OKRs to your team and beyond. We encourage you to communicate them widely, using a variety of media. One method, sharing them in an in-person venue, such as an all hands or town hall style meeting is strongly recommended for a number of reasons. Chiefly, it provides the opportunity for employees who were not directly involved in OKRs creation to ask questions of those who were there when the critical decisions were made. And giving employees this opportunity is vital to ensuring a sense of fairness and being heard, which is dispiritingly absent in most workplaces. In a Harris Interactive poll of 23,000 workers, only 17 percent felt their organization fostered open communication that is respectful of differing opinions and that results in new and better ideas.[18] New ideas are the currency of successful businesses, and when constructed properly OKRs propel those innovations in thought. But to do that, every single person must understand why you chose what you chose, and how they can contribute. If that sounds like a segue, it is. In Chapter 4, we'll show you how to create OKRs from top to bottom, ensuring your entire workforce is focused on what matters most.

 **NOTES**

1. John Beshears and Francesca Gino, "Leaders as Decision Architects," *Harvard Business Review* (May 2015).
2. "How to Make OKRs Actually Work at Your Startup," http://firstround.com/review/How-to-Make-OKRs-Actually-Work-at-Your-Startup. Accessed January 21, 2016.

3. Schumpeter blog, "Management by Goal-Setting Is Making a Comback, Its Flaws Supposedly Fixed," *The Economist*, March 7, 2015, www.economist.com/news/business/21645745-management-goal-setting-making-comeback-its-flaws-supposedly-fixed-quantified-serf.

4. Donald Sull and Kathleen M. Eisenhardt, *Simple Rules: How to Thrive in a Complex World* (New York: Houghton Mifflin Harcourt, 2015).

5. Paul R. Niven, *Balanced Scorecard Evolution: A Dynamic Approach to Strategy Execution* (Hoboken, NJ: John Wiley & Sons, 2014).

6. Perry Hunt, "Never Underestimate the Power of a Paint Tube," *Smithsonian Magazine*, May 2013.

7. Ben Lamorte, "Everyone Should Have OKRs! Q&A with a Googler," *Enterprise Goal Management* (January 21, 2015), http://eckerson.com/articles/everyone-should-have-okrs-q-a-with-a-googler.

8. See for example Edwin A. Locke and Gary P. Latham, *New Developments in Goal Setting and Task Performance* (New York: Routledge, 2012).

9. Teresa Amabile and Steven J. Kramer, "The Power of Small Wins," *Harvard Business Review* (May 2011).

10. "Set Objectives and Develop Key Results," Re: Work, https://rework.withgoogle.com/guides/set-goals-with-okrs/steps/set-objectives-and-develop-key-results/. Accessed January 5, 2016.

11. Michael J. Mauboussin, "The True Measures of Success," *Harvard Business Review* (October 2012).

12. Michael J. Gelb, *How to Think Like Leonardo daVinci* (New York: Bantam Dell, 2004).

13. Christina Wodtke, *Radical Focus: Achieving Your Most Important Goals with Objectives and Key Results* (cwodtke.com, 2016).

14. "Goal Summit 2015: Why Goals Matter with John Doerr," *Better Works* (May 10, 2015), https://www.youtube.com/watch?v=MF_shcs5tsQ. Accessed January 25, 2016.

15. Greg McKeown, *Essentialism: The Disciplined Pursuit of Less* (New York: Crown Business, 2014).

16. Ibid.

17. Susan Cain, *Quiet: The Power of Introverts in a World That Can't Stop Talking*, Kindle edition (New York: Random House, 2012).

18. Stephen R. Covey, *The 8th Habit* (New York: The Free Press, 2004), 3.

CHAPTER FOUR

4

# Connecting OKRs to Drive Alignment

WE'RE GOING TO BEGIN THIS CHAPTER with a story directly from Paul on the importance of connecting goals.

During the summer between my junior and senior years of college, I was living with my retired parents at my childhood home in a small town in eastern Canada. I'd lived in that house my entire life, and while my parents took pride in the property and maintained it well, the rough (some may say savage) Canadian winters had exacted a toll on the roof of our house. It was clearly in need of replacing, and fast. Since my parents were living on a fixed income and I had a bit of time before starting my summer job, I decided I would take it upon myself to fix the roof. This despite the fact that what I knew about roofing you could easily write on a piece of confetti.

The first step was enlisting a team of buddies to help with the project, which I assumed could be completed in a couple of days (faulty assumption number one of many). With the standard college currency of pizza and beer offered, all of my friends agreed to assist. My father advised us on the supplies we'd need, and we dutifully went around town assembling the raw materials for the new roof. We were all set.

On a glittering May morning we began. Up the ladder and on to the roof we shimmied. Tools and materials were hoisted up and we began tearing apart the old roof. Shingles, tarpaper, and the sounds of Billy Idol booming from my ghetto blaster (this was the early 1980s) filled the air. Within a few hours, the driveway next to the house was littered with the roof's remains, emblematic of our early, and prematurely declared, success. The day continued and soon the roof was stripped. All that remained now was putting down the new materials. And that's when things went sideways.

Tearing apart the old roof was easy, but putting on a new one? None of us had any idea of what to do. There was no master plan to follow. Before long, we were stepping into each other, knocking tools from the roof to the ground, and repeating steps over and over again. It was chaos. Even Billy Idol couldn't help us. A near riot broke out because two of the guys could swear that in the chorus of the song "*Eyes Without a Face*" he was crooning "*How's about a date.*" Today, the spat would be settled in about 15 seconds through a Google lyrics search, but back then, it was to remain unsolved and provide yet another conflict dividing us on the roof.

Salvation appeared in the form of another friend who had some previous experience in roofing. He'd been busy the first couple of days and unable to join us, but fortunately, he made his appearance as tempers were reaching the boiling point and confusion reigned. He immediately took stock of the situation and shared with us the key and necessary steps in putting the roof down. He then broke the steps down sequentially and assigned each of us a task that contributed to the overall goal. Within minutes we were competently and happily assembling the roof. I can't suggest any of us were then qualified for a career in the roofing industry, but we did manage to lay down a roof that I'm proud to say kept my parents dry for over two decades.

This story clearly demonstrates one thing: College students don't know what they're doing and should not be trusted. No, that's not it. The story illustrates what can happen when people, even with the best of intentions, don't see how they can contribute to an overall goal. When we started putting down the new roof, each of us was excited to make a contribution to help my parents. But we had no context for our actions. We didn't see how our actions influenced the goals of fixing the roof, because until my friend with real knowledge of roofing arrived there was no big picture strategy we could plug into to make our contribution. We weren't aligned in our actions. The result: Poor productivity, low engagement with the task, and suboptimal results.

##  A CRITICAL LINK

We've previously lamented the pitiful levels of employee engagement here in the United States and around the world, and the staggering costs in lost productivity it leaves in its wake. One of the chief reasons engagement remains so stubbornly low is the fact that employees, not unlike young Paul and his friends, are eager to make a meaningful contribution but lack the context to leave their unique mark.

In one poll of 23,000 U.S. residents employed full-time, only 37 percent said they have a clear understanding of what their organization is trying to achieve and why. The same study discovered that only 9 percent believe their work teams had clear, measurable goals.[1] Other reports have come to similar conclusions. In reviewing the data, one researcher noted: "There is tremendous positive impact to the bottom line when employees see strong connections between company goals and their jobs."[2] As this quote reveals, it's not just engagement that gets a bump when employees have a line of sight from their work to the company's goals; the effects ripple from improved processes to enhanced customer relationships, all the way to the profit and loss statement in the form of improved financial results. It's clear that organizations benefit tremendously when employees see the connection between what they do everyday and how those actions affect overall goals.

##  CONNECTING OKRs

Illuminating that relationship between what employees do and how those actions lead to overall strategy execution is best accomplished with connecting OKRs from top to bottom in your organization. By connecting, we mean creating sets of OKRs throughout the company that align with your highest-level OKRs (could be corporate or business unit, depending on where you're starting) and signal the unique contribution offered from teams and individuals throughout the enterprise.

Connecting confers a number of benefits, among them the ability to foster two-way learning. Every organization today must excel at fast-paced learning in order to make necessary course corrections and keep aggressive rivals at bay. When you connect OKRs, you generate learning opportunities in two directions. First, as business units, departments, and individuals develop their own OKRs, it provides them the opportunity to showcase their unique role in creating overall value for the company. To do this effectively, of course, they must understand the business's strategy in order to create OKRs that align with it. So, as they create OKRs, they're learning more about, and deepening their understanding of, the organization's purpose and strategy. Simultaneously, as OKR scores are analyzed across the company, leaders benefit from the ability to examine results spanning the entire organization. Rather than relying on a small set of indicators that serve as abstractions for the entire operation, executives can perform deep dives into every facet of the company by reviewing OKRs at all levels. This veritable treasure trove of data improves decision making, the allocation of resources, and accelerates learning.

##  HOW TO CONNECT OKRs

When it comes to connecting, you don't want to emulate Paul and his buddies, climbing up to the roof with no plan whatsoever. Not to worry, we've got you covered (like a roof—get it?) with the steps to follow when connecting your OKRs.

### How Deep to Connect

We covered the topic of where to develop OKRs in Chapter 2. As we noted there, ultimately your goal should be to spread the use of OKRs throughout the entire company. The question is one of timing. Do you rush to connect from top to bottom, perhaps in the very first year? Or, do you employ a more measured approach, staggering the implementation over a period of months, or even years?

OKRs can be a transformative device for your business, sparking new thinking that leads to previously uncontemplated levels of success. To fulfill that potential, the framework must be embraced and used at all levels of the company, allowing you to foster fluency in a new corporate language; that of strategy execution. Obviously, the faster you connect, the faster your employees master this new taxonomy, and the sooner results improve.

We firmly believe in momentum, and suggest you move aggressively, but thoughtfully, in connecting OKRs. That sounds like a contradiction, so we'll unpack the key terms. Aggressive is self-explanatory, meaning you connect quickly and deeply to all levels (perhaps to the individual) of the company.

However, we temper that with the word *thoughtfully*, which in this context implies you have contemplated, and can answer in the affirmative, these questions: Do we have executive support for OKRs? Do we have a clearly documented strategy that is reflected in our corporate OKRs? Are we committed to using OKRs, regardless of initial results, to manage our business? If you can successfully overcome those hurdles, then a rapid rollout may be appropriate.

Whether to connect all the way down to the individual level is a question that requires some additional coverage. The pros and cons must be carefully weighed. Let's begin with the potential advantages:

- *Enhanced awareness of OKRs:* This level of connection provides a great impetus to communicate the principles and techniques of the framework.
- *Increased buy-in and support:* Understanding the process and having the chance to be directly involved will likely boost commitment toward it.
- *Drive comprehension of OKRs throughout the company:* In order to construct effective OKRs, employees will be required to thoroughly grasp the OKRs of their team and related units.
- *Grow engagement:* As employees are able to draw a line from what they do to the big picture goals of the company, they may become more engaged and willing to offer the discretionary effort necessary to move the ball a little further down the field.
- *Develops skills:* At the individual level, OKRs will reflect a mix of personal growth ambitions and contribution to the company.[3] The personal growth component can assist employees in furthering their career, which (see above) can lead to enhanced engagement.

Those are compelling arguments for connecting to the individual level. However, there are possible disadvantages as well. They are presented next:

- *Reduced engagement:* OKRs may be viewed by some as yet another corporate-imposed compliance tool that increases complexity and leaves even less time to "get things done."
- *Confusion around variable compensation:* Should your organization utilize a separate incentive compensation system that does not link to OKRs, employees may be confused as to why two separate systems exists (OKRs and incentive compensation).
- *Lack of teamwork:* Individuals may focus too much on their own OKRs rather than the team-level OKRs.

- *OKRs that resemble a to-do list:* Effective OKRs focus on results, not tasks. However, when creating OKRs at the individual level, there is often the temptation to include job-related tasks that, while important for the individual, may not contribute to overall strategy execution.
- *No value-add:* Some teams will likely already have the equivalent of an OKR system in place at the individual level. For example, a call-center team with a staff of a hundred telemarketers probably already has a call-center tracking system in place that provides real-time feedback to every employee. Asking each telemarketer to also write down OKRs and update the metrics could be redundant and simply a waste of time.

Ultimately, the decision will depend on your culture and readiness for such deep connection of OKRs. One possibility that we've seen organizations employ with success is making individual OKRs an optional step. Sears Holding, whose innovative practices you can learn more about in Chapter 7, have chosen this approach, allowing individual associates to decide for themselves whether to opt in to the OKR program.

## Determine the Number of OKRs

In the last chapter we shared the consensus view that your corporate set of OKRs should comprise between two and five objectives each with two to four key results. However, we also noted this was on the very high end of the scale and urged you to follow the well-worn advice of "less is more" when choosing OKRs.

As you plan to connect OKRs, possibly through the entire organization, you must wrestle with the question of whether to impose a limit on the number of objectives and key results each group may select. Those new to the endeavor may be excited by the promise it holds and find their enthusiasm getting the better of them as they catalog a never-ending list of OKRs necessary to propel them forward.

Passion is a trait you're loath to impinge upon, but once the number of OKRs reaches a certain level you quickly reach a point of diminishing returns, as it proves impossible to manage and you achieve a bloated list of priorities. There is no magic number. However, we'll once again admonish you to keep the volume low, especially at the outset as your teams become accustomed to using, and managing by, OKRs. If people insist on a numerical range, rather than identifying a specific number, consider focusing instead on a not-to-exceed number.

## Preparing Your Groups for Connecting

Even the fittest among us wouldn't lace up their running shoes and hit the trail for a demanding run without first stretching: loosening their muscles to prepare them for the challenge that lays ahead. Consider the following two items the connecting equivalent of stretching—putting your groups in the best possible position to create effective OKRs.

In Chapter 2 we discussed the importance of a mission statement, which conveys your core purpose as an organization. All groups that are going to create connected OKRs should create a mission that clearly outlines their raison d'être: Why they exist and how they add value to the organization. We've used the word context at several points in the text and are repeating it here because once again, the exercise of creating a mission will provide context for the connecting process to follow. As group members debate potential OKRs, they can continually look to the mission to ensure what they're proposing fits with their overall purpose.

Armed with their own mission statements, each connecting group must then answer this fundamental question: "How do we support the organization's mission and strategy?" In broad strokes, how does the group contribute to the company's success? As you'll learn shortly, the concept of influence is the key to connecting, and this question primes groups for that task by having them enumerate, in advance, how they support the company's overall strategic goals.

## Ensure Everyone Understands the Highest-Level OKRs

Do you remember that game children used to play at birthday parties, called telephone? The kids would be seated around a table or assembled in a line and a parent would whisper a phrase in the first child's ear. Maybe something like, "All little kittens love milk." The first little boy or girl would then turn to the next and whisper the message in their ear. On and on it went until the short missive finally arrived at the last child, who was to then repeat it aloud to the entire group. Inevitably, by that time the phrase was garbled and bore no resemblance whatsoever to what had been transmitted to the first child just moments before. In the example above, the proud young boy or girl who had the privilege of sharing with the entire group might announce, "Olive and Kenny love Mike," prompting a chorus of laughter from the others.

Connecting OKRs is basically a more sophisticated version of the telephone game, albeit one with much greater stakes. You're starting with the corporate-level OKRs, the equivalent of what is whispered in the first child's ear, and betting/hoping that by the time that message is conveyed to business units, down to departments, and ultimately received by individual employees it's clear enough that they have understood it and, thus, created OKRs that define their part in meeting strategic goals.

As you communicate your corporate OKRs, it's absolutely imperative that everyone in the organization understands them; what they specifically mean, why they were chosen, and why they are so vital to the company's success. Even if what you've constructed at the top seems relatively straightforward and obvious in meaning and intent, never forget that others will be refracting that message through their specific lens of experience, and may draw completely different conclusions, which could potentially lead to connected OKRs that are horribly misaligned. Communication is not something that can be overdone in an organization. Many change experts suggest there is a vast tendency to under-communicate key priorities, often by orders of magnitude. Here's a quick guideline: At the point you've become utterly weary, bordering on ill, from communicating the how and why of your corporate OKRs, that's when you might just be getting the message across. One of our clients understands this necessity of repetition. The CEO begins each companywide monthly meeting by reciting the mission and top-level OKRs. It only takes about 5 minutes, but in our attention-deficit driven society, that's often about 4 minutes and 30 seconds too long for some employees, who begin rolling their eyes at hearing the mission and OKRs yet again. But the CEO is quite content with this. He knows that only through repeating the message again and again can he ensure it occupies the mind space necessary for effective execution to take place.

## The Key to Connecting Is Influence

Allowing all groups, perhaps even individuals, to show how they influence overall corporate OKRs is the purpose and goal of a connecting exercise. Let's use Exhibit 4.1 to walk through the process.

As we noted in the previous section, it all begins with the top-level set of OKRs. These are the critical levers of your success, and everyone in the company must possess a deep understanding of them before you begin connecting. We'll assume you're starting from the corporate level. If that's the case, the first actual connection occurs as business units (as described in Exhibit 4.1,

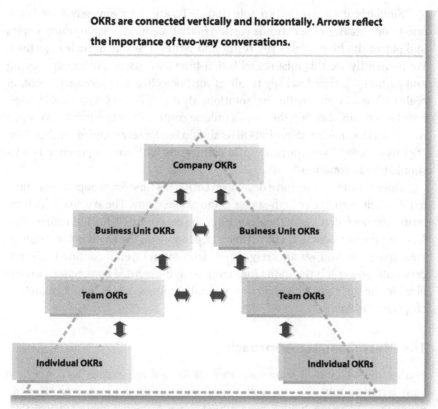

**OKRs are connected vertically and horizontally. Arrows reflect the importance of two-way conversations.**

**EXHIBIT 4.1** The Connecting Process

but your terminology may differ) study the corporate OKRs and ask, *"Which of these OKRs can we influence, and how?"*

It's important to note from the outset that you don't anticipate every group to exert an influence on every corporate objective and key result. That's not the point of the exercise. Some organizations fail to recognize this point and, hence, insist that business units and teams identify OKRs for every corporate objective. This results in force-fitting objectives and key results that are often not relevant to the group and simply divert attention from what truly does matter. Your aim is influence—which of the OKRs can we help move the needle on? Having said that, we would expect every unit to see a link between its work and at least one corporate OKR.

Similarly, it's important to note that OKRs are not seamlessly linked on a one-to-one basis. In the extreme version of that scenario, a team simply copies and pastes the higher-level key result and writes it as one of their objectives. We frequently see this mistake with first-time OKR users. Although copying and pasting a higher-level key result as your objective may seem expedient, in reality it's a lazy and ineffective solution. Most connected OKRs should originate bottom-up, showing the team's unique contribution to success. We agree with John Doerr, who notes that OKRs should be "loosely coupled" rather than "tightly coupled," and the process for connecting with your supervisor's OKRs should be a negotiation.[4]

Once business units have developed OKRs, it's time for groups below them to take their turn in our high-stakes game of telephone. These units, which we term *team level*, don't take their cue from the corporate OKRs, but rather, they focus on the business unit above them. Depending on the levels of hierarchy in your company (and we sincerely hope it isn't many), you'll continue this process until you reach the individual level. A well-executed connection process provides line of sight from every individual employee all the way back to the corporate OKRs.

## The Mass Connect Approach

You've now assembled your corporate OKRs and are excited to connect to your business units. The immediate and most pressing question is: "How do we do that?" The mechanics are outlined above, but what about the logistical side of the equation? Most companies will assign someone (perhaps a member of the executive or strategy teams) to work one on one with business units in crafting their connecting OKRs. That person will facilitate a workshop with each unit, spending the considerable time and effort necessary to ensure they draft a batch of OKRs that align with what has been created at the corporate level. We think there is a better way, we call it the *mass connect* alternative.

This method places a premium on open communication, friendly competition, and camaraderie in building OKRs. Rather than working with each business unit individually, under the mass connect approach you'll bring all groups together at one time to develop a draft set of OKRs. If yours is a large organization, you may be thinking, "Everyone? I'd need something the size of Madison Square Garden to accommodate every person from every business unit!" Obviously, that's not feasible or practical, so we recommend that you select delegates from each business unit (typically two to four people) to represent the group at the session. Outlined below is a standard agenda for a mass connect session. As for the length of the event, we usually book about six hours, allowing ample time for breaks and lunch:

- *Executive briefing on your OKRs journey:* Start the day by having a member of your executive team regale the assembled teams with a stirring (hopefully) narrative of why you embarked on the OKRs path, what you've done thus far, and your expectations for the session. This creates context (there's that word again) for the workshop, provides yet another opportunity to educate everyone on OKRs, and inspires the group to bring their very best to the endeavor.

- *OKRs refresher:* By this time we hope you will have furnished your entire organization with an abundance of OKRs education materials (articles, a certain book perhaps, presentations, etc.) but in the spirit of overcommunication, take the opportunity to ensure that there is a level playing field of knowledge among those assembled for the connecting process. This need not be a comprehensive review of the literature, but simply a light overview of key topics.

- *Presentation of the corporate OKRs:* As with education, we're assuming this is not your first pass at sharing the corporate OKRs. But, once again, it's a chance to reinforce each objective and key result, answer any clarifying questions, and ensure the teams possess the understanding necessary to write their own OKRs.

- *Draft OKRs:* Provide the teams with about 90 minutes to create a first draft set of OKRs for their unit. A facilitator (or facilitators—could be internal, external, or both) will roam the room answering questions, helping ensure that teams remain on track and focused on the task at hand and offering guidance and assistance to help should they get stuck in any potential quagmires. As facilitators ourselves, we've been part of many of these sessions and can attest that this is, no hyperbole here, a fun process. The energy in the room is electric, as you encounter spirited debates mingled with laughter and the euphoria of "aha" moments when teams crack the code and conjure up a perfect OKR.

- *Report outs:* Each team is allotted approximately 10 minutes (again, depending on how many teams you have) to share their OKRs and answer any questions. Be vigilant about the timing in this step. Garrulous presenters who hijack the floor, rambling off on endless tangents, can quickly destroy the momentum and deplete all of the positive energy you've created thus far.

■ *Idea sharing:* This is, dare we say, another fun part of the day. During this step teams move about the room discussing their draft OKRs with other teams on whom they may be dependent to achieve certain OKRs, or who may be dependent on them. This facilitates horizontal alignment (something we'll discuss shortly), cross-fertilization of ideas, and enhances overall knowledge of the important role each and every team plays in the organization's success.

■ *Re-draft OKRs:* Based on the feedback they received from their colleagues, each team now reviews, refreshes, and refines their OKRs.

■ *Report outs:* Each team reports their updated OKRs and answers any questions.

Careful readers will note that we didn't provide timing for all these steps. Again, it's because the amount of time you allot for each step will depend on the number of groups in the room. Obviously, the fewer the teams represented, the shorter the session may be. Following the workshop your OKRs champion, the person or group responsible for shepherding the implementation forward, will follow up with each group to finalize their OKRs.

This mode of connecting not only engenders more positive energy than moving sequentially from group to group, but is also significantly more efficient. By gathering several groups at one time, you can cut the time of connecting, and thereby enhance momentum, considerably.

 **CREATING ALIGNMENT**

Our hope is that this book will find a wide audience and help many organizations improve their performance through the use of OKRs. But, finding an audience is a relative term, and it seems very unlikely this book will have the staying power of Sun Tzu's *The Art of War*. The Chinese military treatise dates to the fifth century BC and is still popular today. Of course the audience has shifted; today's reader is more inclined to study the text's chapters to glean insights on business strategy, rather than defeating a foreign enemy in an armed conflict. Sun Tzu offers many pithy but deceptively complex aphorisms throughout, and one that applies particularly well to our present journey is this: *"He whose ranks are united in purpose will be victorious."*[5]

Ensuring your people are aligned around a common purpose is job number one for any multinational corporation, regional government, local nonprofit, or neighborhood lemonade stand. As we've demonstrated, connecting OKRs provides an outstanding opportunity to drive that alignment through every job and function of your firm. In this section, we'd like to share with you the two types of alignment you'll be fostering during the process: vertical and horizontal.

## Vertical Alignment

This is the type of alignment most people think of when considering the connecting of goals through an enterprise. As the word implies, *vertical* connecting consists of creating OKRs that flow downward, eventually reaching the individual employee level. However, as we've previously noted, it does not mean the executive team dictates a number of obligatory goals that are essentially forced upon lower-level groups regardless of fit or necessity. Instead, vertical connecting is facilitated when teams, departments, or individuals look to the OKRs of the group to whom they report and ask: "How can we influence those OKRs? What can we do, and measure, at our level to drive both our and their success?" Again, the process is one of *loose coupling*. With vertical alignment we're attempting to create a line of sight from what your group does every day to the group to whom you report, and ultimately to the company's aspirations.

What's the nastiest four-letter word that can be uttered in a corporate setting? Not the one you might be thinking. It's *silo*. We're all well aware of the deleterious effects calcified silos can have on a company's performance. Isolated groups focused solely on their own success, with little regard to the organization's overall strategic goals. But, let's give these departmental silos the benefit of the doubt, because it's unlikely they've always harbored an intense desire to remain isolated from the rest of the organization. In fact, a more reasonable scenario is that they've never been given the formal means to demonstrate how they might contribute to the company's priorities. Executives have relied on their functional expertise and, hence, they've focused more intently upon that particular set of attributes. However, experience clearly illustrates that if you give people the opportunity to show how they link in the chain of performance they will gladly take it.

Here's an example of driving vertical alignment from an organization we worked with recently. The CEO of this mid-sized company declared that customer retention was their top priority. Traditionally, customer retention had been the sole domain of their customer success team; it managed ongoing client interactions and renewals. Soon after the CEO's announcement, everyone assumed customer success would just work harder to drive customer retention, and other departments would continue to focus on their current priorities.

However, with OKRs in place they were able to create a culture of alignment across the company.

The product team had traditionally focused on what they felt new customers would want, or what would differentiate them from the competition. But with the advent of OKRs, the product team now asks this question before approving a new feature request: "How does this product improvement drive customer retention?" The marketing team also shifted their outlook because of the OKR implementation. They transitioned from an event-marketing approach of sponsoring channel partner events to launching their first annual user conference, which they were confident would help drive customer retention. They took the time at the user conference to interview customers and gather valuable survey data. Finally, even the sales team changed their paradigm thanks to OKRs. They are now taking time to call on their install base and ask open questions around how they can add more value. They do this to build the relationship and emphasize the importance of working together over the long haul. Again, the goal is to help promote and drive customer retention. Each of the teams profiled above is doing something different, something germane to their specific function, but the common denominator is the identification of actions that help them drive the corporate strategy of increasing customer retention. That's vertical alignment in action.

We'll leave you with one last point to consider regarding vertical alignment. The concept is often represented by the metaphor of a waterfall; goals flow down with the water, throughout your entire company. However, perhaps a more appropriate metaphor is one offered by our friend and colleague Felipe Castro, founder of Lean Performance, who suggests the image of a fountain. The water from a fountain does indeed flow downward from its highest point, but it doesn't come to rest at the bottom. Rather, it is circulated back through the fountain in a never-ending flow. That is a beautiful and apt metaphor for vertical alignment. Goals do indeed drift down, but as we previously illustrated, knowledge, learning, and adaptation flow back up to the top with the aid of connected OKRs.

## Horizontal Alignment

We mentioned in the previous section that when it comes to connecting goals, most people are familiar with the concept of vertical alignment, or cascading down. This familiarity results from the fact that vertical cascading is widely employed in most organizations, and effectively at that. The deeply entrenched notion that execution hinges on alignment has been accepted for decades (at least as far back as Drucker's work on management by objectives in the 1950s). Thus, it has been rigorously studied, with best practices shared and widely used throughout the business population. Why is it then, if organizations are aware of the value inherent in alignment, and have been utilizing vertical cascading for generations, that our rates of strategy execution remain so stubbornly low?

It turns out that there is a second form of alignment, one that has largely been ignored by many companies, that may prove even more crucial in the quest to execute strategy: horizontal alignment (see Exhibit 4.2). The following statistics will swiftly shed a light on why horizontal alignment is so critical. When managers are asked if they can rely on their boss and direct reports most of the time, fully 84 percent reply in the affirmative. However, when asked if they can rely on colleagues in other functions and units all the time, a scant 9 percent reply positively. As we've shared earlier in the text, much of the work in a modern enterprise involves disparate teams coming together to solve customer issues or create new value. When one unit can't depend on another a number of damaging events tend to ensue: duplication of effort, missed opportunities, and escalating conflicts resulting in damage to the company's culture. When asked directly about cross-functional coordination managers do recognize the challenge; 30 percent cite failure to coordinate across units as their greatest challenge to strategy execution.[6] However, they have, to this point, failed to put systems in place to engender the cross-unit cooperation necessary to compete in today's environment. Once again, we believe OKRs can fill this void.

The good news is that creating horizontal alignment is not a complicated endeavor whatsoever. It simply entails having the discipline to hold detailed conversations with other units throughout the company to discover mutual dependencies, and ensure both units then create OKRs that reflect them. The resulting OKRs may be unique for each unit or in some cases they may decide to use "shared" OKRs. These come into play when multiple teams are working very closely to achieve a result, and thus share the same OKR. Shared OKRs help avoid situations in which one team may be celebrating because they completed their component of a project, but another is working frantically on their piece (which relies on the first team), and as a result of this lack of cooperation the company fails to reach its overarching goal. We would expect the shared variety to make up a relatively small percentage of your overall inventory of OKRs.

In the section on mass connecting, we proposed an "idea sharing" step during which teams share their prospective OKRs with others, searching for dependencies that may result in updated objectives and key results that illuminate shared interests. That process represents a highly expeditious method to reveal dependencies and more effective OKRs. However, given time constraints

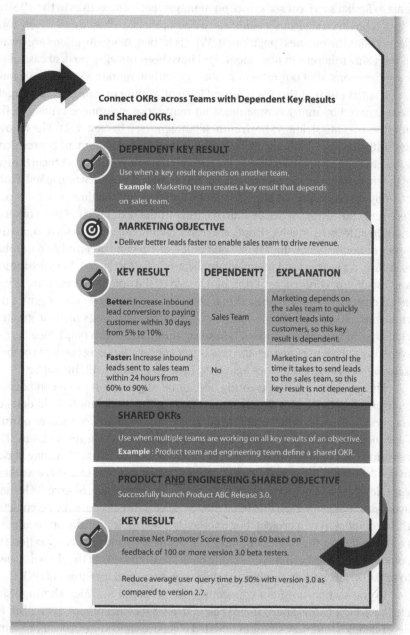

**Connect OKRs across Teams with Dependent Key Results and Shared OKRs.**

**DEPENDENT KEY RESULT**

Use when a key result depends on another team.
**Example** : Marketing team creates a key result that depends on sales team.

**MARKETING OBJECTIVE**

• Deliver better leads faster to enable sales team to drive revenue.

| KEY RESULT | DEPENDENT? | EXPLANATION |
|---|---|---|
| **Better:** Increase inbound lead conversion to paying customer within 30 days from 5% to 10%. | Sales Team | Marketing depends on the sales team to quickly convert leads into customers, so this key result is dependent. |
| **Faster:** Increase inbound leads sent to sales team within 24 hours from 60% to 90%. | No | Marketing can control the time it takes to send leads to the sales team, so this key result is not dependent. |

**SHARED OKRs**

Use when multiple teams are working on all key results of an objective.
**Example** : Product team and engineering team define a shared OKR.

**PRODUCT AND ENGINEERING SHARED OBJECTIVE**

Successfully launch Product ABC Release 3.0.

**KEY RESULT**

Increase Net Promoter Score from 50 to 60 based on feedback of 100 or more version 3.0 beta testers.

Reduce average user query time by 50% with version 3.0 as compared to version 2.7.

**EXHIBIT 4.2**   Horizontal Alignment

it may be necessary to follow up with other units after the event to conduct a final review of horizontally aligned OKRs. Again, as with most things, in the end it comes down to making this a priority and committing the time and energy to see it through.

## CONFIRMING THE ALIGNMENT OF CONNECTED OKRs

It's one thing to create a set of corporate OKRs that can improve focus on what really matters. However, the value of an OKR implementation can increase exponentially when you connect, thereby allowing all participants to announce their contribution to the bigger picture. Connecting may be the most important part of your OKRs process and, therefore, ensuring it is done well and actually serves its purpose is critical. For that reason, once you begin rolling out the program and having lower-level groups develop their own OKRs you can't take it as an article of faith that those OKRs are in fact aligned. You've got to check each and every set to ensure they are in fact drawing a line of sight back to your strategic goals. Outlined below are a number of factors to consider when reviewing connected OKRs:

- *Objective coverage:* As we've previously noted, it's unreasonable to expect groups developing OKRs to be able to influence each and every objective and key result of the group to whom they report. Again, the principle is influence: Which OKRs can we exert an influence on at our level, and how do we track that impact? However, when assessing alignment, it is important to ensure that across the enterprise you're receiving adequate coverage of your most important objectives. As an example, if at the corporate level you've established an objective of improving new product development cycles and see no mention of anything related to that in any of the connected OKR sets, there is a problem.
- *Both vertical and horizontal linkages are present:* Effective OKRs stretch both upward and sideways throughout the company. Especially for groups that have strong dependencies with other teams, you should expect to see a fair proportion of both vertical and horizontal alignment illustrated in the connected OKRs.
- *Reasonable target scoring levels:* Especially for novel OKRs, those you've never considered before, determining appropriate levels for scoring can be difficult and require a good deal of professional judgment. Ensure the

targets represent an appropriate level of stretch but are still within the team's grasp.

■ *Strategic impact:* This is the most common sense attribute of an effective connected OKR; will its achievement make it more likely that the organization as a whole will meet one or more of their OKRs? After all, that's the ultimate purpose of connecting.

■ *Adherence to any "rules" you've established:* If, for example, you've put in place a plan not to exceed number of OKRs that may appear on any connected set, simply check to see that no group has gone over that number. One of the greatest benefits of connecting is allowing individual creativity in OKR design to flourish. However, consistency in approach will help aid understanding and use of the program.

 ## CLOSING THOUGHTS ON CONNECTING

One of the most toxic problems in modern organizations is inconsistency. We've all witnessed it in our careers. Take the boss who endlessly praises the virtues of teamwork and sharing, yet hoards information, keeping employees in the dark and greatly diminishing their ability to make day-to-day decisions. Or, executives who demand high performance from throughout the ranks but refuse to remove poor performers. Those whose noxious attitude and slack performance drag down their entire unit. It's a simple fact of neuroscience that our brains crave patterns, and thus, inconsistencies such as these (and many more we're certain you could catalog) cause a dissonance and frustration that can spill over to our own work.

Connecting may not completely solve this problem, but it can greatly ameliorate the situation. When you develop a set of connected OKRs, you're entering into a pact with your employees and the manager or executive to whom you report. Like any pact or contract, there is a negotiation component. In this case, the negotiation consists of coming to agreement on which OKRs you'll settle on to signal your team's unique contribution. During that process, you have the opportunity to bring any glaring inconsistencies into evidence, sharing with your superior why and how they potentially hamper your performance. This dialog alone is a great benefit of the connecting process. It allows for open communication directed at shedding light on the way things truly are within your four walls, and what can be done to ensure everyone is focused on what matters most to your success. We've sat in on dozens of such conversations, during which a team leader and supervisor negotiate on OKRs, and the feedback on the process has been universally positive. The CIO of one client phoned us shortly after such a conversation and said, "I've known each of my directors for over 20 years, and after hearing them present their OKRs to me, for the first time I felt as if I really understood what was important to them."

We'll leave the topic of connecting with this quote from a book titled *The Amateurs*. The author asked Olympic rowers to describe their best moments, and here's how he captured their responses: "When most oarsmen talked about their perfect moments in a boat, they referred not so much to winning a race but to the feel of the boat, all eight oars in the water together, the synchronization almost perfect. In moments like that, the boat seemed to lift right out of the water. Oarsmen called that the moment of swing. When a boat has swing, its motion seems almost effortless."[7] It's difficult to imagine a more fitting description of the triumph that results when people work together toward a common goal. Through the connecting of OKRs, that same effortless motion the oarsmen felt can be yours as well.

 **NOTES**

1. Stephen R. Covey, *The 8th Habit* (New York: The Free Press, 2004).
2. Stephen Taub, "Dazed and Confused," *CFO.com* (September 2002).
3. Christina Wodtke, *Radical Focus: Achieving Your Most Important Goals with Objectives and Key Results* (cwodtke.com, 2016).
4. From John Doerr interview at Goal Summit, San Francisco, April 16, 2015.
5. Sun Tzu, *The Art of War* (Oxford, UK: Oxford University Press, 1963).
6. The statistics in this section are drawn from Donald Sull and Rebecca Homkes, "Why Strategy Execution Unravels—and What to Do About It," *Harvard Business Review* (March 2015).
7. Quoted in James Surowiecki, *The Wisdom of Crowds* (New York: Doubleday, 2004).

# CHAPTER FIVE

# Managing with OKRs

O NCE UPON A TIME THERE was a man named Gus who got in over his head with debt and was way behind on all his payments. Exhausting every source of credit, and not knowing where else to turn, Gus goes to church one day, kneels at the altar and prays to the Lord that he might win the lottery to right his financial ship. "Dear Lord," he pleaded, "Please let me win the lottery. I'll be a new man, I promise." A week went by with no lottery jackpot for Gus. Back to church he went. "Lord, just let me win this week and you'll see, I'll turn over a new leaf." Another week passes and Gus is no richer. Frustrated and close to tears, Gus returns to church, "Lord, I don't understand, I've prayed, I've promised to change, why won't you let me win the lottery?" Suddenly there came a loud clap of thunder, and the Lord spoke, "Gus, meet me halfway: Buy a ticket!"

Poor old Gus could have spent an eternity praying for relief from his debts, but without taking action the most he could expect were faded hopes and a set of sore knees. Creating OKRs and not rapidly sharing and reviewing results is akin to hoping to hit the lottery without going to the trouble of buying a ticket. You can't "set and forget" goals and hope to achieve any of the OKR benefits we've chronicled throughout the text. The modern business offers countless distractions to divert your attention from what matters most—a hundred fires you can fight every day—but to execute successfully and take your performance to a new level, regular and disciplined reviews of OKR results must become part of your operating rhythm and corporate culture. In the sections that follow we'll provide direction on how to do just that.

## THE CYCLE: MONDAY MEETINGS, MID-QUARTER CHECK-INS, AND QUARTERLY REVIEWS

As we all know, today more than ever (a cliché phrase we know, but one that is utterly appropriate) companies must ride the outer edges of the learning curve should they hope to stay ahead of competitors who may appear overnight from around the corner or the other side of the globe armed with cunning business plans aimed at stealing your market share. In this environment, waiting casually until the end of the quarter to review results, when scores have been tabulated and the opportunity to take action on missed goals has passed, is a critical blunder. You need fresh, current data points throughout the quarter that can be transformed into useful knowledge to be deployed throughout the enterprise. For that reason, we offer a three-pronged approach: Monday meetings, mid-quarter check-ins, and end-of-quarter reviews.

### Monday Meetings[1]

We can practically see your eyes rolling as they passed over the word *meeting*. You're probably thinking, "Another meeting? Really? That's your best advice?" But before you hurl the book across the room, two points in our defense: While we recommend a Monday meeting, it isn't mandatory. We recognize that every organization has its own threshold and tolerance for meetings, and this may or may not work in your culture. Second point: Although we may appear to be adding a meeting to your already bloated schedule and possibly increasing organizational complexity in the process, it is our belief that meetings like this (and the mid-quarter check-in we'll discuss shortly) actually hold the promise of simplifying your life and reducing complexity by highlighting and magnifying what is most important to the success of your business. Once you master the art of these sessions, it's probable that other meetings you currently hold will suddenly pale in a value comparison and can be mercifully jettisoned from your day planner. Ready to reconsider the meeting?

The purpose of the Monday sessions is threefold: Assessing progress, identifying any potential issues before they blossom into significant problems, and, especially as you begin using OKRs, establishing the rigor of incorporating OKRs and a performance-based approach to management into your culture to ensure your team stays focused. Don't consider this session a formal examination of results. Rather, the focus should be on information sharing and generating beneficial discussions.

Here are some topics you may wish to include in your Monday meetings, which should be scheduled for no more than one hour.

- *Logistics:* Especially if the team holding the meeting is senior in nature, a good place to start is simply determining who will be where during the week. Although the number and quality of virtual meetings has increased dramatically over the past decades, there are still times when you need your colleagues in the room with you to make an important decision, debate a controversial issue, share a crucial piece of information, etc. Therefore, knowing each other's schedules is both convenient and practical.

- *Priorities:* What are the key priorities, the things that must get done this week to inch closer to achieving your OKRs? As we alluded to above, it's easy to get trapped in the whirlwind of pressing and urgent issues swirling about in any business, so ensure the priorities discussed are in fact leading to the achievement of OKRs.

- *Status:* In Chapter 3, we shared the advice of OKR expert Christina Wodtke, who suggested that when setting key results at the beginning of the quarter you assign a confidence level of 5 out of 10. During the Monday meeting, you can gauge the team's current level of confidence. Has it ratcheted up? Gone down? Either way, the most important question is why. If you're progressing as planned, you'll want to put in mechanisms to stay there, but if the team feels momentum is sagging, perhaps it's time to discuss how you can strategically shift resources to put things back on track. Keep in mind that the team's assessment of progress is going to be a subjective evaluation, and that's fine. This is an informal review and shouldn't necessitate team members scrambling to capture and interpret a thousand data points every Monday. Later in the chapter, we'll discuss setting a tone of learning during your OKR reviews, but for now we'll note that it's crucial your team members feel comfortable in sharing difficult news or a loss of confidence in the ability to meet an OKR. If such a revelation is greeted with anger and recriminations from superiors you can be sure that, going forward, such information will be closely guarded, perhaps even concealed until it's too late to act on it, which spells even greater difficulties for the company. Every member of your team should feel confident that when openly sharing even difficult news, it will be greeted by pledges of support and assistance, not reprimands.

■ *Engagement:* As we've noted several times, OKRs should challenge and stimulate people to engage in the breakthrough thinking necessary to reach unprecedented heights. The potential downside of a stretch goal, however, is frustration that can soon travel swiftly down the tracks to burnout. Use the Monday session to gauge the team's mood. Are they still actively engaged in the pursuit of objectives, or are they merely paying lip service with no real intention to invest the discretionary effort the target demands?

■ *The big picture:* Back in Chapter 3 we defined a health metric as something the company will monitor frequently (over years, perhaps), because it is representative of successful execution of their strategy. Well-designed OKRs should ultimately propel the success of health metrics. To that end, use the session to discuss any recent developments or issues related to these critical enablers of strategy execution, and how they may impact your OKRs now, and in subsequent quarters.

Take advantage of the Monday meetings to share information among your peers and generate a dialog on your progress. At the end of the session each member of the team should understand their colleagues' priorities for the upcoming week and be prepared for any collaboration necessary to ensure steady progress.

## Mid-Quarter Check-Ins

If we were to assemble four finance ministers, four chairmen of multinational companies, four Oxford economics students, and four London garbage collectors, and ask them to generate 10-year forecasts on a number of key economic variables, who do you think would offer the best prediction? We don't have to speculate, because *The Economist* magazine actually conducted this experiment back in 1984. The results? The chairmen and Oxford students managed to tie the garbage collectors, and the finance ministers finished in the cellar. But to make matters worse, the average prediction was more than 60 percent too high or too low.[2] Perhaps you're thinking, "Well that was over 30 years ago; we've become much more proficient at making predictions now." Unfortunately, that's not the case. In a recent study, researchers asked hundreds of chief financial officers from a variety of industries to forecast yearly returns for the S&P 500 over a nine-year horizon. Their 80 percent ranges were right only a third of the time.[3] We humans, despite our avid proclivities to offer predictions on virtually any subject, simply are not good at it, and that fact has implications for your OKRs.

As we already mentioned, the weekly confidence rating applied to OKRs by your teams is as much art as science. And, since there is a decent probability that most of your team will be new to this sort of assessment system, the accuracy of predictions may vary widely and could potentially be as poor as the Finance Minister's mentioned above. Despite the team's best intentions, prognostications that are well off the mark can lead to unwelcome surprises come the end of the quarter. To avoid that situation, we recommend you engage in a mid quarter check-in to conduct a slightly more formal review of your progress. You may have noticed the qualifier *slightly* in the previous sentence. As with Monday meetings, at this point in the quarter you're not performing a highly forensic audit of success, but merely seeking directionally correct information. Therefore, while you may dig a bit deeper into the prospects of achieving your OKRs, you don't want your teams spending untold hours gathering data to support their claims one way or the other.

With the possible exception of logistics, each of the topics we outlined for the proposed Monday meetings could find a place in the agenda for your mid-quarter check-in. However, status will take center stage in this gathering. You'll want to calibrate expectations based on any new information you've gathered in order to determine your priority actions for the remaining six weeks of the quarter. Depending on the velocity of change in your industry, circumstances could alter dramatically in the course of a few weeks and it may become clear that a certain objective is out of reach and will have to be abandoned, while others could be elevated and warrant additional resources to ensure success. Additionally, as we highlighted in Chapter 3, you may require a change to OKRs mid-stream due to a major customer demand, supplier issue, strategic pivot, or other issue demanding prompt attention.

Even at this point in the quarter, it's difficult to forecast with certainty whether or not you'll meet your OKRs. However, with several weeks in the rearview mirror and experience mounting you should be able to move beyond mere intuition. Ammunition in the form of actual operating data will enable you to make reasoned estimates of success, thereby allowing you to strategically allocate resources for the remainder of the quarter.

## Quarterly Reviews

The time for sticking a finger in the wind or relying on subjective confidence levels to assess where you are has come to an end, and the moment has arrived to actually grade your performance at the end of the quarter. The two primary components of the review meeting are what and how.

The "what" comprises the grades (scores) you assign for each of your key results. Based on performance during the quarter, each team (or individual should you connect that far into the organization) will determine their final score, and provide the rationale for that determination to their peers, colleagues, and superiors. This wide sharing of results is yet another benefit of OKRs, as it provides all teams the chance to learn more about their colleagues' triumphs and challenges, what works, and what is ultimately possible when the entire organization is working in alignment. Assuming you've been rigorous in holding Monday meetings and also conducted a mid-quarter check-in, providing a final grade to OKRs should be a relatively simple, straightforward, and quick process.

As for the actual presentation of results, you should consider both timing and flow. There is no accepted standard length for the duration of a quarterly review, but we doubt you want to turn it into a marathon session that requires vats of coffee and a pizza run. Let's assume you're targeting a three-hour meeting that will include presentation of results, questions and answers, and general discussion. If you have 10 teams slated to present their OKRs, advise each team they are allotted 6 minutes and will be cut off at 12. This will ensure the presentation component of the meeting does not run over two hours. Regarding the flow of the meeting, consider having each team begin with the key result they are most proud of thus far so that they can start on a high note.

The second component of the quarterly review meeting, the *how*, is what will ultimately drive the success of your OKRs program, and your organization's ability to execute. While the grades you assign are obviously important, what really stokes the flames of learning are the conversations spawned from a deep investigation of what occurred during the quarter. The scores should serve as a launching point for intense discussions that challenge conventional views, unearth assumptions, and test working hypotheses. In our experience, many organizations struggle with these meetings where candor and honesty should be the order of the day. Although some companies are able to engage in passionate discussions, leaving nothing on the table, the well-worn rules of civility hamper others from reaching a level where actual revelations are found. We're not suggesting you need profanity-laced altercations among your team to foster insights; in fact, we urge you to respect your entire team and refrain from ever engaging in verbal assaults that could wound another person's sense of self or impinge on their psychological safety. Recent research into effective teams backs up this assertion by noting that the psychological safety of participants is a vital enabler of group success. What we are saying is that in order to make the best use of your OKRs data (scores), you need to carefully think about how you'll structure your meeting to ensure learning is maximized.

In the sections that follow, we'll provide some guidelines for structuring and running a quarterly review. Let's begin with one key logistical point that cannot be overlooked.

## Schedule the Meetings in Advance

In a study, university students were asked just prior to their Christmas break to name a project they intended to work on and complete during their upcoming vacation. The proposed endeavors varied widely, from writing an important paper to settling a family conflict, to engaging in a challenging sports activity. Participants were also asked whether they had formed intentions on when and where they would get started to work on the projects. When the results were tabulated after the holiday, fully two-thirds of those who had formed "implementation intentions," by noting where and when they would work on the task, had successfully completed it. However, only about a quarter of those who did not form implementation intentions were successful.[4] Hundreds of subsequent studies have replicated this effect, demonstrating that in order for real change to occur, we must move from noble ambitions to specific behaviors that outline in detail when and where we'll do the work.

Scheduling review meetings in advance may appear at first glance as a piece of banal and common sense advice, but we've both witnessed change programs (OKRs and others) that have died on the vine not because of some fatal flaw in the program itself, but simply because when the framework was up and established the organization never followed through on holding regular meetings to discuss and learn from results. In the study cited above, the researchers deliberately chose the Christmas holidays because they knew the students would be bombarded with potential activities that could impede them from completing their stated goal. Parties, shopping, time with family, all of these and many more are enticing alternatives to completing an important project. For most companies, in that sense, every day is like Christmas. There are innumerable issues and activities vying for your attention, and thus it's easy to put a "review meeting" on the backburner in favor of a seemingly urgent need that demands your full response immediately. Clear the change path for your team by scheduling your review meetings in advance and making them a sacrosanct commitment.

We hope we've convinced you to get the quarterly meetings on your calendar and never, ever cancel them. Assuming that's the case, and you've assembled your team to review results at the end of a quarter, let's look at a number of things you can do to maximize that investment.

## Manage Your Expectations

Ulysses S. Grant once sat for a photo shoot with the famous Civil War photographer, Mathew Brady. Finding the studio too dark to work in, Brady sent an assistant up to the roof to uncover a skylight. The assistant slipped and shattered the window. With horror, the spectators watched as two-inch shards of glass, every one potentially lethal, fell from the ceiling like daggers, crashing around Grant. As the last pieces hit the ground, Brady looked over and saw that Grant hadn't moved. He was unhurt. Grant glanced up at the hole in the ceiling, then back at the camera as though nothing had happened at all.[5] Sometimes the results of OKRs will not be what you expected or hoped for. It is in those moments you need to be Grant-like: Steely, resolute (and maybe lucky). Have faith in the process and maintain your commitment to learning. Surprising results may come in two forms, poorer than expected, and, conversely, better than expected.

Scoring low on key results is entirely probable, especially as you begin using the framework. In your zeal to generate breakthroughs you may be overly optimistic in projecting what you can accomplish during the quarter, setting targets that are ultimately unachievable. As we discussed earlier, hopefully any unrealistic objectives will be identified early in the process during either your Monday meetings or the mid-quarter check-in and can be dealt with accordingly at that point. However, it is possible that end-of-quarter results will disappoint. If that's the case, your goal should be to critically examine what happened and learn from any less than desirable outcomes.

At the other end of the spectrum are OKRs scores that all approach a 1.0, at first blush, a stunning accomplishment worthy of wild celebration. But let's not pop the cork on that Veuve Clicquot quite yet. Chances are, again, as you become accustomed to setting and scoring OKRs, there is every bit as high a probability that you will set targets that are too low, as you will targets that are excessively demanding. In this case, a set of 1.0 scores shouldn't signal a party but, again, an opportunity to calibrate and craft more appropriate targets going forward.

According to most OKRs practitioners and clients we've worked with, the sweet spot for results are scores hovering around 0.6 and 0.7. But, regardless of the score, as we argued above, what really takes precedence is not the number but the conversation the results produce. Let's consider some ways to stimulate that discussion.

### Solicit Feedback from Everyone

What is your favorite Pixar movie? *Wall-E* maybe? How about *Finding Nemo*? Or perhaps 2015's *Inside Out*. There are many others to choose from, all exemplars of a standard of excellence that is unprecedented and almost entirely unheard of from a major Hollywood film studio. Pixar's extraordinary success can be attributed to many factors: compelling and universal stories, talented directors and writers, and stunningly imagined and rendered worlds, to name just a few. However, perhaps the most significant contributing factor is their inclusionary process. When Pixar films are in production and screened at the studio, all employees, literally everyone regardless of their field, are asked to send notes to the film's creators. Pixar directors consistently cite this process of soliciting all voices in a film's final version as key to their success.[6]

We encourage you to follow Pixar's lead and, when reviewing results, include your entire team in the process. After all, transparency can be one of the biggest benefits of using OKRs. Cloistering your management team behind closed doors to interpret your quarterly results not only impedes support for the OKRs program but also robs you of one of the greatest sources of potential value at your disposal—the brainpower of your team. Your goal should be to establish a sense of ownership in OKRs from every single employee, regardless of rank or function. The best way to engender that feeling is including all voices in the ongoing OKRs dialog.

### Ask Simple Questions to Get the Conversation Started

The organizational psychologist (among many hats he has worn) Edgar Schein tells a story of how posing a simple question made him a star in the eyes of one CEO client.[7] The executive was concerned that his company's culture had become immovable and frustrating. He noted that just the previous day he had a staff meeting of his top 15 people who always sat in the same place at the table. On this particular day, only 5 people were able to attend and, despite the surplus of available seats, each person sat in his or her usual position, causing them to be scattered around the enormous table. "You see what we're up against?" the CEO lamented to Schein. He then gazed at the consultant expectantly, hoping for affirmation and support (and possibly a magic solution). Schein thought about the situation for a few moments and then, rather than offering any solutions, he simply asked, "What did you do?" The CEO replied that he didn't do anything, and in that moment a light bulb went off in his head. The frozen culture was most likely an artifact of the executive team's inaction. For the next several hours, they explored ways in which they were complicit in their own situation, and how they could improve it. Over the next year, they were able to transform their culture, all the changes stemming from a humble and simple question.

At times, the situations you encounter appear nastily complex, and it's difficult to find your way into the subject. When that occurs, the temptation to offer solutions is second nature to most of us. After all, that's how most "stars" rise through the corporate ranks—by providing answers to anything and everything that ails the organization regardless of how intractable a problem may appear. Any void when a challenge exists, any deafening silence on the part of a leader, can mistakenly be interpreted as a lack of knowledge, impacting the individual's ongoing credibility. No wonder we all talk too much in meetings. But a stream of spontaneous answers can often lead to difficulties when the underlying issues aren't properly understood, or the ramifications of the response haven't been carefully considered. Perhaps Peter Drucker said it best when he noted, "The most serious mistakes are not being made as a result of wrong answers. The truly dangerous thing is asking the wrong questions."[8]

As appealing as it may be to rattle off solutions for every issue the business faces, upon deeper deliberation, it's usually evident that most problems are immune to simple solutions. Always start with questions—the simpler the better—when reviewing OKRs results, before proceeding to possible answers. The deeper you burrow into a challenge or issue, the more elements of it you expose. With the problem's dimensions standing in bold relief, you're much more likely to then generate insights.

### Diagnose Issues Using the "Five Whys"

Consistent with the advice offered in the preceding section, one very simple question you can ask, one that inevitably provokes careful thought and yields results, is "why." And in the spirit of "You can never get too much of a good thing," we suggest you ask it five times in order to resist the gleam of surface issues and get to the root of the problem at hand, which is typically buried much deeper. That was the original intention of the method as conceived by Sakichi Toyoda and used at the Toyota Motor Corporation. Today, the technique is employed in many forms (some people prefer three whys) and for numerous purposes, including strategic visioning, but we feel it is best suited to assist you in diagnosing issues when reviewing key results.

In his book *The Lean Startup*, Eric Ries describes how using the five whys led to the development of an important employee training initiative.[9] His firm, the metaverse website IMVU (a metaverse is a virtual-reality space in which users can interact with a computer-generated environment and other users), described as the world's largest 3D chat and dress-up community, suddenly began receiving complaints from users after a new version of the product had been released with a key feature disabled. Obviously, a metaverse relies exclusively on active and engaged users, and thus it was crucial that Ries and his team discover what was wrong. So they turned to the five whys:

1. Why was a key feature disabled in the new release? Because a particular server failed.
2. Why did the server fail? Because an obscure subsystem was used in the wrong way.
3. Why was it used in the wrong way? Because the engineer who used it didn't know how to use it properly.
4. Why didn't the engineer know how to use it? Because he was never trained.
5. Why wasn't the engineer trained? Because his manager didn't believe in training new engineers because he and his team were "too busy."

Ries and his team began their inquiry fully anticipating that a technical fault was to blame for the customer discontent. However, on using the five whys their assumptions were shattered when they determined the true cause of customer complaints could be linked to a very human managerial decision. This was undoubtedly a startling, but equally insightful and beneficial, revelation. As a result of their analysis, IMVU launched a training program for all new engineers. Whenever you face a perplexing issue, one that defies easy, off-the-shelf solutions, challenge your team to answer *why* five times to uncover the more likely root cause at play.

### Learn from Mistakes

Back in August 1928, Alexander Fleming was anxious to go on vacation. So much so that the Scottish biologist left a pile of dirty petri dishes stacked up in his hospital lab. When he returned, most of the dishes had, of course, been contaminated, as you might expect. Fleming discarded most of the dishes in a vat of Lysol, but when he came upon one containing staphylococcus, he hesitated. The dish was covered in bacteria except where a blob of mold was growing. Around the mold was an area free of bacteria, as if the mold had blocked the bacteria from spreading. Fleming had a flash of insight that it could be used to kill a wide range of bacteria, and from his "mistake" of leaving petri dishes out during his vacation, penicillin, one of the most widely used antibiotics today, was born.

Today, "We need to encourage risk taking and learn from our mistakes" is as common a sound bite from executives in the corporate world as the "We're going to take it one game at a time" refrain echoed by athletes of every sport around the globe. It's become popular, of course, because it's true. The only sure path to success in any endeavor is to tolerate and learn from failure, sometimes repeated failure. So it is with OKRs. We encourage you to embrace a spirit of inquiry as you review your results each quarter. What at first glance may appear to be an ignominious and frustrating failure of some sort could be cloaking an innovation that will swiftly differentiate you from competitors.

### Leaders Should Speak Last

In working with executives around the world, we've encountered a vast array of personality traits and leadership styles, but in our experience one thing most CEOs share in common is their stated desire to harness the wisdom of their subordinates when making decisions. We've lost count of how many times a CEO has whispered to us just before the start of an important meeting: "I'm going to just sit back and see what the team has to say."

Whether they are consciously aware of it or not, this inclination to listen before speaking has significant ramifications for the dynamics of the meeting. Research has consistently demonstrated that if a leader contributes an idea first, group members will often unwillingly follow suit, effectively ending contemplation of alternative ideas.[10] To phrase the effect of this much more colloquially, "If something interests my boss, it fascinates me." It's human nature to feel the stifling influence of an executive's comments and fall into line behind them. Therefore, if you're a leader and wish to ensure that you are gathering the best ideas available from your entire team, be sure to listen first and speak later. The team will appreciate your careful consideration of their thoughts and you can use the opportunity to weigh their input before reaching and sharing your own conclusions.

 ## UPDATING OKRs AT THE END OF THE QUARTER

The actual mechanics of OKRs creation are quite straightforward. At the beginning of the year the company creates its highest-level set of OKRs. That exercise may include both annual OKRs and more tactical quarterly OKRs. These high-level "corporate" OKRs provide context for the connecting process we described in detail in Chapter 4, in which business units, teams, and perhaps even individuals create their own OKRs which demonstrate their contribution to overall strategy execution.

At the end of each quarter, OKRs are graded and new OKRs are then developed throughout the organization. As we noted in Chapter 3, some OKRs may remain the same for several quarters, especially those identified as particularly crucial in light of current strategic or operational challenges. You may also carry forward any OKRs that you did not successfully achieve during the quarter, those whose success is of ongoing strategic importance. Any OKRs you *did* achieve will most likely be eliminated, updated with a new crop that once again stretches the team to deliver its very best. Exhibit 5.1 provides a standard timeline for the OKRs process.

 ## SOFTWARE AND OKRs

Do you remember the Apple slogan from a 2010 commercial for the iPhone: "There's an app for that"? We're sure you do, as the phrase exploded right along with the ever-increasing number of apps available in the app store. It became such a part of popular culture that Apple eventually trademarked the phrase. Well, not surprisingly, there's an app for OKRs. Several of them, in fact. Not just apps, but robust and sophisticated software packages that promise unprecedented access to, analysis of, and increased engagement from your OKRs program. In this section of the chapter we'll explore when to look for a software tool and the requirements you must consider. Also, we'll furnish 20 questions to ask before buying a solution.

### When to Look for a Dedicated OKRs Tool

Although it is possible to launch your OKRs program while simultaneously rolling out a dedicated OKRs software application, the vast majority of practitioners begin by leveraging common productivity tools such as Microsoft Office. If you are just starting with OKRs, we recommend a phased approach, conducting a search for a dedicated software solution to manage your OKRs only after your organization has completed at least one full OKRs cycle. Getting through your first cycle with familiar tools allows you to focus on learning about the OKRs process itself, rather than tackling the learning curve associated with a new software tool. However, in the long run, to make the system sustainable most organizations do feel the need to manage OKRs in a dedicated software platform.

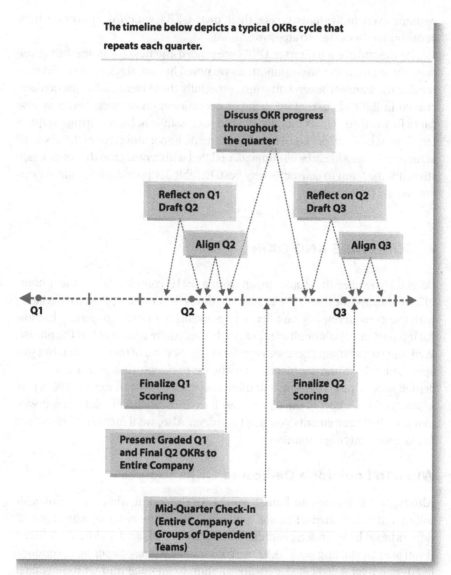

The timeline below depicts a typical OKRs cycle that repeats each quarter.

Discuss OKR progress throughout the quarter

Reflect on Q1 Draft Q2

Reflect on Q2 Draft Q3

Align Q2

Align Q3

Q1

Q2

Q3

Finalize Q1 Scoring

Finalize Q2 Scoring

Present Graded Q1 and Final Q2 OKRs to Entire Company

Mid-Quarter Check-In (Entire Company or Groups of Dependent Teams)

**EXHIBIT 5.1** OKRs Timeline

Large organizations, including Google and Sears Holdings, have developed proprietary systems for defining and tracking the OKRs of thousands of employees. But what if you're not a Fortune 500 company, or don't possess the internal resources to develop an in-house solution? Based on our client work and discussions with hundreds of managers who use OKRs, we feel that small organizations, those with less than a hundred employees, may be well suited to using existing software platforms such as Google Docs, MS Word, Excel, or PowerPoint. As noted above, however, at a certain point, you may feel the need for a more robust solution to capture and track OKRs. If and when that time comes, begin by carefully documenting your requirements. Doing so will help you quickly narrow your search to those vendors whose products are a good match to your specific needs.

## Determining Your Requirements for a Software Solution

In the sections that follow we've supplied a simple framework to assist you in identifying requirements for a software solution. Our advice comes in the form of five questions:

1. How many people will use the OKRs tool?
2. Do you want an OKRs tool designed primarily for executives, teams, or individual contributors?
3. Will you score OKRs based on entering predictive data, or progress-to-date?
4. Do you want software that makes use of gamification?
5. Should your OKRs solution get everyone on a weekly cadence?

Let's look at each in turn.

### How Many People Will Use the OKRs Tool?

As with nearly any software category, different OKRs vendors target organizations based on their size. Let's divide the market into two categories: Large and small/medium. Any organization with more than two thousand employees we'll classify as large. Small and medium-sized businesses are those between a hundred and two thousand employees.

*Large:* Vendors attempting to sell OKRs applications to large organizations may also sell to midsize companies, but typically not to very small firms (those we identified above as numbering a hundred or less), unless there is a strategic reason to acquire the customer. Software offered by vendors targeting large firms is designed to accommodate thousands of users, and the engineering team proactively seeks to ensure the product is available on every platform including mobile phones and even smart watches.

*Small/Medium:* Vendors selling to small and medium-sized companies will often sell to divisions of larger organizations but are, of course, happy to work with organizations of limited size as well. Since these vendors themselves are smaller, their products may not include every bell and whistle the larger providers can offer. However, for smaller firms with tight fiscal constraints, their software may offer the perfect match of functionality and price.

### Do You Want an OKRs Tool Designed Primarily for Executives, Teams, or Individual Contributors?

The software market is also stratified based on primary users of the system. Each solution targets a different key user for the tool, typically skewing toward either top leadership or individual contributors. When we ask vendors whom their software is primarily designed for, they are very quick to answer. Some solutions are clearly designed for the individual contributor, while others are geared for the CEO. Still others may be configured chiefly for team leaders. Exhibit 5.2 outlines how tools designed for the CEO compare with those targeting teams and individuals as key users.

Systems designed principally for the individual contributor seek to enable workers to make measurable progress on goals, see how their goals connect to the bigger picture, and increase employee engagement. Those intended primarily for the CEO, however, may increase employee engagement, but are primarily envisioned to reduce surprises and enable the CEO to take proactive actions such as allocating resources based on early warning alerts. Tools designed for teams strike a balance between the two other approaches.

### Will You Score OKRs Based on Entering Predictive Data or Progress-to-Date?

All OKRs tools we've analyzed require that users enter data to update status on OKRs throughout the quarter. However, when you enter data about progress on your OKRs, what do you wish to communicate? Do you want progress to date or predictive data outlining expected results at the end of the quarter?

Historical data reflect past achievements and progress-to-date. For example, if a user has created a key result to add 20 customers, and 10 are added, the user may enter "50 percent complete" into the system (or may enter "10 customers") and the system automatically translates the input to a progress of 50 percent toward the target.

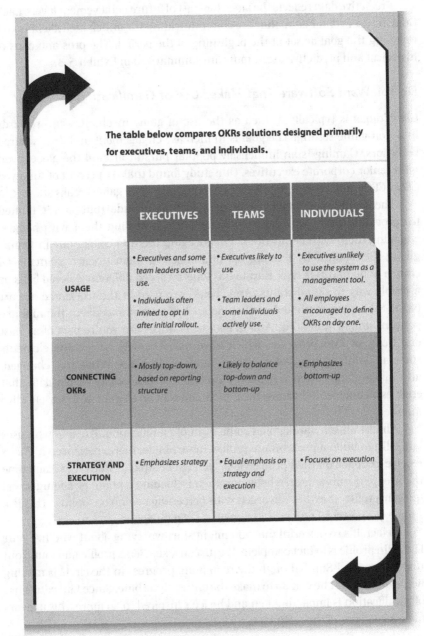

The table below compares OKRs solutions designed primarily for executives, teams, and individuals.

| | EXECUTIVES | TEAMS | INDIVIDUALS |
|---|---|---|---|
| USAGE | • Executives and some team leaders actively use.<br>• Individuals often invited to opt in after initial rollout. | • Executives likely to use<br>• Team leaders and some individuals actively use. | • Executives unlikely to use the system as a management tool.<br>• All employees encouraged to define OKRs on day one. |
| CONNECTING OKRs | • Mostly top-down, based on reporting structure | • Likely to balance top-down and bottom-up | • Emphasizes bottom-up |
| STRATEGY AND EXECUTION | • Emphasizes strategy | • Equal emphasis on strategy and execution | • Focuses on execution |

**EXHIBIT 5.2**   Primary Users of OKRs Solutions

Predictive data reflects the latest forecast of future achievement levels. Each time the users enter data, they are communicating the anticipated likelihood of reaching the goal as set at the beginning of the period. The pros and cons of historical and predictive user inputs are summarized in Exhibit 5.3.

## Do You Want Software That Makes Use of Gamification?

*Gamification* is typically defined as the use of game mechanics and rewards in a non-game setting. The goal is to increase engagement and drive desired behaviors. Gaming is an immensely popular pursuit around the globe, even with senior corporate executives. One study found that 61 percent of surveyed CEOs, CFOs, and other senior leaders say they take daily game breaks at work.[11]

The techniques employed in gamification include (but aren't limited to) providing users with goals to accomplish, awarding them with badges, engaging them with competition, encouraging them to collaborate in teams, giving them status by leveling up, and enabling them to earn points.[12] Of course none of this is new. Karate has long awarded different-colored belts as a visible way to signal status. And "belts" are used in the workforce as part of the Six Sigma methodology. Boy Scout badges and medals in the military perform similar functions. And of course, chances are you're part of at least one frequent flyer program, which have relied heavily on gaming elements such as point accumulation, status, and leveling up. What has changed, and made gamification a growing force, is the availability of big data that enables businesses to harness these techniques in an elegant and cost-effective manner.

Almost all software applies some form of gamification. Anyone who uses LinkedIn to build a professional profile, for example, has experienced it. Users receive feedback on their profile via a "percent complete" status bar. Each time the user performs a desired behavior, such as loading a photo or adding a skill to their profile, they are rewarded with percentage complete points. This is a simple but powerful and well-designed use of gamification.

In fact, it's so powerful that you might start worrying about whether your LinkedIn profile is in fact complete. We just checked Ben's profile and found out that he's an "All-Star," though the remaining progress in the circle is making Ben wonder what he can do to make the entire circle blue. Since LinkedIn's use of gamification is impacting Ben and he feels inspired to do more, this appears to be a good use of the technique.

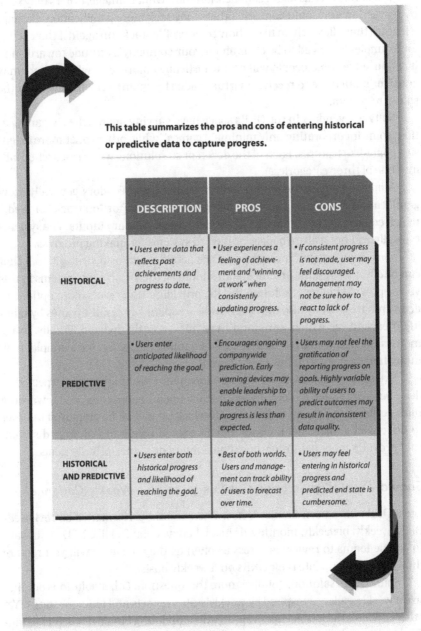

This table summarizes the pros and cons of entering historical or predictive data to capture progress.

| | DESCRIPTION | PROS | CONS |
|---|---|---|---|
| HISTORICAL | • Users enter data that reflects past achievements and progress to date. | • User experiences a feeling of achievement and "winning at work" when consistently updating progress. | • If consistent progress is not made, user may feel discouraged. Management may not be sure how to react to lack of progress. |
| PREDICTIVE | • Users enter anticipated likelihood of reaching the goal. | • Encourages ongoing companywide prediction. Early warning devices may enable leadership to take action when progress is less than expected. | • Users may not feel the gratification of reporting progress on goals. Highly variable ability of users to predict outcomes may result in inconsistent data quality. |
| HISTORICAL AND PREDICTIVE | • Users enter both historical progress and likelihood of reaching the goal. | • Best of both worlds. Users and management can track ability of users to forecast over time. | • Users may feel entering in historical progress and predicted end state is cumbersome. |

**EXHIBIT 5.3** Data Entered into OKRs Solutions

While we find this use of gamification somewhat valuable, others may see it as distracting and confusing. Still others may seek more gamification. Perhaps a feature that allows them to see how their profile stacks up against their peers, for example. You need to be clear about your company's attitude toward gamification since some people will enthusiastically embrace it, while others may consider it offensive to receive a virtual badge for taking certain actions in the software system.

Software vendors in the OKRs space have varying approaches to gamification, some incorporating only minimal "games" while others offer more extensive game-like features. Each of the dozen or so solutions we've researched falls into one of three categories.

*Minimal gamification*: A distraction is how these vendors generally view gamification. Users may be able to flag goals as "green" or "on track" or "red," which equates to "not on track." These are basically binary inputs. The systems typically will not feature badges or reward systems for making progress.

*Some gamification*: These vendors see gamification as a strategic tool that can be effective in some instances, but should be used sparingly. Systems in this vector provide higher resolution inputs, providing users with more options to define progress. They also may encourage frequent key result updates by making it easy to see which were (and were not) recently updated. Finally, usage metrics may be employed at this level of gaming, showing, for example, how many times a key result has been viewed.

*Extensive gamification*: In this instance game techniques are expected to drive behaviors such as defining key results, updating progress, and rewarding high performers. Points, badges, and leveling up will all be employed in order to drive goal achievement. OKRs may be scored using an automated system that provides more points for more challenging or higher-priority goals.

## Should Your OKRs Solution Get Everyone on a Weekly Cadence?

Once OKRs have been finalized, how often should performance be reviewed? Daily, weekly, biweekly, monthly, or just whenever you feel like it? Do you want to enable teams to review progress as often as they see fit or will you require that every team update their OKRs on a weekly basis?

Some OKRs solutions totally ignore this question. Other solutions emphasize a weekly cadence inspired by weekly status reports and team meetings. Yet others offer features that encourage frequent updating but do not define a standard cadence. Should you choose to evaluate OKRs applications, we advise you first to think about whether you'd like to require a standard cadence across the organization. Software with a minimal focus on cadence does not encourage users to adopt a review standard and update goal progress. These tools may enable users to check a box in order to request reminders to update goal progress on a weekly basis. The tools that are built on a weekly cadence require all users to update status each week. They frequently include charts that visualize progress on goals week over week.

Once you've considered requirements, it's time to get on the phone and start arranging product demonstrations with software vendors. We're sure they'll love to drive the product demonstration. However, we recommend writing a list of questions that are important to you prior to the product demo so that you can control the discussion. After all, it's your money! So . . .

##  LET'S PLAY 20 QUESTIONS!

Although we recommend starting with simple tools that your employees are currently familiar with, such as MS Office, at some point in your OKRs journey you're likely to consider a dedicated software tool. With the use of OKRs spreading quickly to organizations of all sizes around the globe, dozens of sophisticated software solutions are emerging to manage the framework.

Armed with hands-on experience using OKRs for at least one cycle, and having cataloged your rough requirements for a potential dedicated OKRs platform, you're ready to craft a list of key questions you'll want answered during your initial solution demo. We've created the following queries with the help of OKRs software users, vendors, and prospective buyers:

1. Does the software support bottom-up origination of OKRs as well as top-down processes to connect OKRs?
2. Can OKRs cross teams to enable horizontal alignment or identify cross-team dependencies? Or, does the system require OKRs be connected only to higher-level OKRs?
3. Does the system allow you to visualize how OKRs connect?
4. Does it include social features that permit colleagues to add comments to OKRs that they don't manage?
5. Is your OKRs deployment optional for employees or does the software agreement specify that all employees must purchase a license?
6. Can you update and access OKRs from a mobile device?
7. How does the system encourage users to define and update scores for key results?

8. Can you click a button to create a summary report detailing a team or individual's progress on OKRs that can be used to inform a performance review meeting?

9. Does the tool include a dashboard that can be used to present and summarize progress on OKRs at a board meeting?

10. Does the OKRs software allow users to enter anything for a key result or is there technology that ensures key results are measurable and have a set timeframe?

11. What kind of OKRs coaching services and support does the software vendor recommend or provide?

12. Does the software support all five types of key results (i.e., baseline metric, positive target metric, negative target metric, threshold target metric, and milestone)?

13. Does the system have a "draft mode" whereby users can enter their OKRs but not make them visible until finalized?

14. Does the system support Single Sign On (SSO) or does it require the user to memorize a password in order to login?

15. System of record data integration: Can data be extracted from external systems such as a CRM (e.g., Salesforce.com), general ledger (e.g., Oracle Financials), or a business intelligence tool (e.g., Information Builders) to automatically populate standard metrics that are already tracked in a system of record?

16. How easy is it to add or remove an employee? Does this require technical support from the vendor?

17. Does the system keep track of OKRs from prior time periods so that users can go back and compare current OKRs to prior OKRs?

18. What type of information or metric is the tool capturing? Do users enter historical progress to date, predictive scores, or both?

19. Does the system enable individuals to assign a standard status to key results (e.g., "on track" could be green, "behind" may be red) or does the software system automatically indicate the status?

20. What gamification elements does the software provide?

 **NOTES**

1. Portions of this section are based on material in Christina Wodtke, *Radical Focus: Achieving Your Most Important Goals with Objectives and Key Results* (cwodtke.com, 2016).

2. Michael E. Raynor, *The Strategy Paradox* (New York: Doubleday, 2007).

3. Jack B. Soll, Katherine L. Milkman, and John W. Payne, "Outsmart Your Own Biases," *Harvard Business Review* (May 2015).

4. Peter M. Gollwitzer, "Implementation Intentions: Strong Effects of Simple Plans," *American Psychologist* (1999).

5. Ryan Holiday, *The Obstacle Is the Way: The Timeless Art of Turning Trials into Triumph* (New York: Portfolio, 2014).

6. Ed Catmull and Amy Wallace, *Creativity Inc.: Overcoming the Unseen Forces That Stand in the Way of True Inspiration* (New York: Random House, 2014).

7. Edgar H. Schein, *Humble Inquiry: The Gentle Art of Asking Instead of Telling* (San Francisco: Berrett-Koehler, 2013).

8. Quoted in Robert Simons, "Stress Test Your Strategy," *Harvard Business Review* (November 2010).

9. Eric Ries, *The Lean Startup: How Today's Entrepreneurs Use Continuous Innovation to Create Radically Successful Businesses* (New York: Crown Business, 2011).

10. Steve J. Martin, Noah Goldstein, and Robert Cialdini, *The Small Big: Small Changes That Spark Big Influence* (New York: Grand Central Publishing, 2014).

11. Jane McGonigal: *Reality Is Broken: Why Games Make Us Better and How They Can Change the World* (New York: Penguin, 2011).

12. Rajat Paharia, *Loyalty 3.0: How to Revolutionize Customer and Employee Engagement with Big Data and Gamification* (New York: McGraw-Hill, 2013).

# CHAPTER SIX

# Making OKRs Sustainable

 **DON'T THINK OF OKRs AS A PROJECT**

When you think of the word *project*, what comes to mind? Probably something along the lines of a planned undertaking utilizing both human and financial resources that has a defined beginning, finite scope, and anticipated end date. In the corporate world, projects—sometimes referred to as initiatives—typically reflect all of those characteristics, and are a common accompaniment to your daily work life.

OKRs reflect many of the attributes noted above, with the primary exception of one, and that is "anticipated end date." Your OKRs program will have to begin on some unique day, it will entail the use of financial and human resources, and the implementation will be carefully planned. What you should not do, however, is assign an anticipated end date. Projects come to a natural end, whether successfully completed or not; at some point the endeavor is terminated. OKRs on the other hand should be ingrained in your culture, and ultimately become part of the way you do business on an ongoing basis.

An OKRs implementation is never really complete because your business is never finished. Is there ever a point at which you can confidently declare victory? A glorious day when you've vanquished your competitors far and wide, achieved complete domination of the market, and surpassed all of your customers' wildest hopes and expectations? Of course not, because the environment in which you operate is constantly shifting under your feet. Macro elements such as the overall state of the economy and the political landscape will impact your decision making and success, while closer to home the effects of competition, your ability to master core processes, attract the right talent, leverage the latest technology, and a host of other issues will necessitate constant strategic course corrections. Your partner in this sometimes perilous, always challenging, journey should be OKRs. As conditions inevitably change, your OKRs must reflect the fluctuating reality in which you work, providing a compass of sorts for employees to ensure that, while there may be uncertainty, everyone is focused on the most important goals to move the business forward.

Someone once asked the prolific British playwright, novelist, and short story writer Somerset Maugham if he wrote on a schedule, or only when inspiration struck. Maugham replied, "I write when inspiration strikes. Fortunately, it strikes every morning at nine o'clock sharp."[1] That is a quintessential example of commitment and the discipline it takes to do something well. The same applies to your OKRs program. Creating OKRs can be arduous, especially if your organization has no history of goal setting. Ensuring there is alignment throughout the company is also challenging. But perhaps most difficult of all is finding the energy and requisite passion, when faced with the constant whirlwind that is modern business, to keep using the system day in, day out, week in, week out, and quarter in and quarter out. However, with every OKR cycle you're building a skill, one of learning and insight, and as you continue the process with rigor the revolutions of the flywheel come faster and the odds of success accelerate rapidly. Stick with it!

 ## WHO OWNS THE OKRs PROCESS?

We hope the previous section convinced you that OKRs should never be considered a temporary project, but must instead be embroidered into the fabric of your culture. One of the ways to imbed the process is to designate just a couple of key ownership roles, which are discussed in the paragraphs that follow.

In Chapter 2 we argued that executive sponsorship is an absolute must for any change initiative, OKRs included. Therefore, the first role that needs filling is that of executive sponsor. Ideally, your CEO will assume this responsibility, but in their absence any member of the C-suite will suffice. What matters in the end is having a senior executive who is willing to vocally advocate for and support the OKRs implementation from its humble beginnings as just another good idea, through the rocky shoals when momentum stalls and doubt creeps in, to the promised land of a process fully ingrained as part of your management practices.

Regardless of the nature of a change initiative, the sponsoring executive must have a partner. We'll term this person the *OKRs champion*. The champion works at the front edges of the implementation, working with those impacted, liaising with consultants if necessary, and providing logistical support. Perhaps the champion's most important function is that of in-house OKRs expert. When team members have a question on the theoretical or practical aspects of the model, it's the champion's number they'll dial. This individual will be an indispensable ingredient to OKRs success. Someone with a background in OKRs is obviously an attractive candidate for the role, but we believe a superior trait is enthusiasm. Find someone for whom the passion of OKRs burns bright—someone who instantly grasps the potential of the model and is anxious to share it with colleagues. The champion is typically a mid-level manager who is gifted with exceptional communication skills and enjoys credibility throughout the organization. Expect the champion to devote 50 (or perhaps a little more) percent of their time during the 3- to 5-week period when OKRs are scored for one period and created for the next. In the intervening time their commitment, depending on how you decide to structure the role, will likely entail just a few hours per week.

One final consideration is where to "house" the OKRs process. Should it be a denizen of the finance function? HR? Strategy? Operations? When we researched this topic and shared notes on our findings and personal experiences, no single corporate office predominated. For some the finance group, which often serves as the reporting hub of the organization, assumed ownership of OKRs. For others it was HR. Still others housed OKRs under the strategy mantle. In the end the name on the door doesn't matter so much as a commitment to the principles embodied by OKRs. Having said that, it's imperative to avoid a situation in which one single department is seen as driving the OKRs process to the exclusion of any other groups. The last thing you want is people thinking or saying: "OKRs are just an HR thing," or "Finance is shoving OKRs down our throat." While one group may ultimately be recognized as the custodian of OKRs, there must be a shared belief throughout the organization as to the value of OKRs. You're looking for a home in which the executive sponsor believes in the merits of OKRs and is willing to support, develop, and constantly evangelize the tool.

## OKRs AND PERFORMANCE REVIEWS

In his book *High Output Management*, the father of OKRs, Andy Grove, devotes an entire chapter to the topic of performance reviews.[2] He begins it by posing a basic question to a group of his managers: Imagine yourself to be a supervisor giving a review to a subordinate. What are you feeling as you're doing this? The responses were telling: anger, anxiety, guilt, discomfort, embarrassment, and frustration were frequently mentioned. Next, he asked the group to think back to some of the reviews they had received and what, if anything, was wrong with them. They were only too happy to oblige and quickly rattled off a number of shortcomings, including comments that were too general, mixed messages, poor feedback on how to improve, and only recent work considered.

In our experience, few corporate relics are as quick to produce eye rolls and grimaces as the not so esteemed topic of performance reviews. They're a required activity in virtually all organizations, large and small, yet as a recent survey from Deloitte discovered, 58 percent of managers feel they don't serve their purpose well.[3] Outlined below are just some of the criticisms aimed at performance reviews. Most are general in nature, but one is directly related to OKRs:

- *Performance reviews focus on the past:* Most reviews dwell almost exclusively on goals set in the past, often the distant past. By the time an employee and manager sit to discuss the goals they've become stale and largely irrelevant. As you know, performance isn't an annual event, it fluctuates; based on changes in the field and required adjustments. Performance reviews should reflect the dynamic nature of business.
- *They are susceptible to biases:* When we meet with our boss to go over our performance, it's an emotionally charged experience for both parties. And, unwittingly we're both bringing unconscious biases to the meeting that will likely increase the emotional tension even more. The person being reviewed will in all probability fall prey to the effects of "illusory superiority." English translation: We all think we're above average. But when we're reviewed, and undoubtedly criticized, that unexamined and invisible self-perception of superiority is challenged, leading to frustration and alienation. On the other side of the desk is the reviewer, who is the unsuspecting sufferer of "idiosyncratic rater effect." Another English translation: When reviewers rate qualities such as "potential" (which often surface in a review), they are driven not so much by who you are,

but more by their own idiosyncrasies: How they define potential, how much they think you have, and how tough a rater they generally are. Studies show that as much as 61 percent of a rating is a reflection of the reviewer and not the person being reviewed.[4] Little wonder Grove heard adjectives like frustration, anger, and anxiety when he asked about performance reviews.

■ *They are an enormous time drain:* We mentioned a Deloitte study on the effectiveness of reviews above, and we're wondering if they included themselves in the research. We ask because the company determined it was spending around 2 million hours a year on performance reviews. And, no, it wasn't time well spent holding frequent one-on-ones to provide fast feedback and learning to employees. Rather, it consisted of primarily bureaucratic headaches such as filling in forms, holding meetings, and deciding on ratings. No organization has the luxury of devoting time to pushing paper while ignoring the feedback employees need and crave.

■ *Linked to OKRs, they can produce sandbagging:* As we've discussed throughout the book, OKRs are designed to tug at the edges of organizational capacity, stretching people to deliver their very best. Linking OKRs to performance reviews holds the very real potential to diminish this most vital of the tool's attributes. It's simple human nature; if you know that your next job, a tantalizing new project, or even a bonus or raise (something we'll cover a bit later) hinges on your ability to meet OKR targets, then of course you're going to scale back on your aspirations and avoid unnecessary risks. Who wouldn't? Our intention is not to impugn you or your team's integrity with that assertion; it's a simple matter of self-preservation. But even those bold enough to aim high and take risks when setting OKRs will ultimately suffer if, despite deploying Herculean efforts, they fall short and therefore must suffer the consequences in a formal review. It is for this reason that the vast majority of organizations we've worked with, studied, and spoken with do not formally align OKRs with performance reviews.

The purpose of this section is not to vilify the performance review process, although it has been widely pilloried in the business literature for some time now, and a number of high profile companies, including Accenture, Adobe, and the aforementioned Deloitte are eliminating them in favor of tools that provide more frequent feedback.[5] In fact, when performed with diligence and care, performance reviews remain a valuable exercise for both reviewer and employee. Andy Grove acknowledged this when he said, "The fact is that giving such reviews is the single most important form of task-relevant feedback we as supervisors can provide."[6] What is necessary, given the current realities of both the workforce and the business environment, is a fundamental alerting of the seemingly antiquated process.

One very positive development, that has ramifications for the use of OKRs, is the transition underway in many leading companies from stale, end of year performance reviews to real-time tracking, coaching, and mentoring that seeks to constantly shape an employee's development. Rather than doling out praise or criticism in one big bureaucratic chunk at the end of the year, organizations are now encouraging regular feedback between employees and managers, fostering an ongoing dialog designed to accelerate skill development and minimize the debilitating impact of festering poor performance. OKRs, with their quarterly cadence, beautifully facilitate this tempo of review, allowing managers to regularly assess a contributor's performance and offer feedback on a much more timely basis. Additionally, our dramatically shifting workforce demographics support this evolution, as 79 percent of millennials state that they want their bosses to serve as a coach or a mentor.[7]

Even if yours is one of the enlightened organizations moving to more frequent one-on-one conversations between managers and employees, we don't recommend formally linking OKRs to the process. The potential downside of "sandbagging" through weak targets outweighs the benefits conveyed by using OKRs to judge performance. However, because OKRs operate on a more frequent cadence and ideally represent what is most important to the company, they should set context for, and inform, the frequent one-on-ones between employees and managers. Once again, as we've done several times in the book, we can refer to the groundbreaking work of Peter Drucker on this topic. He recommended employees write what he referred to as a *manager's letter*. In the letter, the employee begins by defining the objectives of his superior's job, and of his own job as he views them. Next, he outlines the performance standards he believes are being applied to him. He then documents the things he must do to attain those standards of performance, and lists any potential obstacles in his path. The letter also includes an inventory of things the company does to assist him in his efforts, and the items that hamper him. Finally, he drafts what he proposes to do the next year to meet his goals. If the superior accepts the letter it becomes the charter under which they operate.[8]

We can draw on the essence of Drucker's manager's letter to outline a number of items that you can use in order to ensure OKRs—while not directly linked to—are informing your performance reviews. We'll pose them in the form of questions an employee can answer before and/or during the review:

- What are the company's OKRs? This provides an opportunity to ensure the employee is aware of, and understands the nature of, the highest level OKRs.
- Which key results do you feel you contributed to the most, and how did you do so?
- Which of your team's OKRs did you help define?
- Which of your team's OKRs did you contribute to, and how?
- How did you apply what you learned from last quarter's OKRs to the present quarter?

If you're holding regular status meetings and have been diligent in reporting results, compiling responses to these questions shouldn't be a burden for any employee, and it will go a long way in enabling a productive dialog on performance.

## OKRs AND INCENTIVE COMPENSATION

Let us ask you perhaps the single most fundamental question possible: Why do you work? Are you motivated by the challenge of exceeding expectations, the fulfillment derived from cracking what was considered an inscrutable problem? Or, does your drive stem primarily from collecting a fair salary and perhaps a monetary bonus for reaching previously negotiated targets? That doesn't make you a bad person. After all, you have to put food on the table and try to squirrel away a few dollars each month for retirement and your kids' college funds.

The basic principle in play here, one we're confident you're aware of as it has been the subject of intense inquiry for literally decades, is intrinsic versus extrinsic motivation. The former, pursuing an activity for the inherent joy it brings, may produce fulfillment and a sense of pride, while the latter, engaging in a task to receive promised rewards, holds the possibility of sharpening our focus on what must be done in order to succeed. Most of the academic research on the subject suggests that extrinsic (incentive-based) rewards have the net effect of reducing intrinsic motivation, and actually lowering performance.

Author Daniel Pink in his popular book *Drive* supports this theory, noting the potential unintended consequences of employing monetary incentives, including extinguishing intrinsic motivation, lessening performance, diminishing creativity, encouraging unethical behavior, and fostering short-term thinking.[9]

The debilitating effects of extrinsic rewards seem particularly caustic to endeavors requiring creativity and innovation, which of course every business in the world relies on for success. So, given the apparently overwhelming evidence condemning the use of extrinsic rewards, how popular are they in actual practice? In a word: extremely. In one recent study of incentive pay practices, the researchers reported that 99 percent of organizations surveyed used some form of short-term incentive program to reward employees.[10]

## Pros and Cons of Linking Incentives to OKRs

As a leader using OKRs to drive focus and alignment on what matters most, you face an important decision: In spite of the findings presented in most research on motivation, should you link incentive compensation to the achievement of key result targets? In the following lists we've laid out some of the pros and cons of each alternative. Let's start with the pros, why you might consider making the link from OKRs to incentives.

- *Laser-like focus on goals:* This is the obvious and most significant benefit of aligning bonus plans with OKRs. You'll ensure everyone covered by the plan is not only aware of your OKRs, but will likely become obsessed with their achievement should the carrot you dangle be sizable enough.
- *Honor perceived fairness:* Research has demonstrated that when employees impacted by downsizing understand that the decision was made fairly they are much less likely to hold negative feelings such as anger and frustration.[11] Fairness is a virtue we all cling to and rely on in our lives, from our days swinging on the jungle gym with our playmates as kids to our time in corporate meeting rooms attempting to understand why a strategic decision is being made. Living in a world that appears unfair affects people's cortisol levels, their well-being, and even their longevity. If your organization preaches teamwork, for example, and holds employees accountable with OKRs that stress working collaboratively, yet all monetary rewards are derived from profits, you can be sure this will set off unfairness alarm bells in everyone affected, leading to frustration, disenchantment, and lower engagement with both OKRs and the organization.

When you link OKRs with compensation it may appear to employees that their discretionary efforts are fairly aligned with potential rewards.

■ *Simplicity:* We've both worked with, and been part of, organizations whose incentive compensation schemes are so bewildering and complicated they make a tax form look simple by comparison. By connecting OKRs and incentives you draw a straightforward and clear line of sight from the vital enablers of strategy execution to the monetary prizes that await high performance. There is little to no guesswork involved; everyone understands at the outset what he or she must accomplish in order to receive a bonus.

Now let's look at the other side of the incentive coin, considering some of the potential cons of tying bonuses to OKRs:

■ *Sandbagging:* Yes, our old nemesis rears its ugly head once again. As with performance reviews, the greatest risk in aligning incentives with OKRs is that employees, potentially even star performers, will negotiate easy to accomplish goals in order to pad their pockets at the expense of the organization's success, sacrificing untold value that slips away as a result of their modest targets. Ironically, sandbagging is the "evil twin" of perceived fairness noted in the Pros section. Employees who witness peers receiving fat bonus checks for mediocre accomplishments will surely, and justifiably, cry foul.

■ *Reduces the likelihood of "leading" indicators:* Consider a sales rep whose OKRs are focused exclusively on deals closed and revenue generated. This person may recognize that certain selling skills are lacking in his team, but does he then take time away from meeting with customers and selling in order to create and administer a training program that will likely only produce results in some distant period? Of course it depends on the individual, but probability suggests he would not, simply because sacrificing the time could potentially reduce his bonus in the current period. Training may be vital to his team and the company's ongoing success, but perversely, because of the OKR/incentive link in the short-term he is not incented to act in the long-term best interests of either.

■ *Could be inconsistent with new business realities:* We noted earlier that extrinsic rewards (such as incentive compensation) may be particularly harmful when associated with tasks requiring creativity and innovation. Stanford professors Jeffrey Pfeffer and Robert Sutton concur, positing that when work is complex and requires collaboration, incentive compensation may prove ineffective.[12] We've previously noted (way back in Chapter 1) the changing landscape of organizations, along with the rise of teams that are formed to address specific business problems, and once the challenge has been successively resolved, the team disbands and its members are reassigned to other squads. Thus, as organizations continue to adapt their structures, incentive compensation may hamper rather than assist a smooth transition.

## Case Studies and Client Experiences

The OKRs field, when examined from an academic perspective, is still relatively nascent. Therefore, it's difficult to point to validated research on any OKRs-related topic that advocates one course of action as absolutely correct in all circumstances. However, what literature that does exist on the topic of linking incentives to results is clear in its admonition: Don't do it. Virtually all of the case study companies you'll hear from in Chapter 7 have avoided the link, as have the vast majority of clients we've worked with around the globe. Having said that, we can't say with certainty that you should not make the connection at your firm. The old cliché is true: Every company is different, and what doesn't work at another company may be perfectly suited for the culture and business practices you've fostered.

From our client work, we've observed some organizations that allocate a small percentage of an employee's potential bonus (typically between 10 and 20 percent) to a more subjective and discretionary "Use of OKRs" component. For example, an employee who was initially reluctant to engage with OKRs but later became a *champion* and regularly updated progress at team meetings might receive the full discretionary component of the bonus. Conversely, an employee who, after being advised not to create multiple key results, goes on to create a list of 20, vastly overextending himself in the process and clearly not adhering to the spirit of OKRs, may not receive any of the bonus.

If you do determine a bond between OKRs and incentives is appropriate, we urge you to carefully consider the timing aspect of the link. While you might be eager to unite pay and performance, OKRs, like any change initiative, require the ascent of a learning curve, and you can be sure there will be bugs in the system you'll want to work out during your initial foray into the framework. We suggest you perform several OKR cycles, ironing out the kinks in your implementation as it were, before tying incentives to results.

Whether OKRs figure in the equation or not, it's overwhelmingly likely that some form of incentive system resides in your company. Similar to our suggestion in the examination of performance reviews, you might consider including OKRs as part of the discussion that informs any cash awards you do allocate to your employees.

The conversation will include not only the percentage of OKRs achieved, but also the degree of difficulty associated with each. Subjectivity is unavoidable whenever judgment is involved, but by at least "loosely coupling" OKRs to the compensation process, you're honoring your commitment to the program and demonstrating to employees that it is an important piece of their success.

 ## TOP 10 OKRs ISSUES

Throughout this book, we've done our best to provide a comprehensive guide, outlining what it takes to successfully implement objectives and key results. We're confident that if you follow the advice offered in these pages, your organization will be able to avoid the hazards that inevitably appear as part of any change-related initiative. However, based on our experiences and extensive research, there are a number of issues that are so pervasive we feel they warrant additional attention before you launch your campaign. Listed here are our top 10 OKRs issues. We've broken them down into three chronological sections: Before you begin creating OKRs, developing OKRs, and once you've created OKRs.

### Issues to Consider Before You Begin Creating OKRs

#### Understanding Why You Are Implementing OKRs

This topic was covered in Chapter 2. However, because we've witnessed the debilitating impact of no guiding rationale for an OKRs program so many times, it merited a place on our roster of the top ten issues.

OKRs are quite prevalent in Silicon Valley, but the tool is quickly emerging on the global stage as well (as you'll see from some of the case study companies profiled in Chapter 7). As the framework continues to ascend in popularity you can be certain it will reach the radar screens of companies large and small in virtually all industries that have heard of the many benefits it confers and are anxious to claim them for themselves. But before embarking on this journey, you must determine why OKRs are right for you at this moment in your history. Penicillin is unquestionably a good thing, but we're not going to administer it to ourselves everyday just because we know it has health benefits. There has to be a specific reason to utilize it. We're stretching the analogy somewhat, but it's the same for your OKRs. The tool in and of itself is a positive device (who would argue with the value of setting ambitious goals to focus and drive alignment?), but unless you know why you're using it you're unlikely to achieve the benefits it offers.

Today's employees are overwhelmed with data points and other stimuli at home, at work, and with the rise of smart phones, watches, and Fitbits, increasingly at play. To separate the signal from the often cacophonous noise requires a filter dedicated to determining why some things should enter your cognitive space and others be denied entry. It is incumbent on you, as a leader, to impart that signal and clearly articulate why OKRs are the appropriate tool to enhance your business right now. Without a clear rationale, OKRs risk suffering the ignominious fate of being just another "flash in the pan," "This too shall pass" initiative that most employees will blithely ignore.

### Obtaining Executive Sponsorship

A detailed review of this critical enabler was also supplied in Chapter 2, including a number of suggestions on how to influence sponsorship. We encourage you to review those carefully should you feel a lack of executive support is present as you begin your OKRs implementation.

As we discussed earlier in the chapter, OKRs should not be considered a finite project, but must be considered a dynamic and fluid approach to management, helping you surf the waves of change that flow towards any business. Given that OKRs are intended to be by your side for the long-term, the implementation involves many stages. First you develop (perhaps, depending on your particular rollout plan) high-level OKRs. Later you connect to groups throughout the enterprise. You establish a reporting rhythm to ensure OKRs become part of the heartbeat of the operation, and down the line you may devise methods to cleverly align the tool with performance reviews, compensation, budgets, and other key processes inherent in running any business. The common thread running through all of these disparate events is the necessity of executive sponsorship. Without an enthusiastic leader present at every juncture, the effort can quickly lose momentum and eventually stall out altogether. Ambivalence cloaked in faint support won't cut it. Simply put, nothing substitutes for a devoted and knowledgeable executive leading the charge.

### Providing OKRs Training

One of the questions we're most asked by newcomers to OKRs is: "What is the difference between this model and other corporate performance management tools?" There are a number of differences of course, but one of the first things we mention is the model's relative simplicity and ease of understanding. When we say simple, we certainly aren't implying simplistic, but rather noting a key benefit of OKRs, which is that the general concepts can be grasped quickly, and that is an enormous advantage when it comes time for implementation.

Relative simplicity can prove to be a double-edged sword, however. Some organizations will be introduced to the topic and feel it is so straightforward that no training is required for employees who will soon be using the tool to manage their businesses. It's as if they rely on managers to somehow magically know how to define great OKRs from the start. It is conceivable that a small portion of leaders may not need any OKRs training. They may have used OKRs previously or be endowed with excellent critical thinking skills that enable them to intuitively know how to communicate effectively and ensure everyone is helping shape the direction of the team. But chances are, most people will either be new to the model or not be graced with the genetic disposition to take to it naturally. Therefore, we recommend training all of your staff on the fundamentals of the approach prior to creating any OKRs. Doing so serves a number of purposes. Practically, it allows for a level playing field of knowledge, ensuring there is a shared understanding of what OKRs are, and what they are not. Training is also akin to planting a seed that will soon blossom into the flower of more effective, well thought out, and strategic OKRs.

### Ensuring There Is a Strategy in Place

Very early in the book we noted global executives' obsession with strategy execution. As you'll recall, we cited a recent survey of 400 leaders in which execution topped a list of some eighty items in importance. We're going to go out on a limb, but not venture very far out, in assuming that if you're reading this book, execution is important to you as well. If that's the case, there is an inherent assumption that you currently have a strategy in place. After all, how can you possibly execute something that doesn't exist?

Sadly, however, many organizations don't have a true strategy in place. They may have some ideas floating around in the head of their CEO, or corporate values gracing framed posters in the foyer, but that's not strategy. Strategy entails the articulation and communication of fundamental business priorities, such as Who are our Customers (target markets)? What do we sell (must have a core offering)? And, why will customers buy from us (value proposition)?

You can develop OKRs without the aid of a strategy in place, but what you create is a very shallow imitation of what the model can potentially offer. The principal benefit of having a strategy to draw from before you develop OKRs is context. The strategy provides a lens through which to judge each and every objective and key result from top to bottom throughout the company. If the OKRs being recommended don't in some way move you closer to the execution of your strategy, while they may provide a quick operational boost, in the long run they won't lead to sustainable success.

## Issues to Consider When Creating OKRs

### Setting Quantitative Objectives

We've included this as our first of the "when creating OKRs" issues because of its fundamental nature. Plato once observed, "The beginning is the most important part of any work." And so it is with OKRs. Getting off to a good start is vital, and to do so you must master the fundamentals of the model, one of which states that objectives are aspirational and not quantitative. Objectives are meant to inspire the team, capturing their shared imagination and propelling them to new heights. Numbers come later, when we gauge success with key results. If you miss or ignore this distinction and begin your work by creating objectives that are basically metrics themselves you'll immediately create confusion and greatly hamper the odds of a successful implementation.

### Avoiding All "Top-Down" OKRs

OKR rookies will often make the mistake of copying company-level key results and establishing them as their objectives. In some isolated cases, this could be appropriate, but for the most part, OKRs should be as much a bottom-up as top-down effort. If you're running a department or business unit your OKRs should connect to those of the group to whom you report, but signal your unique contribution to overall success. Copying and pasting OKRs stifles creativity and substantially reduces the chance of driving alignment through the organization.

### Addressing Problems with Key Results

That's a very broad description, we know, but it serves as an umbrella for a number of problems we see with key results, including:

- *Too many:* There is an old story from Mark Twain that is possibly apocryphal, but a fitting preface to this discussion. As the tale goes, Twain wrote a long letter to a friend that opened with the line, "I tried to write a short letter, but it was too hard so I wrote a long one." When it comes to key results, we're all like Mark Twain. We'd like to confine them to a short list but often that's too difficult, so we end up recording every possible metric we can brainstorm. Of course that approach is in complete contradiction with the spirit of OKRs, which demand a focus on the critical few enablers of success.

■ *Poor quality:* This includes key results that are poorly defined, ambiguous, or difficult to understand and act on. One quick test: If you have more than one acronym in a key result it may be time to reconsider it.

■ *An abundance of milestone key results:* Milestone key results can often add value within a broader set of OKRs. However, if all your key results are of the milestone variety, with no metrics to actually help you keep score, you're defeating the purpose of the OKRs process, which focuses on results and not tasks.

### Using Consistent Scoring Systems

We recommend a simple system consisting of four scores: 0, 0.3, 0.7, and 1.0. That is our advice, but it's totally acceptable if your organization adopts a different system. However, the system you agree on must be the same for every team. We've encountered organizations that, for example, allow some teams to score OKRs, while others don't. Some teams use color-coding, while others rely on numerical values. Predictive scoring is employed by some, progress to date by others. The last thing you want is a patchwork quilt of scoring. It drives inconsistency, confusion, and frustration. Leadership must choose a single scoring system, clearly define it, and then use it consistently throughout the organization. This will create the most effective learning experience and avoid the inescapable confusion that emerges from disparate scoring systems.

## Issues to Consider Once OKRs Have Been Created

### Avoiding the "Set It and Forget It" Syndrome

If you set OKRs and then act as if it were a one-time exercise that you revisit at the end of the quarter, you're missing out on the ongoing discipline component of the process that we noted in our original definition of OKRs. By neglecting to review and discuss OKRs progress throughout the quarter, we'd argue that by definition, you're not actually utilizing OKRs in their intended manner, which is to serve as a dynamic real-time learning aid. One surefire way to avoid the set it and forget it trap is to commit to both the Monday meetings and mid-quarter check-ins we discussed in Chapter 5.

### Failing to Connect OKRs to Drive Alignment

If yours is a very small organization, or you represent one business unit in a larger entity, then a single set of OKRs may be sufficient for guiding the actions of your entire workforce. Organizations of any appreciable size, however, should endeavor to connect OKRs up, down, and across the enterprise to gain the exponential benefits from having your entire employee base focused on distinct but aligned goals.

Front-line employees are often so far removed from high-level strategy that a corporate set of OKRs, while providing a modicum of guidance, does little to spearhead daily activities. Our belief, based on empirical research, experience, and plain old common sense, is that most people want to make a difference, to contribute to the greater purpose embodied in the organization's mission. Connecting OKRs unleashes employee creativity and allows you to harness the only known power source we'll never exhaust: brain power.

 ## HOW NOT TO IMPLEMENT OKRs...AND WHERE CONSULTANTS CAN HELP

If you're a business leader responsible for shepherding the implementation of OKRs in your organization, after reading this book you might think, "This seems pretty straightforward, I can hammer our OKRs out over the weekend." Let's say you do that. On Sunday night after getting the kids to bed you sit down, maybe with a cup of coffee (or something stronger) and draft what you think are the perfect set of OKRs. Monday morning rolls around and you announce them to your team. Depending on your unique style you may note that the OKRs reflect intense deliberation on your part and are therefore basically set in stone, or you act in a more benevolent fashion and invite comments. Either way the message is pretty clear: I'm the leader, here are the OKRs, any questions? We doubt any hands will spring into the air. Your team is defensive from the start and you've failed to take advantage of one of the system's chief benefits: receiving bottom-up input in creating effective OKRs.

The story above is of the extreme variety and we don't expect you would actually engage in that sort of behavior . . . would you? In practice, a more likely scenario when developing your initial OKRs is for the team leader to, rather than unilaterally set the OKRs, facilitate the creation process with no outside assistance. We understand and applaud your enthusiasm and commitment to be directly involved by leading the facilitation process, but believe it's a bad idea for a number of reasons:

1. Roles quickly blur. Are you a facilitator, a participant, or both? Your answer will greatly impact how you act in the workshops.
2. We all fall prey to unconscious biases, and without knowing it's possible you may steer the discussion of OKRs in a direction that reflects your own thinking, rather than collecting input from, and synthesizing the collective wisdom of, your team. You may feel great after the meeting ("Those OKRs are terrific!"), but your team, who had no say in what was crafted, will likely be grumbling (or worse) about how OKRs are just another way of dishing out more work.
3. The team loses your valuable input as a leader and arbiter of key decisions. Your role as a leader is to weigh the opinions of the team, and when disagreement fogs the air, use your professional judgment and experience to render a well thought out decision.

If going it alone isn't the answer, then what is? It's difficult to not sound self-serving as we write this because we are consultants. However, we're convinced that a well-trained and experienced consultant can add tremendous value to, and rapidly accelerate the success of, your OKRs implementation.[13] Especially if you're new to OKRs, a consultant brings something you simply don't possess at this time: implementation experience and proven methodologies for completing the work in a timely fashion.

Consultants also offer objective advice. As a neutral facilitator or *naïve coach*, someone who is not an expert on the team's work and therefore not immersed in the minutia of what keeps the team up at night, a consultant can pose questions that often unearth basic assumptions, forcing everyone to take a step back and revisit their core mental models. Finally, consultants offer a quality sometimes in short supply during an implementation period—credibility. It's a sad but undeniable fact that senior management may be more receptive to OKRs when they are co-developed by an outside expert with legitimate bona fides in the field.

Should you feel a consultant's assistance may be right for your OKRs work, here are a number of factors to consider when selecting a firm or individual:

■ *OKRs experience:* As OKRs continue to make their way into the mainstream of strategy execution and performance management they will undoubtedly draw the attention of consulting firms large and small, eager to capitalize on a growing trend and potential source of untapped revenue. You may think step one for you, as a client, is to discuss a prospective consultant's track record of success, but we actually see that as the second step. Your first order of business is to ensure their definition of OKRs and yours are consistent. Again, as the tool rises in prominence you can expect more and more firms to offer OKRs services. But are they really OKRs? They may be peddling not-so sophisticated dashboards, KPIs masquerading as OKRs, or an irrelevant software solution. Ensure their working definition of the framework is in alignment with your expectations. With that condition satisfied, you can examine their past client engagements to determine how they work, typical scope, and of course, how their clients have benefited from their intervention.

■ *Look for a range of skills:* Talented consultants must wear a lot of hats. They must be skilled in communication and able to present concepts clearly and cogently, while liaising comfortably with all levels of the company. Facilitation skills are obviously a must, as much of the work will involve leading conflict-filled workshops to craft and refine OKRs. Analytical skills are also necessary for combing through data and materials in order to properly prepare to effectively facilitate. Ensure the consultant you're considering possesses the requisite skills to confidently and competently lead the engagement.

■ *Knowledge transfer:* A key component of every work plan devised by consulting firms will be sufficient and timely knowledge transfer from the consultants to the employees of the contracting organization. Knowledge transfer implies just that—a passing of knowledge on key concepts and techniques from the consultants to the clients. However, in their zeal to complete their work on time and on budget, consultants may inadvertently sacrifice knowledge transfer activities in favor of more tangible work efforts. Organizations pay a heavy price when this occurs. As the consultants are walking out the door they leave behind an organization bereft of the skills and knowledge necessary to sustain the momentum that was so difficult to achieve. Ensure any consultants you work with will devote the necessary time to a comprehensive sharing of OKRs knowledge.

■ *Cultural fit:* When one of us (Paul) was still in the corporate world, he had an interesting experience when the company he was working with hired a well-known consulting firm to assist with a restructuring project. The culture at the company was very open, collegial, and chummy. Some meetings actually started a minute or two late because of participants hugging one another. The consulting team assigned to the company couldn't have been more different in their approach. They cloistered themselves in a meeting room, barely made eye contact in the hallways, and spoke with no one but the senior executive team. They may have considered themselves professional, but to the staff, their cool demeanor appeared standoffish, aloof, and even condescending. This conflict of style had an impact on the engagement, as staff members weren't comfortable working with, and certainly wouldn't be candid with, the consultants. The rift quickly became irreparable and the firm was let go. Cultural "fit" is an often-overlooked attribute when considering a consulting partner, but one that should stand on even ground with knowledge and experience. While you won't be wedded to your consultants, they will be an extremely important part of your organization during OKRs development. Look past the lavishly illustrated brochures or websites to the real people you'll be dealing with every day. Will they be compatible with the culture of your organization? Will executives and frontline staff alike be willing to work shoulder to shoulder with them? If the answer is no, keep looking.

 ## CONCLUDING THOUGHTS

While some old business irritants never seem to fade away, office politics come to mind for example, for the most part this is a very exciting and rewarding time to be working in organizations. In the past several decades we've witnessed stratospheric gains in an array of fields—change management, organizational structure, the application of neuroscience to the work world—that have elevated the practice of management to near art form.

Despite the prodigious theoretical and practical advances, however, many organizations continue to struggle with the most basic of challenges: Communicating and executing their unique strategy. We believe execution results from a workforce armed with knowledge of the company's top priorities, aligned around a common purpose, and motivated to succeed. OKRs serve each of these functions in an elegantly simple and utterly effective fashion.

As we chronicled early in the book, the model's origins can be traced to the middle of the past century, but we're confident its greatest period of growth and development is just beginning to gather around us. One of the boons of our digital age is the lightning fast spread of productive ideas, and OKRs certainly fall into that category. As more organizations around the globe become aware of, and begin to harness, the framework's potential, we expect their experimentation, tinkering, and modifications to advance OKRs to new and previously unheralded heights of efficacy. We feel privileged to lend our voice to this revolution in organizational effectiveness, and thank you for allowing us to be your guide during this portion of your OKRs journey. We wish you great success.

## NOTES

1. Steven Pressfield, *The War of Art, Break Through the Blocks and Win Your Inner Creative Battles* (New York: Black Irish Entertainment, 2012).
2. Andrew S. Grove, *High Output Management* (New York: Random House, 1983).
3. *Impraise* blog, "Deloitte Joins Adobe and Accenture in Dumping Performance Reviews," Steffen Maier, May 3, 2015, http://blog.impraise.com/360-feedback/deloitte-joins-adobe-and-accenture-in-dumping-performance-reviews-360-feedback.
4. Marcus Buckingham, "Most HR Data Is Bad," *Harvard Business Review* (March 2015).
5. http://blog.impraise.com/360-feedback/deloitte-joins-adobe-and-accenture-in-dumping-performance-reviews-360-feedback. Accessed May 2, 2016.
6. Grove.
7. *Impraise* blog.
8. Peter Drucker, *The Practice of Management* (New York: HarperBusiness re-issue edition, 2010).
9. Daniel Pink, *Drive: The Surprising Truth About What Motivates Us* (New York: Riverhead Books, 2011).
10. See WorldatWork and Deloitte Consulting, "Incentive Pay Practices Survey: Publicly Traded Companies," February 2014.
11. David Rock, *Your Brain at Work: Strategies for Overcoming Distractions, Regaining Focus, and Working Smarter All Day Long* (New York: Harper Business, 2009).
12. Impraise Blog.
13. Portions of this section draw on Paul R. Niven, *Balanced Scorecard Step-by-Step: Maximizing Performance and Maintaining Results*, 2nd edition (Hoboken, NJ: 2006).

# CHAPTER SEVEN

# Case Studies in OKRs Use

A S A RESULT OF GOOGLE'S highly publicized success with the model, OKRs are often associated exclusively with the Silicon Valley. However, the highly malleable framework is actually applicable to any organization, anywhere. We've been fortunate enough to work with companies large and small in a variety of industries around the globe. It's their stories we wanted to share with you. But how?

If you've ever read a business book (and we doubt this is your first foray into the genre) you know that showcasing companies to illustrate key points is a standard practice. And we're no different in that regard. Before we began writing the book we contacted a number of organizations with which we're familiar (mostly from our consulting work, but not always) and asked them to complete a questionnaire documenting their experience with OKRs. Our intent was to then sprinkle in quotes from the cases throughout the book to add color and context to our primary recommendations. As you've seen from reading the book, we did do that to some extent, but probably not as liberally as you may have experienced with other books. It turns out that the responses we received were so good, and so informative, we felt it would prove much more beneficial for you to read them in their entirety. Parsing them across chapters would have diminished their overall message.

On the pages that follow you'll hear the inspiring and educational stories of a number of companies, ranging in size from around 100 employees to over 33,000, and located around the world.[1] We encourage you to read each one carefully and apply the many lessons they offer to your own OKRs implementation. Enjoy.

## FLIPKART

Launched in 2007, Flipkart is India's leading e-commerce marketplace, offering more than 30 million products in over 70 categories. The company's 33,000-plus employees serve 45 million registered users who clock over 10 million daily visits. That's a lot of numbers and they all add up to Flipkart becoming India's first billion-dollar e-commerce company. We were pleased to speak with Niket Desai, the company's former chief of staff.

*Why were OKRs introduced? Did you consider any other program?*

We had a highly complex organization that spans logistics, core technology, and ads. Each individual component, alone, would be a massive company fraught with its own complications. That all three had to run in unison made it more difficult.

OKRs were implemented as a cross-company endeavor to first and foremost align core Flipkart initiatives. The practical components of OKRs, like numerical assessments, pre-alignment before codifying goals, were major benefits for an organization that was in silos.

*Who initiated OKRs (who brought them to your attention; how did they get on your radar screen)?*

Punit Soni (chief product officer) and I brought them up, primarily to use in our division only as we had been trained on, and used the model at Google and Motorola with great success.

*Who sponsored the implementation?*

Punit sponsored it within the product organization.

*Where in your organization did you develop OKRs? At the corporate level? Or at a business unit level, and why?*

Initially it was our business unit level because we were trying to make sense of our allocation and use of resources as well as provide focus. It turns out these benefits were wanted by the rest of the organization as well, and since

OKRs "play nice with each other" it was widely adopted. OKRs have since been deployed to over 10,000 employees, but affect 33,000.

**What was your process for developing OKRs? Executive training, retreats, workshops, etc.?**

At first, in our business group, the rollout worked like this:

- A wide note was sent out explaining what OKRs were, and why we'd be adopting them.
- We published examples of OKRs that were organization specific as examples.
- We held an All Hands meeting to dive into them further (our purpose in using OKRs).
- We asked direct reports to the chief product officer to provide their draft OKRs.
- We held conflict sessions for different groups to agree on what would and would not make good OKRs (and handle dependencies up front).
- We published these to a public site and spread them organization wide. We felt it was important that everyone should know what we're working on.
- Finally, we held another All Hands meeting to review the finalized OKRs.

Initially, it was rough. It took us about three quarters to get the kinks and confusion of OKRs out. The most common problems were:

Too much work and not enough focus (what really matters!).

A tendency to use the OKR as a binding document (carrots vs. stick). The challenge with OKRs is that they sometimes look like contracts. Objectives and key results is an iterative process, one in which there is negotiation and stretch goal setting. This requires tremendous trust across and within the organization. An example is allowing teams to do bottom-up assessments of not only what they think they should do, but also what outcomes they think they can make. If it were top-down only, and the outcomes were "directly" tied to performance, OKRs becomes more like contracts that teams will ultimately use to strong arm one another into getting their work done. OKRs actually help complex organizations work together by showing the larger picture and complicated interactions across services and teams. The belief in the larger picture drives the groups towards convergence and fair triaging (and reprioritization) when necessary. If OKRs are used as sticks—that is, pure contractual obligations without empathy for the existing work at hand (business as usual), the true power of alignment and stretch thinking that OKRs are capable of will never be realized.

*How do you ensure your OKRs reflect the organization's strategy—so that you have people focused on doing the right things?*

We did a few things. First we recommend you take time. That's the major mistake I see from people using OKRs. It makes sense so they just do it. But nothing simple is easy. It's simple because it contains tremendous complexity—and the work to embed that complexity allows it to seem easy (especially when OKRs become effective).

It's also very important to listen. OKRs should be at least partially bottom-up. Groups should say what they plan on doing and roll that up. Leadership should take that opinion and guidance and mix it with their own intentions to create a mix of strategic and ground-level realities.

Finally, let people vigorously debate. When people escalate, ask them for a recommendation instead of giving an answer. That's where the best ideas and real initiative show up.

*How do you score your OKRs?*

Once mid-quarter and at the end of the quarter, using a 0–1.0 scale.

*Do you have a limit on the number of OKRs?*

We supply this guidance: we recommend three to five objectives. And approximately the same or a slightly higher number of key results per objective.

*Who manages the OKRs process on an ongoing basis?*

We had a team of chiefs of staff representing major sections of the organization that would operationally run the process. Leaders in the company were expected to get their drafts, scoring, and dependencies done on their own. Leadership would set up review dates and actually give feedback.

*Have you rolled OKRs out to lower levels of the organization?*

We go at least three to four layers of teams deep, but at that point we do not mandate. It's a process to get full deployment of OKRs (all the way to individual) and in our experience the major benefits occur at approximately the first three layers (chief, VP, director). That creates the heavily sought after alignment and focus.

*How do you ensure there is alignment among all OKRs?*

At first, we recommend dedicated sessions for people to come and resolve issues (especially cross-team). The truth is, well-designed organizations where functions and ownership are well understood, and jive with the organizational direction, make it easier. OKRs become complex when the complexity of the business is mirrored by the organization setup.

Defining measurable results is easy if you understand what you should be measuring, and what matters for your business. I find that the quality of OKRs has a good correlation with a person's understanding of their business. Blindly going for growth without understanding the key reasons behind specific metrics (revenue drivers, hypothesis testing, etc.) can be misleading.

Our OKRs were complex to align at first, but over time became easier as people handled their own dependencies and negotiations along with some organizational shaping that aligned things naturally. OKRs tell you where the future of your organization is going. By definition, the dependencies show converging or diverging efforts—and over time can hint at organizational changes that will be required.

**What has been your approach to communicating and educating the organization on OKRs?**

We feel it's vital to over communicate. Provide resources, and make them easy to find. And it's not just e-mails. We developed "Practical Guides" to OKRs, example documents, presentations for other leaders to use, and did a number of brown bag sessions across the company to evangelize, explain, and implement OKRs.

We also have a single place for all OKRs and resources. Having one place for all of this makes it easier for people to find information, which is a key component to a successful implementation.

We were insistent about timelines and OKR sharing. We broadly shared OKRs and encouraged other teams and groups to share their own for feedback, review, and understanding. Also, we had leaders engage with OKRs to show it wasn't something to be considered "busy work" for everyone else in middle management to handle. We held one-on-ones with major teams to ensure we captured the strategic direction within OKRs and helped them understand deeply where we were trying to go.

Finally, we also relied on All Hands and Town Hall meetings. In the ultimate show of support and sponsorship, our highest levels of leadership presented the company OKRs as well as the driving forces behind each one. These events are also a great avenue to apply context to how OKRs and groups interact.

**How do groups report on and review OKR results?**

We hold reviews at the end of each quarter for scoring and drafting OKRs for the following quarter. Then, early in the new quarter we hold an All Hands meeting for presentation of OKRs. We also hold mid-term OKR checks, but these happen mostly online.

**Do you use a technology system for OKRs?**

We are building our own OKR tool to manage OKRs, dependencies, and automated communication company wide.

**Did technology make new benefits possible?**

Definitely. It's proprietary and helps far beyond OKR management.

*Have you, or did you ever, consider linking OKRs to compensation? Why or why not?*

No, and loosely at best. OKRs do not provide context of conditions or work, just outcomes. Decision and outcomes should be separated (basic decision-making theory) and so, similarly, a direct tie to compensation could be easily gamed. It's more important people stretch and try and fail, than hit their numbers to ensure compensation.

*Have you linked OKRs to performance reviews? Why or why not?*

It may, again, provide context but performance reviews are specifically about development and feedback.

*What specific benefits have you achieved from OKRs?*

There are several:

■ Company-wide transparency, and convergence toward alignment.
■ More outcome focused than "hard-work" focused.
■ Forced thought and better articulation of ideas and strategies.
■ It's becoming part of the culture. I helped introduce the program but have subsequently left the company. However, OKRs remain, showing the power of the framework itself.

*How do you ensure ongoing momentum for OKRs?*

■ It has required a top-down push.
■ Showcase OKRs in meetings, presentations, and manifestations of strategy in action.
■ Make them widely available and easy to find.

*What were the major surprises in your implementation?*

They were used as bats. There's a tendency to view them as contractual obligations versus desired outcomes.

*What would you do differently?*

■ Focus. Less is more.
■ Start at the highest level and slowly go down levels for OKRs instead of all at once.
■ Talk more about "standard business" work that needs to happen versus OKRs. Absence of the maintenance work doesn't mean you drop it.

*Would you recommend using OKRs to other companies? Why or why not?*

Absolutely!

##  CAREERBUILDER

Each month, more than 24 million visitors go to CareerBuilder, the largest online job site in the United States, to find new jobs and career advice. The company, which is a global leader in Human Capital solutions, works with employers around the world, including 92 percent of the Fortune 1000. The company is committed to matching the right talent with the right opportunity more often than any other site. Andy Krupit, CareerBuilder's Manager of Agile Development walked us through their OKRs implementation.

***Why were OKRs introduced? Did you consider any other program?***
We didn't consider any other program. We chose OKRs primarily because the model provides:

- More focus on what we say is important to us
- Better alignment with business and across teams
- Accountability: The "positive" tension from business

***Who initiated OKRs (who brought them to your attention; how did they get on your radar screen)?***
Sonia Madan, who works with me as an Agile Coach, brought the concept to my attention. I quickly saw the opportunity to leverage this framework as a tool to facilitate filling the needs we were seeing. We discussed at an offsite with IT Leaders and reviewed the Rick Klau Google video. We collectively agreed to introduce and seek buy-in with our business partners.

***Who sponsored the implementation?***
Our Chief Information Officer (CIO), Roger Fugett.

***Where in your organization did you develop OKRs? At the corporate level? Or at a business unit level, and why?***
We introduced it at the "team" level (business unit & IT team). We are an Agile/Lean shop. This is embedded in our culture. We wanted to explore using OKRs at the team level first to understand the framework's impact and effectiveness prior to introducing it at additional levels.

***What was your process for developing OKRs? Executive training, retreats, workshops, etc.?***
Initially, we held a three-day workshop with technology leaders, product owners, and business leaders. There were multiple three- to four-hour sessions for each "team." Prior to the workshop each team was introduced to OKRs by Ben Lamorte.

The diagram below represents our quarterly OKR Process:

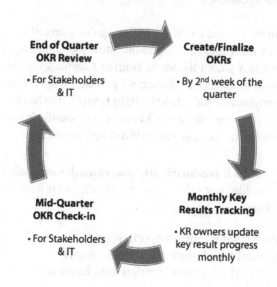

**End of Quarter OKR Review**
• For Stakeholders & IT

**Create/Finalize OKRs**
• By 2nd week of the quarter

**Monthly Key Results Tracking**
• KR owners update key result progress monthly

**Mid-Quarter OKR Check-in**
• For Stakeholders & IT

Create/Finalize—Teams will *Draft* (mission, one to two objectives with two or more key results); *Align* (alignment check with other teams they work with); *Refine*—through refinement sessions with OKR coaches (three of us facilitating as a neutral third party allowing others to think critically); *Finalize*—with senior leadership from business.

Key result owners will track, update, score, and report on key results at mid-quarter check-in (team, business present).

Product owners with key result owners hold end-of-quarter review of OKRs, roadmap, etc. Scoring of key results revisited.

***Did you use the Google model? If so, did you modify it to fit your organization?***

Yes. We liked and kept the Google model of scoring. But we felt it was too big a change all at once to implement OKRs at the individual level, so we have delayed that portion.

***How do you ensure your OKRs reflect the organization's strategy—so that you have people focused on doing the right things?***

Our OKR coaches held facilitation sessions with our business groups and IT leaders on drafting their top OKRs for the quarter. Often using the "5-Why" technique until we got our businesses to focus on the "Why" and not the "How."

### How do you score your OKRs?
Like Google, on a scale of 0–1, using 3 main grading points (0.3, 0.7, 1).

0.3—This is what we expect to achieve in the quarter.

0.7—"A stretch." Some dependencies, and not everything is in our control.

1—This would rock everyone's world. Not impossible, but seemingly. Also known as "super stretch"?

### Do you have a limit on the number of OKRs?
We didn't the first time, but in retrospect, we should have. Perhaps, given the number of teams we were working with, limiting them to one objective. We will continue to take an iterative approach as to how we should handle this going forward. We do recommend that no team has more than three objectives overall.

### How long did it take to develop your initial set of OKRs?
One month (workshops, draft, align, refine, finalize).

### Who manages the OKRs process on an ongoing basis?
Our OKR coaches with the primary focus being led by our product owner manager, Sabrina Pickeral.

### Have you rolled OKRs out to lower levels of the organization?
No.

### What has been your approach to communicating and educating OKRs to the organization as a whole?
As we began to engage with and train the businesses that work with IT, many of those business units have begun to spread the word in terms of the value. We now have other areas of our organization wanting to work with the same framework.

### How do you ensure there is alignment among all OKRs?
Part of our OKR drafting process is an "Alignment Check." This is about involving the dependent business/teams and ensuring that we are not working against each other. Also, we initially published our OKRs in a simple Excel document in a public location for all to see. We know this is not ideal, in terms of understanding relationships between the OKRs, etc., but it was a start. We are currently looking into alternative methods for making the OKRs more transparent and easily consumable.

### How do groups report on and review OKR results?
Right now, we are leveraging our cultural value of *Disciplined Freedom* for this. Teams/key result owners are using their own methods to ensure transparency.

*Do you use a technology solution for OKRs?*

We started with a home-grown solution that allows for easy updates to scoring, but have put that on the back burner for now as we felt introducing that in addition to the concept of OKRs with our business was too much. Therefore, we went with Excel at first just to get started.

*Did technology make new benefits possible?*

We're not in the technology implementation phase yet.

*Have you, or did you ever, consider linking OKRs to compensation? Why or why not?*

No. We tried that with other metrics and realized we were driving the wrong behavior. Ultimately, we want to keep OKRs aspirational. Being tied to compensation eliminates that.

Not for direct salary compensation or bonus potential. However, we are considering the pros and cons of how OKRs might influence our reward programs. To us, it is not entirely realistic to believe that the performance of an individual whose effort is directly reflected in the impact to a KR can be completely divorced from incentives. This is analogous to having "skin in the game" like sales and their numbers tied directly to their rewards. However, ultimately we want to keep OKRs aspirational, and we realize that linking OKRs directly to compensation does work against that. In the past, we explored having other metrics tied to compensation (i.e., bonus) and the result was that is ultimately drove the wrong behavior. I also feel that there is always a danger of driving the wrong behavior when something is transparent and competitive. We are in search of the "right" balance. It will be key for us with OKRs to insist on a collaborative KR setting with transparency—this aligns well with our Agile approach to the way we work, and should help drive out the low-balling and sandbagging.

*Have you linked OKRs to performance reviews? Why or why not?*

OKRs influence the performance rating, not determine them. We use OKRs as a tool to facilitate continual improvement, having them as part of the conversation during performance evaluation.

*What specific benefits have you achieved from OKRs?*

We are still new to the process but the biggest benefit we have seen so far is having strategic/visionary conversations around the *why* of what we do versus just doing. This has helped us achieve great focus and purpose on what we do every day.

*How do you ensure ongoing momentum for OKRs?*

We have to keep it in the day-to-day conversations with our business partners. Once it becomes a part of the CareerBuilder vocabulary, we have reached utopia.

*What were the major surprises in your implementation?*

Operational parts of the business did not think there would be much value in adopting OKRs, but they have found tremendous value in focusing on their *why*. Also, another major surprise was that these conversations quickly led to many teams collaborating on an initiative when that might not have happened previously. They realized they had a shared objective and joined forces!

*What would you do differently?*

We tried to change the vocabulary overnight across the company and that was hard. We started this movement in IT so people automatically assumed OKRs was something for IT and not for their benefit. I would've chosen one main business unit to focus our efforts on for a quarter to get the wins and then share that across the company and slowly bring more units into the framework.

*Would you recommend using OKRs to other companies? Why or why not?*

I would recommend using OKRs to other companies for sure. This critical-thinking framework has set us up for future success by ensuring we are focused on why we do the things we do and helps bring teams together by talking with the same terminology. It increases collaboration, confirms/defines strategy, and sparks innovation.

## ZALANDO

Zalando is Europe's leading online fashion platform for women, men, and children. Founded in 2008 in Berlin, it now serves 15 countries, offering a wide variety of fashion products from more than 1,500 brands. The company employs over 10,000 people in Europe and had revenue of almost 3 billion euros in 2015. Christoph Lange, Vice President of Brand Solutions, was kind enough to share the Zalando story with us.

*Why were OKRs introduced? Did you consider any other program?*

We received very good feedback from companies that are using OKRs (Google, for example). The system provides global alignment, full transparency, and is based on trust and collaboration. We also appreciate that it is an easy to understand framework.

***Who initiated OKRs (who brought them to your attention; how did they get on your radar screen)?***

I visited the Google headquarters, and many people mentioned how strong OKRs as an instrument are. During the visit I had the chance to meet with Rick Klau, who was referring to his You Tube video (this was August 2013).

***Who sponsored the implementation?***

We are very fortunate within Zalando to enjoy a lot of freedom to try new things. I was setting up a new department, Zalando Brand Solutions, and decided to use OKRs from the outset. Our board was very supportive of the decision.

***Where in your organization did you develop OKRs? At the corporate level? Or at a business unit level, and why?***

We started in one department, Brand Solutions. Brand Solutions enables its fashion partners to connect to their customers through the Zalando platform. In the beginning, the team focused on providing an easy way to publish a brand's digital content in its own brand shop, including a CMS and Analytics tool. Brand Solutions is now set to fully integrate stock inventory to the Zalando platform from every fashion business—be it brands, retailers, or pure offline players—to make their products available to consumers.

There we used OKRs at the department, team, and individual level for three quarters. For the fourth quarter, the program was rolled out to the whole company, starting at the senior management level, and then to our larger departments and teams.

***What was your process for developing OKRs? Executive training, retreats, workshops, etc.?***

We started by conducting a lot of research on the topic. As I noted above, we spoke with people from Google, but also read a lot of blogs, articles, and relied on other sources of information.

As for implementation, within Brand Solutions, we created our OKRs with small groups of leaders and presented to teams.

When it was time for the broader company rollout, we had external support from Ben Lamorte and conducted a series of training sessions and workshops for leaders and OKR experts to learn the basic theory of OKRs, how to ask questions, and to support the teams in OKR drafting sessions. Now we have an established OKR expert roundtable to discuss learnings and challenges to evolve the OKR approach at Zalando.

***Did you use the Google model? If so, did you modify it to fit your organization?***

Mainly, yes. But we adapted it to fit our specific needs.

***How do you ensure your OKRs reflect the organization's strategy—so that you have people focused on doing the right things?***

The majority of OKRs should connect to higher-level OKRs within our company. We create company-level OKRs on both a yearly and quarterly basis to reflect our overall strategy.

***How do you score your OKRs?***

We use a 0 to 1.0 scale, where 0.7 is the "sweet spot." Our OKRs are publicly graded, and we don't link them to either bonuses or people's performance.

***Do you have a limit on the number of OKRs?***

Yes. To ensure we drive focus, we began with a maximum of five objectives, each with a maximum of four key results. We are now exploring the possibility to reduce the number of OKRs even more in order to increase focus.

***How long did it take to develop your initial set of OKRs?***

For Brand Solutions, it took us eight hours per person (for the full team) to develop our very first quarterly OKRs.

***Who manages the OKRs process on an ongoing basis?***

We have an OKR committee at company level to ensure enough bottom-up OKRs and to set and review the company-level OKRs on a quarterly basis, but there is no central process for OKRs; the teams own them. We do, however, have central support to assist employees. Where possible, we encourage our OKR experts to help facilitate OKR drafting sessions.

***Have you rolled OKRs out to lower levels of the organization?***

Yes. By the end of 2015, OKRs were fully rolled out down to the VP level and OKRs were optional for teams below this level. Taking this phased approach let us focus on learning. However, starting in 2016, all teams are participating in OKRs.

***What has been your approach to communicating and educating OKRs to the organization as a whole?***

We've used a number of methods to communicate and educate our employees about OKRs, including:

- zTalks: Live streaming of our company OKRs and grades each quarter to all employees
- Presenting OKRs in departmental All-Hands meetings
- Keeping OKRs transparent so that everyone has access to everybody's OKRs

■ Team OKRs on posters, hung in their departments
■ Training sessions, videos, and presentations

### How do you ensure that there is alignment among all OKRs?

Every OKR owner has to meet with all teams on which either he or she is depending on or vice versa to get buy-in from the other team before finalizing—we call that *alignment week*. We also insist on full transparency throughout the process of creating OKRs so that everyone is aware of what is being developed.

Within Brand Solutions, we conduct an end-of-quarter OKR workshop with our full team to come up with a draft of department OKRs that gets us 80 percent of the way there. In the past, the input was collected in single teams, but getting all of the teams that comprise Brand Solutions together to draft OKRs from the start gets us 80 percent complete much more efficiently than having our teams draft OKRs in silos.

In order to ensure OKRs enabled more alignment across teams, we recently implemented a Zalando wide OKR alignment week. This week is intended to keep calendars mostly free for the time to meet with all necessary teams and departments to align with overarching OKRs. This week is at the beginning of the quarter.

### How do groups report on and review OKR results?

It varies by department. But, some of the ways are All-Hands meetings where OKR grades are shared, biweekly grading meetings that are open for all to attend, and the use of shared documents in Google Drive. In Brand Solutions, we now also do a mid-quarter review with all teams where the teams demonstrate their results, to make them tangible.

### Do you use a technology solution for OKRs?

We are about to implement a dedicated solution to manage OKRs (mid-2016). We actually did quite well for a full year simply by leveraging Google Drive.

### Did technology make new benefits possible?

Yes, technology allows for simultaneous collaboration, which makes things fast and easy. It also facilitates rights and role management (i.e., everybody can comment, but only the team can edit). Finally, with technology, OKRs become mobile and are accessible from anywhere.

### Have you, or did you ever, consider linking OKRs to compensation? Why or why not?

No, we believe the biggest motivator is not money, but a challenging goal. Employees should never face the conflict of deciding between a personal reward and the company's success; this should always go hand-in-hand.

*Have you linked OKRs to performance reviews? Why or why not?*

No, OKRs are not a performance management tool. However, we believe OKRs should, in the long-term, be consistent with employee and/or team performance, so they can be included as one point when it comes to performance discussions. But there's no direct linking, no.

*What specific benefits have you achieved from OKRs?*

Given we present company-level OKRs each quarter, everyone at Zalando understands the direction of our company. We saw a major increase in alignment within the Brand Solutions team. In fact one of our early key results was to increase alignment across Brand Solutions teams and we did just that.

*How do you ensure ongoing momentum for OKRs?*

We have created a community of OKR experts and these experts meet regularly to discuss questions and share best practices and ultimately to ensure that we're constantly improving our use of OKRs. We expect the upcoming rollout of our OKR tool in 2016 to help increase momentum as well.

*What were the major surprises in your implementation?*

At first, most of us felt we needed a standardized, dedicated tool for OKRs in order to make the process work, but we managed quite well with Google Sheets for a full year.

*What would you do differently?*

There is not much we would do differently. However, we did start assigning owners to the company-level key results. This is important since it doesn't work well to just assign all company key results to a few executives.

*Would you recommend using OKRs to other companies? Why or why not?*

Absolutely, it's a simple and powerful approach for generating alignment and staying focused on what's important.

## SEARS HOLDINGS CORPORATION (SHC)

Sears Holdings Corporation is a leading integrated retailer focused on seamlessly connecting the digital and physical shopping experiences to serve members—wherever, whenever, and however they want to shop. The company, with 2015 revenues in excess of $25 billion, operates through its subsidiaries, including Sears Roebuck and Co. and Kmart Corporation, with full-line and specialty retail stores across the United States. Holly Engler, the Director of Strategic Talent Management, outlined their OKRs journey for us.

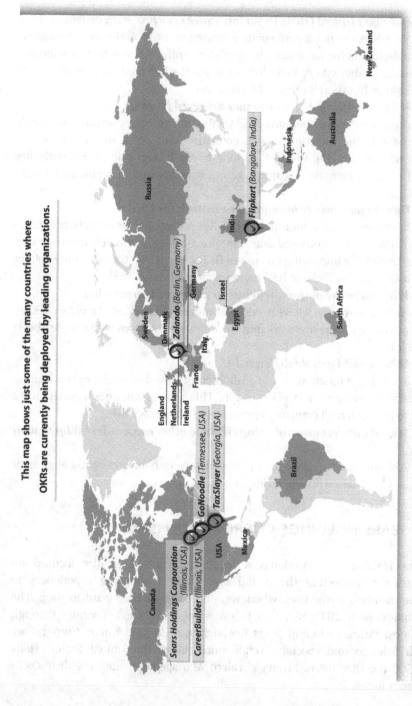

This map shows just some of the many countries where OKRs are currently being deployed by leading organizations.

**EXHIBIT 7.1** OKRs ARE A GLOBAL PHENOMENON

*Why were OKRs introduced? Did you consider any other program?*

As a large, complex organization consisting of about 34 business units, an executive leadership team of over 290 individuals, an associate base of almost 200,000, and an array of business departments ranging from support functions to merchant groups, we struggled to maintain focus and transparency of our key objectives across the entire business. It was difficult for any single associate to understand how their personal contributions were tied to broader strategic initiatives. In addition, we consistently struggled to identify how we could better work *across* business units as opposed to simply *within* business units.

As a company in transformation, it was obvious we needed a process that would allow us to be more agile, flexible, and have the ability to adapt throughout the year to continue driving business results in response to market and customer needs, and changes in our strategy and execution. OKRs seemed like the right tool for the job and after a pilot with our executive team, we didn't need to explore other options. We were confident that we had found something that fit our needs.

*Who initiated OKRs (who brought them to your attention; how did they get on your radar screen)?*

Our CEO and Chairman, Eddie Lampert, had introduced our Chief Human Resources Officer (CHRO) and Talent Management team to OKRs in early 2013. He had seen the Google Ventures video and was intrigued about the possibility of revisiting our goal-setting practices to incorporate more frequent, measureable, and transparent objectives that could help us work more efficiently across the organization to achieve meaningful outcomes.

*Who sponsored the implementation?*

Since Eddie introduced SHC to OKRs, he has continued to be a strong sponsor and advocate of the methodology. In fact, he regularly uses our internal social media platform to communicate advantages and insights he obtains from reviewing OKRs of our senior most leaders in the organization.

Our CHRO at the time, Dean Carter, as well as Chris Mason, the head of Talent Management, were fully on board and championed the approach as well as we continued to create buy in across the organization. As we piloted OKRs with our executive leadership team, they, in turn, became advocates of the more frequent goal-setting process and continued to support OKRs in their respective businesses.

*Where in your organization did you develop OKRs? At the corporate level? Or at a business unit level, and why?*

We initially piloted OKRs with our executive leadership team for two quarters. After collecting our findings and determining that this was not only a viable, but logical thought process for goal setting, we expanded OKRs to roughly 20,000 associates. We continue to expand OKRs to select hourly populations and are always exploring the opportunity to continue expanding the scope.

*What was your process for developing OKRs? Executive training, retreats, workshops, etc.?*

We started our OKR journey by making sure we could fulfill rule #1: create complete transparency of OKRs in the organization. So we quickly partnered with our development team to utilize our internal social media platform as a home for entering, rating, and sharing OKRs. Within a matter of weeks, we had created our initial OKR "platform." We initiated a pilot with our executive leadership team and asked them to simply enter a few objectives that they were working on this quarter, and at the end of the quarter to log back into the platform and self-rate their key results.

We leveraged an OKR expert to provide executive coaching to our senior most leaders to help support understanding of *why* we are utilizing OKRs and *how* to write meaningful objectives and key results. Our Talent Management team also provided individual support to leaders in helping to translate business strategies into measureable OKRs. In addition, we conducted personalized onboarding sessions related to OKRs and performance management to our senior most leaders. Live sessions were conducted for associates at our corporate office to support the education and practice of setting and rating OKRs. These sessions were recorded and are ongoing across the organization.

*Did you use the Google model? If so, did you modify it to fit your organization?*

For the most part, yes. We did make some modification to ensure it fit our business needs. For instance, we don't necessarily set OKRs at the team level for every team in the organization. We put a lot more emphasis on setting individual OKRs. We modified the approach a bit to include broader individual priorities and visibility to Business Unit priorities that in turn support the associate in aligning their OKRs to organizational strategies.

*How do you ensure your OKRs reflect the organization's strategy—so that you have people focused on doing the right things?*

After utilizing OKRs for almost a year in the broader organization, we made the decision to formally introduce them as part of a complete overhaul of our performance management processes. As a result, OKRs became the primary goal-setting technique in the new dynamic performance approach. Due to the size and complexity of the SHC organization, we wanted to ensure that associates were clear on their ability to appropriately align their personal OKRs to broader business objectives. To that end, we layered in what we call *Individual Priorities.*

Priorities represent broader buckets of work, core units of your role, or key projects that span longer periods of time (maybe 6 months, 12 months, or even longer). This created additional alignment at the individual level but didn't necessarily solve for the Business Unit and company level. So we asked each of our approximately 34 Business Unit leaders to publish their strategy in the internal platform in which we host the OKRs technology. Business Unit Priorities represent the two-to-five broader outcomes that the organization is aiming to achieve in a given year, priorities that the majority of associates can and will contribute to at an individual level. These Business Unit Priorities are directly aligned to our company strategy. This creates a direct line for each associate in aligning their personal OKRs with their broader Priorities, which are tied to Business Unit Priorities, and thus aligned with the overall organizational strategy.

### *How do you score your OKRs?*

Associates self-rate their personal OKRs at the end of each quarter using a scale of 0.0–1.0. A rating of 1.0 signifies that you "nailed it" or in other words, made really great progress on that particular objective. On the contrary, a rating of 0.0 means you didn't make any progress at all. Most individuals think about their progress, and thus their respective rating, as a percentage of their progress. For instance, if my objective is to increase sales by 10 percent, and I've increased sales by 5 percent at the end of the quarter, I rate myself a 0.5.

It is important for us that associates utilize these self-ratings not as a direct measure of performance, but instead to develop insights about what they achieved, what progress they can continue to make, and how to apply those learnings in the next quarter. For instance, if an associate is consistently rating themselves a 1.0, it should be an indication that they are not utilizing OKRs to set stretch goals; they are more than likely setting objectives that they know they can achieve. OKRs are meant to be ambitious. Ideally, we like seeing ratings in the 0.6–0.7 range, which is an indication that the associate is stretching themselves and still making good progress throughout the quarter.

### *Do you have a limit on the number of OKRs?*

We do. In fact, we limit associates in the tool to entering five objective each quarter. Within each objective, an associate can identify up to four k results (but certainly are not forced to enter all four). Focus is a key eleme of OKRs—thinking about the few objectives that you can make significant progress on in a specific quarter that results in meaningful progress on your broader priorities. In 2015, we discovered that OKRs are an excellent tool to also remain focused on personal or professional development objectives. In the current state, we give the option to associates to utilize one of their five objectives as a "Development OKR" and to identify the key results that can help them continue progress in developing a particular skill, capability, cultural belief, behavior, etc.

### How long did it take to develop your initial set of OKRs?

Surprisingly, longer than you would think. When you come to realize the difference between a task and a true objective, it makes you think differently about how you set your goals and become confident that you can measure it in a meaningful way at the end of the quarter. I think we, as professionals, take goal setting for granted and don't realize until we are utilizing a thought framework such as OKRs how ineffective our goal setting may have been. That being said, it may take a while to get your senior leadership team aligned on a *good* set of OKRs at the company or team level, and our added complexity of managing 34 Business Units doesn't help facilitate that process any quicker. For individual associates, we ask them to utilize the last week of the quarter and the first week of the quarter to get their OKRs rated and drafted. By the end of the first month of the quarter, associates should have their OKRs refined, aligned, and have begun working toward their progress.

### Who manages the OKRs process on an ongoing basis?

Our culture at SHC is one of personal accountability, and we build tools and processes to encourage our associates to own their performance and productivity with the guidance and support of their managers. OKRs are a tool designed *for* associates, and thus, the individual associate is responsible for managing their OKRs (rating them, entering them, aligning them, and discussing them with their manager).

### Have you rolled OKRs out to lower levels of the organization?

Initially, OKRs were rolled out to our entire salaried and exception hourly population. After integrating OKRs into our redesigned approach to performance management, we started to extend the methodology to other parts of the organization. Since then, we have expanded OKRs to our hourly store supervisors, hourly asset protection managers, and are currently rolling them out also to our retail lead population. Other areas of the business have also expressed interest and we plan to continue to provide additional hourly populations with the ability to utilize OKRs either as a primary goal setting mechanism, or a supplemental personal productivity tool.

*What has been your approach to communicating and educating OKRs to the organization as a whole?*

We utilize several communication channels to inform associates about OKRs. At the end of each quarter, we distribute a centralized communication from our SHC communications team to the entire audience reminding them that it's time to revisit and self-rate their OKRs and begin entering OKRs for the new quarter. They are reminded to do this in preparation of their quarterly check-in conversation with their manager, and to utilize that conversation to align objectives for the quarter. As an added "nudge," the technology we use automatically distributes a reminder on the day that new OKRs can be entered into the system.

Each quarter, we offer live and recorded workshops around topics such as "Aligning OKRs to Your Priorities," "Leveraging OKRs for Effective Check-Ins," or "Writing GREAT OKRs: Tips and Tricks" that continue to educate users on the features, benefits, and best practices of effective OKR writing. These targeted sessions ensure that content is business specific and meaningful to the audiences that attend. In addition to targeted coaching and training, broad communications in the form of short videos or vignettes are used to drive engagement, awareness, and to share success.

*How do you ensure there is alignment among all OKRs?*

Due to the size of the organization, it is difficult, if not impossible to centrally ensure that there is full alignment of OKRs. We rely heavily on the quarterly check-in conversations that associates and managers conduct at the start of each quarter to facilitate a conversation about an individual's OKRs and their alignment with team, business, and organizational priorities or objectives. The transparency of everyone's OKRs helps create the alignment as well, and associates have a personal accountability to ensure that they are aligned to the right outcomes.

Many of our teams and business leaders have integrated OKRs so deeply into their day-to-day practice that often, OKRs are a main topic of discussion and progress reporting in weekly staff meetings. Sharing OKRs at the team level on a regular cadence helps to make sure that team members are consistently reminded of what the team has set out to achieve, and how their individual contributions or OKRs come into play.

*How do groups report on and review OKR results?*

To start, OKRs for each individual are publicly displayed in our internal platform. Managers have direct access and visibility to the OKRs of their direct reports and vice versa, and *all* SHC associates are searchable so that their OKRs can be found. In return, we display usage data for individuals in a feature we call the "Actions Summary" which visually represents their progress on rating and entering OKRs. Managers see this at the team level, and leaders can also see this at an organizational level (viewing their direct *and* indirect associates). This ensures that progress on usage is prominently displayed and available to continue driving awareness and usage.

At the start of each new quarter, managers and associates meet for a quarterly check-in. These check-ins are a repurposed 1:1 and are associate-driven conversations around: What did I work on? How did it go? What's next? Associates are asked to come to the conversation with their self-ratings for the previous quarter completed, and new OKRs drafted. During the course of the conversation, the associate shares with their manager how they feel they did with regards to accomplishing their objectives in the previous quarter and share what they hope to achieve in the new quarter. The manager coaches and supports the associate, helping to provide additional direction or detail as well as to refine the OKRs of the associate and ensure alignment to broader team initiatives. After the conversation, associates make any necessary changes and begin working toward their desired outcomes.

### Do you use a technology solution for OKRs?

We do. We are lucky enough to have *awesome* developers within SHC that have been great partners in launching OKRs to our teams. We utilize an internal, gamified platform that hosts our entire homegrown talent management suite (including goal setting, check-ins or performance conversations, our instant feedback tool, talent review, etc.).

### Did technology make new benefits possible?

Having a technology that supports OKRs is hugely beneficial to us, especially in a large and complex organization like SHC. It provides complete transparency of objectives and key results to other associates across the organization and in other businesses that we would not have had beforehand. With the added benefit of being able to add additional components to the platform with respect to our performance management platform, associates now have a single place to go to review *what* they are working on, and *how* they are making progress against those objectives. In addition, as we continue to develop insights, learnings, and best practices, we are equipped to continuously evolve the technology to meet our needs.

### Have you, or did you ever, consider linking OKRs to compensation? Why or why not?

At SHC, we do not link compensation and performance exclusively. In fact, we intentionally position OKRs as a personal productivity tool to help drive execution and growth, and do not mandate that associates utilize OKRs (however, more than 70 percent of associates use them each quarter utilizing the opt-in approach). Compensation at SHC is discretionary and is a factor of *several* inputs including performance, potential, length of time in role, pay to market, and many other inputs. OKR self-ratings are just that . . . self-ratings. We do not aggregate them into any magical HR database and store them as a measure of performance. We encourage associates to utilize their self-ratings instead to conduct meaningful conversations around their performance and forecast their work to help them achieve results.

### Have you linked OKRs to performance reviews? Why or why not?

If we had performance reviews, we may have. However, in 2014 we eliminated the performance review and performance rating for our salaried and exception hourly associates (the population primarily utilizing OKRs).

### What specific benefits have you achieved from OKRs?

Personally, I benefit greatly by simply forcing myself to pause at the end and start of each quarter (at a minimum) and take a deep breath to think about how I did in the previous quarter, did I make progress in the right areas that I needed to be focused on, and what do I need to achieve next quarter? It helps me break down my bigger bodies of work into bite-sized chunks, and I find that this method helps me achieve more and feel more productive. It also helps that I have developed a habit of checking in on my OKRs *throughout* the quarter to help me prioritize my next steps and ensure I am aligned to my desirable outcomes. We continuously work with our business partners to understand how they are benefiting from OKRs and consistently hear positive feedback. Some of the feedback from our associates is:

- "I like that I have set goals that I revisit several times a year instead of just once a year . . ."—Market Manager
- "Determining how I will grade my OKRs, as I write them, allows me to really think about what I want to achieve and how to craft a great OKR."—Manager
- "It's easy to allow our day to get completely swallowed up by the 'whirlwind' and still not get everything done that I would like to. OKR's bring the focus back to what is really going to drive positive change for the business."—Territory Manager

### How do you ensure ongoing momentum for OKRs?

Having key leaders, and a passionate CEO and chairman, certainly helps drive the continued momentum around OKRs. Our centralized Talent Management team, in partnership with the broader HR generalist community and leadership team, continues to support the progress around OKRs across the business. Broad visibility to data, illustrating where OKRs are and are not being utilized, helps our leaders to understand where there are opportunities to continue driving adoption. In addition, this data identifies strong users of OKRs that we continuously leverage to help advocate the advantages of the methodology to others. The data also helps us to drive insights and determine relationships among OKR users that continue to highlight the benefits of using OKRs. For instance, we now know that each quarter, roughly 45,000 objectives are created resulting in approximately 125,000 key results across the organization. That's a lot of data! We then have the ability to correlate usage of OKRs with other talent practices in our ecosystem to understand how usage can impact performance for individuals. In turn, we know that associates who utilize OKRs and simply stop each quarter to reflect on their progress and identify ways that they can continue making progress in the new quarter, are 11.5 percent more likely than non OKR users to improve their performance year over year. That's the difference between being a middle of the road performer and a high performer. These insights are consistently shared back to associates in the organization to illustrate the value of the OKRs methodology to performance and productivity measures.

**What were the major surprises in your implementation?**

I would say that one of the surprises we had was the number of individuals who simply would begin using the tool without driving the process through compliance. We rolled OKRs out to the organization with an "opt-in" approach and relied on communication, education, and value proposition to drive usage. With over 70 percent of users setting OKRs each quarter, we were pleasantly surprised.

**What would you do differently?**

Initially, we were almost solely focused on driving usage and simply asking associates to "try it out." Our strategy was to drive use of the methodology and technology and then come back to educate on quality and effective goal setting. I wouldn't say that this was the wrong way to do it . . . In fact, I think it helped a lot of people simply develop the habit and certainly benefited those who struggled to think about their goals prior to the launch. At this time, we are making a significant investment in developing our associates by helping them understand what a *quality* OKR looks like now and how to appropriately align them, best practices for rating them, and how to know if you have written a strong and measureable OKR.

*Would you recommend using OKRs to other companies? Why or why not?*

Absolutely! I couldn't imagine relying on annual goals any longer when thinking about my own work and the progress that I make throughout the year. It's hard to imagine many organizations that wouldn't benefit from this thought framework.

 **GONOODLE**

GoNoodle gets kids moving to be their best selves. Short, interactive movement videos make it simple and fun to incorporate movement into every part of the day with dancing, stretching, running, and even mindfulness activities. At school, teachers use GoNoodle to keep students energized, engaged, and active inside the classroom. At home, GoNoodle turns screen time into active time, so families can have fun and get moving together. GoNoodle is used by millions of kids and in 75 percent of United States elementary schools. The company's Co-Founder and Chief Product Officer, John Herbold, shared their OKRs story.

*Why were OKRs introduced? Did you consider any other program?*

It was fall 2015. We had just closed on a round of capital and were looking ahead at 2016. The growth plan was aggressive. We knew it would introduce a new level of complexity and potential chaos to our business. How would we manage that growth and scale well? How would we stay focused on the right things? How would we define and communicate our most important work? And how would we measure it and hold ourselves accountable?

I went off and started reading, searching for any clues that could be helpful in showing us how other companies have successfully solved the challenges we were facing. In the course of that research, I came across OKRs. The concept was immediately compelling. It looked like a proven framework that would provide us with the focus, clarity, transparency, and accountability we needed.

*Who initiated OKRs (who brought them to your attention; how did they get on your radar screen)?*

As noted above, I discovered OKRs through my research.

*Who sponsored the implementation?*

I did, with the full support of our CEO. It was important to show our entire team that I was committed to this from the beginning.

***Where in your organization did you develop OKRs? At the corporate level? Or at a business unit level, and why?***

We started with the company and business units. Getting to individual OKRs seemed like too big a step, and our consultant strongly advised against it so early in the implementation. Conversely, we didn't believe company-level OKRs were adequate for us. We already had company goals. (They weren't as well-defined as they are now due to OKRs, but they were directionally accurate.) What we needed was a clear bridge from those strategic, high-level goals to the work of each business unit or team. The connecting nature of OKRs was a very compelling part of our decision to start with both company and team OKRs.

***What was your process for developing OKRs? Executive training, retreats, workshops, etc.?***

We implemented OKRs at a nearly insane pace. I had researched the concepts and had a pretty good grasp of the theory. But I knew the devil would be in the details. To make sure we started this well, I engaged an OKRs consultant to help. An experienced coach seemed like a no-brainer to help us avoid common pitfalls. The upside of OKRs was huge for us, and failure to launch them well could jade the staff and undermine the whole effort. We had to get it right.

The consultant and I had our first call on January 11, 2016, and we rolled out OKRs to the company on January 29, 2016. Again, a nearly insane pace. During those 18 interim days, we worked with the executive team to define our company's 2016 OKRs. The objectives came pretty easily, but we were beginning to realize writing good key results is an art. This is where the consultant was a huge asset.

After we had a working version of our company OKRs, I worked with each department lead to start drafting team-level OKRs in service of the company's OKRs. We had a marathon coaching session with our consultant, going back-to-back with each team lead to again drive us to establish solid key results.

While I worked with each team lead to finalize their OKRs, the consultant and I were in regular contact. We were probably meeting two to three times a week, reviewing progress, answering questions, drafting our internal OKR FAQ document, and discussing best practices for rolling them out to the staff. It all happened at record pace, but we got it done. By our first OKR staff meeting, we had 33 key results defined across the organization, complete with full scoring criteria, and shared in a Google spreadsheet visible to everyone in the company. The rollout was a great success, and it seemed like the fledgling initiative had taken flight.

***Did you use the Google model? If so, did you modify it to fit your organization?***

Yes, we did OKRs at the company and team level and adopted the 1.0, 0.7, and 0.3 scoring system. It is worth noting that we set the scoring criteria for every key result as part of defining the key result. This was both difficult and extremely valuable.

***How do you ensure your OKRs reflect the organization's strategy—so that you have people focused on doing the right things?***

Through a number of means:

- Company and team vision statements—these were a great suggestion by our consultant. What is the reason each team exists within the company? Is the reason in service of the company's vision and annual OKRs? Are each team's OKRs directly in service of their vision?
- Weekly review—every Monday morning, the executive team goes through every OKR and notes an update in the shared document.
- Mid-quarter check-in—we do a mid-quarter staff meeting to review progress, going team by team to share what is working, what isn't, and what we are learning.
- End-of-quarter scoring and review—we do another staff meeting at the end of the quarter to formally score our progress and roll out the next quarter's OKRs.
- OKR onboarding—every new employee gets an overview of OKRs: what they are, why we use them, what the scoring means, etc.

These all help reinforce OKRs as a foundational part of our culture and operating DNA.

***How do you score your OKRs?***

We use the 1.0, 0.7, and 0.3 scoring criteria. Each key result is scored at the time of creation. For our first mid-quarter review we didn't formally score every key result. We simplified by choosing one "green" and one "red" from each team and had the key result owners talk about them. At the end of the quarter, we formally score every key result.

***Do you have a limit on the number of OKRs?***

We aim for two to four objectives with three to five key results for each objective. Some smaller teams have only one objective with one or two key results. Larger teams have more.

***How long did it take to develop your initial set of OKRs?***

A very rapid 18 days!

*Who manages the OKRs process on an ongoing basis?*
I do.
*Have you rolled OKRs out to lower levels of the organization?*
Teams/departments. No individual OKRs yet (We're piloting individual OKRs with my team in Q2).
*What has been your approach to communicating and educating OKRs to the organization as a whole?*
We've used a number of approaches:

- All-hands meeting at the beginning of each quarter to review results and roll out the next quarter OKRs
- All-hands meeting mid-quarter to review progress
- Shared Google Sheet visible to everyone in the company
- Teaching new employees about OKRs when they join the company
- Weekly review of OKRs by exec team, with status updates in a shared document

*How do you ensure there is alignment among all OKRs?*
During the drafting process, we look for dependencies across teams. If they are significant, we make sure they are captured in the OKRs. I also review all the team-level OKRs with our CEO and CFO each quarter to make sure they are aligned with what we most need to accomplish.
*How do groups report on and review OKR results?*
The company's management team reviews progress every week. Team leads provide status updates on their team's OKRs in that meeting.
*Do you use a technology solution for OKRs?*
No. Just Google docs and Google sheets.
*Have you, or did you ever, consider linking OKRs to compensation? Why or why not?*
No. We want OKRs to encourage big ideas. They are intentionally aspirational, and we don't want people to constrain their thinking of what's possible by considering how success or failure will impact their compensation. We believe compensation is an incentive that runs counter to the spirit of OKRs and will negatively affect their impact.
*Have you linked OKRs to performance reviews? Why or why not?*
No. We are very new at this. Our biggest goal is to make OKRs an integral part of our culture, to get our teams comfortable with the process, and to get them to buy into the benefits they provide our company. Introducing a formal

connection to performance reviews adds another layer of complexity we have to manage, and it introduces the possibility for perverse incentives similar to those possible from tying OKRs to compensation.

***What specific benefits have you achieved from OKRs?***

Clarity of our most important work, more focused execution, transparency around what we are focused on, accountability around results, quantification of progress, rallying around ambitious key results, and improved company culture.

***How do you ensure ongoing momentum for OKRs?***

Weekly status meetings at the executive level set the tone for the organization. Given we're using a shared Google Sheet, we can always see who's accessing the OKRs document. There is always someone in the file reviewing the OKRs. Our board reports are communicated using OKRs. The mid-quarter reviews with all staff combined with the end-of-quarter scoring really ensures we maintain momentum. Given we're in rapid growth mode, it's important to note that OKRs are now an essential part of our onboarding process. Our challenge will be to continue to stretch ourselves to think big as the process of OKRs becomes more routine.

***What were the major surprises in your implementation?***

The biggest surprise was how difficult it was to write good key results. It's like an art. In theory, it's simple, but it wound up being much more difficult than expected. The learning curve was steep, but it paid off. As we wrote OKRs, we become better at thinking more critically about what we want to accomplish, how we define and measure success, and how we hold ourselves accountable.

***What would you do differently?***

I would have started the process in December for the first quarter rather than mid-January. We were not able to finalize OKRs until the end of January. It would have been better to finalize OKRs earlier in the quarter.

***Would you recommend using OKRs to other companies? Why or why not?***

Absolutely! As noted in my response to the first question, we now have a level of operating rigor that we never had before. You can get your most important work defined with results that are monitored and transparent for everyone to see. Scoring is really a valuable piece. It's admittedly a little geeky and can be met with some strange looks, but it's awesome to look at a quarter and say, "Here's how we did in an objective way based on scoring criteria that we all agreed to up front." There's no arguing about how successful we were.

## TAXSLAYER

An income tax preparation business dating to 1965, TaxSlayer has evolved into an innovative tax preparation and filing software development company that retains its founder's commitment to a family-owned business and its employees, customers, and community. Today, the company prepares millions of federal and state tax returns annually. Devin Sherman, Director of Corporate Planning, shared the story of their OKR implementation with us.

### Why were OKRs introduced? Did you consider any other program?

We were looking for a goal framework that would help us plan and execute our work. We had used the SMART method: Set annual goals for the year and that's it. But we had never focused on objectives and the results we want to achieve. OKRs made perfect sense to us. The model allows us to add accountability to our work, set a cadence for greater urgency and better planning, and focus on what's really important. The only other system we really considered was KPIs/Balanced Scorecard.

### Who initiated OKRs (who brought them to your attention; how did they get on your radar screen)?

After watching the Rick Klau Google Ventures video and conducting some other research, I (Devin) brought OKRs to the company's attention in 2015. I had conversations with the President and VP of Product about the history of OKRs, how the model was born out of Intel, the simplicity of using OKRs, what they were all about, and how we could really benefit from implementing them here at TaxSlayer.

### Who sponsored the implementation?

I sponsored the implementation.

### Where in your organization did you develop OKRs? At the corporate level? Or at a business unit level, and why?

To start with OKRs, we felt that developing at the corporate and division level would be our best course of action. We wanted to wait until management really understood OKRs before rolling it out to our employees.

### What was your process for developing OKRs? Executive training, retreats, workshops, etc.?

We began by holding an onsite retreat that included seven workshops for our products and specific divisions that would be creating OKRs. We felt it was important to have an OKRs coach/consultant assist us to get started, and we utilized Ben's services.

We wanted to make sure our directors came to the workshops prepared to discuss their goals for the year. So I met with each of them to begin the initial drafting of division-level OKRs that could then be reviewed at the retreat and refined further.

Following the retreat, I met again with each director to wrap up final drafting of division OKRs and set the first quarter key results and scoring for each team. We then had an all-hands meeting at the end of March (right before the new goal year began April 1st). We used that meeting to show the organization that we had a plan for the year, what it was, and how we were measuring ourselves (accountability).

**Did you use the Google model? If so, did you modify it to fit your organization?**

I think we basically did use the Google model. The main difference I see is that our organization and all divisions are setting both annual OKRs and quarterly key results. Our quarterly key results are what's driving the annual OKRs.

**How do you ensure your OKRs reflect the organization's strategy—so that you have people focused on doing the right things?**

We're in a growth mode and expanding our reach in many ways. If OKRs are driving growth and revenue, then we must question why, and learn from what the results are telling us. Everyone understands that OKRs are the most important things they're doing, and that should be moving the organization forward.

**How do you score your OKRs?**

Scoring has been paramount to our use of OKRs, and I believe our directors would agree with that. To set expectations and determine what's aspirational we conduct scoring while setting our key results. This often leads to conversations and debate around what's challenging and what's not. It forces us to have conversations with aligned teams about various targets and measures, which has been extremely helpful.

**Do you have a limit on the number of OKRs?**

We follow the best practice of setting three to five objectives, each with two to four key results. There are a handful of exceptions where necessary, but for the most part everyone is very focused on setting just the most important objectives and key results for them.

**How long did it take to develop your initial set of OKRs?**

For about a month we conducted what I called "Pre-OKR Workshop Planning." I met with each division head to explain what we were doing with OKRs, what level of clarity I was expecting this year before the workshop, and that

OKRs were going to be set in the upcoming workshop. Between the start of these meetings and when we finished drafting and published our first set of OKRs, two months had passed.

*Who manages the OKRs process on an ongoing basis?*

In my role as Director of Corporate Planning I focus on two things: execution using OKRs (or short-term planning), and long-term three- to five-year strategic planning.

*Have you rolled OKRs out to lower levels of the organization?*

Not at this time. We're waiting until we have a year under our belts with OKRs at the company and division levels before rolling it out to the employee level. Even then, we'll consider it carefully given that some other technology companies have moved away from individual OKRs in order to focus on the team level.

*What has been your approach to communicating and educating OKRs to the organization as a whole?*

We've used our monthly company meetings to communicate OKRs to the entire organization. Going forward, I'd like to use some internal Microsoft 365 tools we have to develop a training and feedback site on our OKR process.

*How do you ensure there is alignment among all OKRs?*

We've designated parts of our master spreadsheet to record alignment to corporate objectives as well as cross-functional alignment between divisions.

*How do groups report on and review OKR results?*

Reporting can be done weekly through the weekly OKR status report e-mail each director sends to our executive team but also at mid-quarter check-ins. I am holding an end-of-month OKR chat with each director to also review and get a quick update on status.

*Do you use a technology solution for OKRs?*

The only technology solutions we use at this time are Microsoft Excel, PowerPoint and OneDrive to house documents and our master spreadsheet. Our thought process is let's really learn what OKRs are and how to write great OKRs first, then look at possible software solutions to help manage the process.

*Have you, or did you ever, consider linking OKRs to compensation? Why or why not?*

We have not yet considered the linkage.

*Have you linked OKRs to performance reviews? Why or why not?*

By the end of the year, OKRs will be part of our managers' quarterly performance reviews, in terms of how they are using OKRs. Have they really adopted OKRs, are they using them to their fullest potential, have they met with their team, are they updating their team, etc.

*What specific benefits have you achieved from OKRs?*

I think the specific benefits we have achieved are: (1) More communication—especially conversations that OKRs forced, that we wouldn't have otherwise held. (2) Accountability is at a new level at TaxSlayer. We've set expectations by scoring up front and I think this has really changed the mindset of our managers to being results focused.

*How do you ensure ongoing momentum for OKRs?*

We make it fun and interactive for the management team. For example, it could be an offsite planning retreat for two days where we get 80 percent of our OKRs set. I also think it's a mindset change. We think of the best ways to reward results, and celebrate as a group.

*What were the major surprises in your implementation?*

There were no real surprises, but we did have "Aha" moments with scoring and the distinction between a task and a key result.

I'm exaggerating just a little, but setting scoring criteria for key results upfront rocked our world and that was common feedback from our workshop groups. Not only can our president hold us accountable for our expectations, but also so can the managers themselves. The scoring can be a discussion tool if there is disagreement in the numbers.

Being able to distinguish the difference between a task and a key result was also huge. In the past, we had been run over by tasks and actions and not focused on the real results we're looking to achieve.

*What would you do differently?*

Alignment! We didn't have our company OKRs really nailed down before the OKRs planning retreat and that hurt our alignment efforts to the top. We also didn't really force cross-functional alignment in the workshops, so I'm having to ensure we're communicating the interdependencies between teams and realizing that some are just business as usual support and not key results. Next time we set OKRs, we will have the alignment checks right from the start, when we're in the same room.

*Would you recommend using OKRs to other companies? Why or why not?*

Absolutely. It's a framework that has a long track record so we know it's not another management fad. Google has used OKRs for over 20 years, and I believe Intel still uses OKRs.

If you want a workforce focused on achieving results and working on the right things, use OKRs. They will focus the work and effort and give you measurable feedback every 30 or 90 days. If you just want to cross things off your list and keep employees busy, never knowing what direction you're headed in, don't use OKRs.

## NOTE

1. Please note: While we asked the same questions of all respondents, not everyone answered all questions. Also, some responses were edited for clarity. All edits were subsequently approved by the responding company.

# About the Authors

PAUL R. NIVEN IS A MANAGEMENT CONSULTANT, AUTHOR, and noted speaker on the subjects of OKRs, strategy, and strategy execution. He has written five previous books, which have been translated in to over 15 languages.

BEN LAMORTE is an internationally recognized OKRs coach who has consulted with organizations around the world. He holds a graduate degree in Management Science & Engineering from Stanford University.

Join the global OKRs community led by Niven and Lamorte, and continue the conversation at www.okrstraining.com.

# Index

Adobe, 145
Advancement opportunities, lack of, 24
Agility, 21–22, 25
Alignment:
  about, 108–109
  confirming, 113–114
  cross-functional, 23
  execution versus, 14–15
  horizontal, 73, 111–113
  key results and, 70, 73
  vertical, 73, 109–110
Align phase, 91, 93–94
Amabile, Teresa, 72
Amazon, 48
Apple, 58, 129
Art of War, The (Sun Tzu), 108
Aspirational nature of key results, 70, 71
Attainability, 63, 65

Baby boomers, 16–17
"Back to the Future Visioning"
    exercise, 52
Baseline key results, 76, 77, 78
Bazerman, Max, 34
Beer, Michael, 41
Benefits of OKRs:
  about, 20, 25
  agility, 21–22, 25
  communication, 21, 25
  engagement, 23–24, 25
  focus, 22–23, 25, 148
  transparency, 23, 25
  visionary thinking, 24, 25, 26
Biases in performance reviews, 144–145
Bossidy, Larry, 32

Brady, Mathew, 124
Brainstorming, 66, 90, 92
Brin, Sergey, 5
Buckingham, Marcus, 29
Business units:
  company-level OKRs and, 34–35
  pilot projects, 35, 38
  team level, 106

Cadence:
  dual, 86
  weekly, 136–137
Cain, Susan, 90, 92
Capacity/capabilities, 55
CareerBuilder, 33, 167–171
Carter, Dean, 177
Case studies:
  about, 161–162
  CareerBuilder, 167–171
  Flipkart, 162–167
  GoNoodle, 185–189
  Sears Holdings Corporation, 175,
    177–185
  TaxSlayer, 190–194
  Zalando, 171–175
Castro, Felipe, 110
Challenges, organizational:
  about, 13–14
  disruption, 18–19
  engagement, 19–20
  executing strategy, 14–16
  growth, sustaining, 17–18
  organizing to meet new realities,
    16–17
Champion, OKRs, 143

Change:
  inspiring, 45
  lessons for, 41–42
  in OKRs during quarter, 89–90
  in OKRs from quarter to quarter,
    88–89
  pace of, 13
  reinforcing through formal
    mechanisms, 41
Charan, Ram, 32
Clarity, 75
Coca-Cola, 51, 55
Collaboration, employee, 7
Communication:
  of corporate OKRs, 104
  as OKRs benefit, 21, 25
  understanding versus, 15–16, 21
Company-level OKRs, 10, 34–35, 38
Compensation, incentive, 147–151
Competitive strategy, 57–58
Confidence level, 83, 119, 121
*Confronting Reality* (Charan and
    Bossidy), 32
Connecting OKRs. *See also* Alignment
  benefits of, 99–100, 114–115
  depth of, 100–102
  failure to, 156
  influence as key to, 104–106
  mass connect approach, 106–108
  number of OKRs, determining, 102
  preparing groups for, 103
  understanding, ensuring, 103–104
*Connections* (television show), 1
Consultants, 157–159
Contributions, measurable, 8
Controllable objectives, 64, 65
Corporate goals/objectives, 15–16,
    30, 99
Corporate-level OKRs, 40
Cost, competing on, 57
Costolo, Dick, 22
Coupling, loose, 106, 109, 151
CRAFT (acronym for setting OKRs),
    90–95
Create phase, 90, 91, 92
Critical-thinking framework, 7

Cross-functional alignment, 23
Cultural fit, 158–159
Culture, performance, 16
Customer intimacy, 76, 79, 88
Customers:
  identifying, 57
  as propelling force, 55
CW, The (television channel), 56–57
Cycle, OKRs, 128–129, 130

Data:
  historical, 132, 135
  predictive, 134, 135
Davis, Angus, 63
Deloitte, 17, 22, 144, 145
Dependency between teams, 94
Depth of connecting OKRs, 100–102
Desai, Niket, 70–71, 162–166
Descriptions for objectives, 68–69
Development phase, 39–40
Differentiation, 58
Diffusion of responsibility, 76
Disruption, 18–19
Dissent, 93
Doerr, John, 5, 85–86, 106
Drafting OKRs, 107, 108
Driving the right behavior, 70, 73
Drucker, Peter, 2–4, 7, 45, 110–111,
    126, 146
Dual cadence, 86
DuPont, 55
Dweck, Carol, 24

Education, 32–33, 40, 152–153
Employee engagement. *See* Engagement
Employees:
  collaboration among, 7
  goal awareness, lack of, 15–16,
    30, 99
  manager, relationship with, 23–24
Engagement:
  connection and, 99, 101
  as Monday meeting topic, 120
  as OKRs benefit, 23–24, 25
  as organizational challenge, 19–20
Engler, Holly, 175, 177–185

Ephron, Nora, 86–87
Estée Lauder (company), 57
Excess access, 22, 29
Execution:
  alignment versus, 14–15
  myths of, 14–16
  as organizational challenge, 14–16
Executives:
  quarterly reviews, role in, 128
  software usage by, 132, 133
  top-down execution by, 16
Executive sponsorship:
  gaining, 32–33
  implementation and, 34
  importance of, 31–32
  obtaining, 152
  ownership and, 142–143
Expectations, managing, 124
Extrinsic motivation, 147–148

Failures, 16, 127–128
Fairness, 148–149
Fast food restaurants, 73, 75
Feedback, soliciting, 125
Finalize phase, 91, 94
Financial lens, 59
Fit, cultural, 158–159
"Five whys," 126–127
Fixed mindset, 24
Fleming, Alexander, 127
Flipkart, 162–167
Focus, 8, 22–23, 25, 148
Forces, propelling, 55–56
Fountain metaphor, 110
Freda, Fabrizio, 57
Frequency:
  of reviewing performance, 136–137
  of setting goals, 21–22
  of setting OKRs, 85–86
Fugett, Roger, 33, 167
Future lock-in, 34

Gallup, 20
Gamification, 134, 136
Gelb, Michael, 76
Global phenomenon, OKRs as, 176

Goals, corporate, 15–16, 30, 99
Goal setting, frequency of, 21–22
GoNoodle, 185–189
Google, 5–6, 22, 48, 131
Grant, Ulysses S., 124
Grove, Andy, 4–5, 144, 145–146
Growth, sustaining, 17–18
Growth mindset, 24, 26

Hawthorne Effect, 2
Health metrics, 79–80
Herbold, John, 185–189
*High Output Management* (Grove), 144
Historical data, 132, 135
Homkes, Rebecca, 14–16
Horizontal alignment, 73, 111–113
Housing OKRs process, 143
*How to Think Like Leonardo Da Vinci*
    (Gelb), 76
Human lens, 59

Idea sharing, 108, 111
Idiosyncratic rater effect, 144–145
Illusory superiority, 144
Implementation:
  company and business unit/team,
    34–35
  company-level only, 34, 38
  intentions, 123
  organization, entire, 35, 38
  pilot at business unit/team, 35, 38
  projects, 35–36, 38
  teams, multiple, using single set of
    OKRs, 37
  teams, two, using single set of
    OKRs, 36
IMVU (metaverse website), 126–127
Incentive compensation, 147–151
Inclusionary process, 125
Individuals:
  OKRs for, 12
  software usage by, 132, 133
Influence, 104–106
In-N-Out restaurant, 21
Inspiration, 62–63, 65
Intel, 4–5, 85

Intrinsic motivation, 147, 148
Issues, top ten:
    after creating OKRs, 155–156
    before creating OKRs, 151–154
    creating OKRs, 154–155
IT teams, 36

Johnson & Johnson, 55

Kent, Muhtar, 51
Key results. *See also* Objectives and
        key results
    alignment and, 70, 73
    baseline, 76, 77, 78
    characteristics of effective, 69–73
    creating, tips for, 73–76
    defined, 8–9, 69
    examples, 9
    health metrics, 79–80
    metric, 77, 78
    milestone, 77, 78–79, 155
    number of, 74, 154–155
    problems with, 154–155
    progress-based, 70, 72–73
    quantitative, 69–71
    scoring, 80–84, 122
    threshold target, 77, 78
    types of, 76–80
Klau, Rick, 6, 21, 172
Knowledge transfer, 158
Krupit, Andy, 167–171
Kruse, Kevin, 19

Lampert, Eddie, 177
Lange, Christoph, 171–175
Language, 66, 68, 74–75
Large organizations, 131–132
Leads, journalistic, 86–87
*Lean Startup, The* (Ries), 126–127
Lenses, 58–59
LinkedIn, 24, 134
Listening, 128
Lock-in, future, 34
Logistics, 119

Loose coupling, 106, 109, 151
Lowest total cost, 57

Madan, Sonia, 167
Management by objectives (MBO), 3–4
Manager-employee relationship, 23–24
Manager's letter, 146–147
Managing with OKRs. *See also* Software
        cycle, OKRs, 128–129, 130
    importance of, 117–118
    mid-quarter check-ins, 120–121
    Monday meetings, 118–120
    quarterly reviews, 121–128
Manning, Peyton, 61, 62
Marketing team, 47, 49, 50
Markets, 55
Mason, Chris, 177
Mass connect approach, 106–108
Maugham, Somerset, 142
MBO (management by objectives), 3–4
McDonald's, 57
McKinsey survey, 41
Medium organizations, 132
Metric key results, 77, 78
Mid-quarter check-ins, 120–121
Milestone key results, 77, 78–79, 155
Millennials, 16, 146
Mindset, 24, 26
Mission/mission statement:
    about, 40, 42–44, 43
    connection and, 103
    effective mission statements, 45
    evaluating existing mission, 47
    examples, 48
    importance of, 44–45
    mission objectives and key results, 47,
        49–50
    template for mission statement, 46
    vision and, 51
Mission objectives and key results
        (MOKRs), 47, 49–50
Mistakes, 16, 127–128
Monday meetings, 118–120
Monitoring OKRs, 40

Motivation, 147–148
Movie analogy, 17

National Semiconductor, 85
Negative metrics, 77, 78
Net Promoter Score (NPS), 80
Nike, 48
Nohria, Nitin, 41
Nordstrom, 58
Number:
  of key results, 74, 154–155
  of objectives, 4
  of OKRs, 86–88, 102

Oarsmen, 115
Objectives. *See also* Objectives and
      key results
  characteristics of powerful, 62–64
  controllable, 64, 65
  corporate, 15–16, 30, 99
  creating, tips for, 64–68
  defined, 8, 62
  descriptions for, 68–69
  example, 8
  number of, 4
  qualitative, 64, 65
  quantitative, 154
  scoring, 84
Objectives and key results (OKRs).
      *See also specific topics*
  changing during quarter, 89–90
  changing from quarter to quarter,
      88–89
  company-level, 10, 34–35, 38
  corporate-level, 40
  defined, 6–8
  drafting, 107, 108
  frequency of setting, 85–86
  as global phenomenon, 176
  history of, 1–6
  individual-level, 12
  mission, 47, 49–50
  monitoring, 40
  number of, 86–88, 102

ongoing nature of, 7, 141–142
  presenting, 40
  process of setting, 90–95
  reasons for implementing, 29–31,
      151–152
  shared, 111
  support for, 93
  supporting, 93
  team-level examples, 11
  top-down, 154, 156–157
Oil companies, 56
OKRs. *See* Objectives and key results
Ongoing nature of OKRs, 7, 141–142
Openness, 75
Organization-level OKRs, 35, 38
Ostroff, Dawn, 56
Ownership:
  assigning, 76
  of key results, 70, 72, 76
  of OKRs process, 142–143

Page, Larry, 5
Paint tubes, 67
Passion, 32, 33
Penicillin, 127, 151
Performance, frequency of reviewing,
      136–137
Performance culture, 16
Performance reviews, 144–147
Pfeffer, Jeffrey, 149–150
Pilot projects, 35, 38
Pink, Daniel, 148
Pixar, 125
Planning, 15, 37, 39, 40
Positive language, 66, 74–75
Positive metrics, 77, 78
Possibilities, opening up to all, 75
*Practice of Management, The* (Drucker), 2
Predictions, proficiency at making,
      120–121
Predictive data, 134, 135
Presenting OKRs, 40
Priorities, 87–88, 119
Problems, overcoming, 67–68

Problems with key results, 154–155
Product and engineering teams in
    software space, 36
Products and services:
  determination of, 56–57
  as propelling force, 55
Progress-based key results, 70, 72–73
"Progress Principle, The," 72–73
Projects, 35–36, 38, 141

Qualitative objectives, 64, 65
Quantitative key results, 69–71
Quantitative objectives, 154
Quarterly reviews:
  about, 121–123
  expectations, managing, 124
  feedback, soliciting, 125
  "five whys," 126–127
  as inclusionary process, 125
  listening by leaders, 128
  mistakes, learning from, 127–128
  questions, asking, 125–126
  scheduling in advance, 123–124
  scoring/grading of key results, 122
Questions:
  fundamental, 55–58
  objectives, 65–66
  quarterly reviews, 125–126
  Roadmap Strategy, 55–58
  software, 137–138
*Quiet* (Cain), 90

Rand, John Goffe, 67
Raw materials, 56
Reasons for implementing OKRs, 29–31,
    151–152
Refine phase, 91, 92–93
Renoir, 67
Reporting results, 40
Responsibility, diffusion of, 76
Results, key. *See* Key results
Ries, Eric, 126–127
Roadmap Strategy:
  about, 53–54

lenses, 58–59
  questions, fundamental, 55–58
Rogers, Todd, 34
Role modeling, 41
Rules, simple, 66–67

Sales and distribution channels, 56
Sandbagging, 145, 146, 149
Schein, Edgar, 125–126
Scientific Management, 1
Scoring:
  consistency in, 155
  historical data for, 132, 135
  key results, 80–84, 122
  objectives, 84
  predictive data for, 134, 135
  software and, 132, 134, 135
Sears Holdings Corporation (SHC), 24,
    131, 175, 177–185
Services and products:
  determination of, 56–57
  as propelling force, 55
"Set it and forget it" syndrome, 3,
    7, 155
Setting OKRs:
  align phase, 91, 93–94
  create phase, 90, 91, 92
  finalize phase, 91, 94
  refine phase, 91, 92–93
  transmit phase, 91, 95
Shared OKRs, 111
Sherman, Devin, 190–194
Shipping companies, 19
Silos, departmental, 109
Simms, Charlie, 86–87
Simplicity, 75
Small/medium organizations, 132
Smartphone adoption rates, 13
Social/cultural lens, 58
Social loafing, 92
Software:
  gamification, 134, 136
  historical data as scoring basis,
    132, 135

large organizations, 131–132
number of people using, 131–132
performance, frequency of reviewing,
    136–137
predictive data as scoring basis,
    134, 135
questions to ask, 137–138
scoring OKRs, 132, 134, 135
small/medium organizations, 132
timing for acquiring, 129, 131
type of people using, 132, 133
Software space, product and engineering
    teams in, 36
Soni, Punit, 161
Specialists, 2
Specificity, 70, 71–72
Squads, 37
Stanford, 75
Starbucks, 48
Status quo, avoiding, 64–65
Status updates, 119–120
Stonecutters, 2
Strategic plans, 15
Strategy:
    about, 40, 43, 53–54
    competitive, 57–58
    importance of, 153–154
    lenses, 58–59
    questions, fundamental, 55–58
    Roadmap Strategy, 53–59
Stretch, 5
Sull, Charles, 14–16
Sull, Donald, 14–16
Sun Tzu, 108
Superiority, illusory, 144
Support for OKRs, 93
Sustainability:
    consultants, 157–159
    incentive compensation, 147–151
    issues, top ten, 151–156
    ongoing nature of OKRs, 7, 141–142
    ownership of process, 142–143
    performance reviews, 144–147
Sutton, Robert, 149–150

Talent and skills, developing, 41
Tasks, 74
Taxi industry, 18
TaxSlayer, 190–194
Taylor, Frederick Winslow, 1
Team level units, 106
Teams:
    company-level OKRs and, 34–35
    connecting OKRs, preparing
        for, 103
    dependency between, 94
    objectives, controllable, 64, 65
    OKR examples, 11
    OKRs shared among many, 37
    OKRs shared among two, 36
    in organization, 17
    pilot projects, 35, 38
    product and engineering, 36
    software usage by, 132, 133
Technological lens, 59
Technology, 55
Telephone game, 103–104
Template for mission statement, 46
Thinking:
    critical, 7
    visionary, 24, 25, 26
3D printing, 19
Threshold target key results, 77, 78
Timeframe, 63–64, 65
Top-down execution, 16
Top-down OKRs, 154, 156–157
Total cost, lowest, 57
Total shareholder return
        (TSR), 55
Toyoda, Sakichi, 126
Toyota Motor Corporation, 126
Training, 32–33, 40, 152–153
Transmit phase, 91, 95
Transparency, 23, 25
TSR (total shareholder return), 55
TV shopping networks, 56
Twain, Mark, 154–155
Twitter, 22
Tyson, Mike, 15

Uber, 18
UCLA men's basketball team, 37
Understanding:
  communication versus,
    15–16, 21
  fostering, 41
  of highest level OKRs, 103–104
U.S. Census Bureau's Center for
    Economic Studies, 20

Value, business, 64, 65
Verb, starting objectives with, 67
Vertical alignment, 73, 109–110
Visionary thinking, 24, 25, 26

Vision/vision statement:
  about, 40, 43, 50
  developing, 52
  effective, 50–52
  mission and, 51

Wal-Mart, 45, 57
Weekly cadence, 136–137
"Whys," diagnosing issues using,
    126–127
Wodtke, Christina, 83, 119
Wooden, John, 37

Zalando, 171–175